Simon Wilde

Simon Wilde has been cricket correspondent at the *Sunday Times* since 1998. He was twice previously shortlisted for the William Hill Sports Book of the Year: in 1990 for his biography of the Indian cricketer Ranjitsinhji and in 1994 for *Letting Rip*, a study of modern fast bowling. He is the only author to have made the shortlist three times.

Shane Warne

Portrait of a Flawed Genius

SIMON WILDE

JOHN MURRAY

First published in Great Britain in 2007 by John Murray (Publishers)
An Hachette Livre UK company

First published in paperback in 2008

3

A CIP catalogue record for this title is available from the British Library

ISBN 978-0-7195-6941-8

Typeset in Monotype Bembo by Hewer Text UK Ltd, Edinburgh

Printed and bound by Clays Ltd, St Ives plc

John Murray policy is to use papers that are natural, renewable
and recyclable products and made from wood grown in sustainable
forests. The logging and manufacturing processes are expected to
conform to the environmental regulations of the country of origin.

John Murray (Publishers)
338 Euston Road
London NW1 3BH

www.johnmurray.co.uk

To Gayle

Contents

I
Chess

THE FIRST THING that strikes you is how much he's spinning the ball. He's turning it bloody miles! OK, this pitch is pretty dry but it's only the second evening of the match. Yet he's still managing to rip it as far as you've ever seen anyone rip it in your short life. You've watched the tapes of course, and the team talk two nights ago went over the problems of facing leg spin for the benefit of newcomers like yourself. But even so. Close up, it's simply startling.

Your mind is jolted even as the ball – pitched outside leg stump – darts across the face of your cautiously outstretched bat and rips past the off stump. Goosebumps burst across the back of your neck. To turn the ball like this, his fingers must be amazingly strong – as strong as anyone's in the game. You hear the keeper and slip yelp delight at this conjuring trick. The keeper thuds his gloves together in applause, shouts words of encouragement down the pitch.

You follow their path to squash some imaginary stray piece of turf six or seven yards away just to give yourself time to think and calm down. How do you prepare for this sort of stuff? How *did* you prepare for this sort of stuff? You used Merlyn, England's wizard spin-bowling machine, which replicates pretty well most types of slow bowling, but those visits to the indoor nets were a good few weeks ago now.

In any case, it was only four days ago that you got the call to get yourself over from Perth, the base for England's reserves, on the next available flight. So you've been out of the loop. But no amount of technological gizmos can prepare you for this. The coach did say it would be difficult the first few times.

The next two balls are also his signature ball, big-spinning leg breaks that fly harmlessly past your off stump. Perhaps sensing your vulnerability, and the fact that this Sydney ground has been the scene of many of the bowler's greatest triumphs, the crowd has quietened in anticipation and you're able to hear the snap of the fingers and the ball buzz through its arc. The second ball bounces so much you don't have to play a shot and it easily clears the stumps.

The bowler's face has so far been a study in fierce concentration, but when this little baby takes off his eyes illuminate enough to power the Sydney Cricket Ground floodlights. Were that necessary. Even in late afternoon, the light in Australia is much brighter than in England. There's really no excuse for not seeing what's happening, though when he's ripping it so far it's hard to fathom in even the best light. If only you'd had the chance to face this guy in county cricket. But that's the problem with two divisions. No guarantee you'll face everyone.

Of course you knew he was good. He's been around a long time – he's nearer forty years old than thirty – and knows plenty of tricks. Even as a kid, bowling the ball flat out of the front of the hand, he could get purchase off most pitches; he was strong and intelligent. OK, his overexuberance got him into trouble once or twice, but he was a good listener and a fast learner. But, as with every leg-spinner, control was the key. The very act of wrenching the right arm over and rotating the wrist is hard to repeat precisely, so landing the ball on the same spot is fiendishly difficult. Master control and the keys to the kingdom of heaven are yours.

You're still hoping for a nice juicy four-ball to be served up. If it is, you've got to be ready to cash in. Already, though, it's clear that run-scoring is going to be a lot harder for a while. Before this over, you and Andrew Strauss, your opening partner, who's currently studying the ground at the other end of the pitch, had scored 72 from fifteen overs from the fast bowlers. But the ball has softened now and, with a spinner on, it suddenly seems like a completely different game.

The fourth ball's a back-spinner, a ball that goes on straight and is the classic follow-up to big-spinning leg breaks. But you spot it and play it back down the pitch. The fifth is a googly. It's a beauty, too. You don't pick it at first, and by the time it's registered it has rapped into your front pad.

Bowler and fielders all go up as one. Your skin pricks with sweat. Shit! Was that in line? Surely just going down leg. For a moment the umpire doesn't move, doesn't really look at the figure before him bent on one knee in supplication. Then – sweet Jesus – he gives a little shake of the head. Not out. Yes, definitely just going down leg. Just.

The bowler is not happy, though, and stands with hands on hips glowering anywhere but at the umpire, which suggests it's him he's pissed off with. You hear him chuntering away to himself, and Strauss, who can obviously hear him as well, offers you a conspiratorial quarter-smile. You've spoken about this. The leg-spinner with the fast bowler's temperament. Another Bill O'Reilly. No great surprise he didn't enjoy the Australian cricket academy. He wouldn't have liked the discipline.

Trying to look unfazed, you step back to survey the field.

You catch sight of the sweeper on the midwicket fence. He's waving in the direction of the bowler, as though seeking confirmation he's standing in the right position, but the bowler, at the end of his mark, doesn't seem to see him, and merely wipes his right hand on the towelling tucked into the top of his trousers. He's too busy thinking about the next ball to worry about his field. The fielder shrugs, as if to say, 'Sod him.'

Maybe this isn't going too badly after all. You start to feel a little more positive. You remind yourself to play the ball, not the reputation. When the last ball comes down you definitely feel better about things. It's a leggie on off stump but is fractionally overpitched, and you get a stride in down the pitch, take it on the full, and drill it down the ground for four. It's come right out of the middle. Lovely. It takes your score into the thirties. Maybe you can play Test cricket after all.

You scurry down the pitch to punch gloves with Strauss, and are just about to tell him how pleased you are with that shot when you catch sight of the big screen down on the south side of the ground, pretty much where you've just hit the ball. These big screens really are big, and often command the attention of the crowd more easily than anything that happens out in the middle.

You're quite keen to see the replay of your shot, but the camera is trained on a figure filling the frame of one of the home dressing-room windows. He's bent forward and his face is partly obscured by a floppy white sunhat and a tendril of smoke. His large forearms rest on the window ledge while a pair of physio's hands work deep into his massive right shoulder. All the time he's keeping a careful eye on the field. Momentarily the figure lifts his head; an earring glints. When he – whose fame has owed so much to television –

catches sight of himself on the big screen, he drops the hand cupped round a cigarette out of sight.

The New Year crowd have now seen him on the screen too, and a cacophony of drunken noise goes up from them. The Australians applaud, while a small group of English supporters strike up a chorus of sheep noises. A shiver runs down your spine.

'Look out,' says Strauss, under his breath. 'You've survived an over of Stuart MacGill. Now things are going to get interesting. Looks like Warney's going to have a bowl.'

A few minutes later, Shane Warne, probably the greatest bowler the world has ever seen, has returned to the field and is standing just a couple of yards away from you, lifting his floppy white hat by its centre to avoid bending the brim and handing it with what seems unnecessary solicitousness to the umpire, with whom he proceeds to exchange a few pleasantries.

He spends the next two minutes adjusting his field; Stuart MacGill may not care much about where his fielders are situated, but Warne does – to the inch. By setting his field so precisely, he immediately gives the impression that he knows the batsman's game far better than the batsman does. Why is it necessary that midwicket stand a few yards further to his right? Is that where Strauss hits the ball? 'No one has the unwavering confidence in his ability, and the iron will to affect the course of a game by his own actions that Shane Warne has . . .' Strauss once wrote. 'He gives you the impression that he has already bowled the over to you in his head long before the first delivery comes down.'

It's all very well them telling you in team meetings to be positive against him. Your stomach is knotting just because you're standing near him. And you're not even on strike.

As he prepares himself, Warne is obviously thinking mainly about Strauss but at one point he does fire you a quick glance, which you guess is the start of him trying to sniff out any sign of weakness or negative body language in England's new boy. You instinctively try to make yourself stand a couple of inches taller, then feel slightly foolish for doing so.

You have two early impressions of Warne. One is his sheer physicality. He's not exactly the perfect athletic specimen – he's carrying quite a few too many pounds for that – but there's a menacing power in the massiveness of his upper legs, forearms and shoulders. His fingers and wrist may apply the final revs on the ball, but there's plainly a lot more to the Warne engine than that.

The second thing is the sense of brilliant whiteness. Warne's entrance has almost literally lit up the centre of the pitch. Everything about him seems to be bright. There's the white floppy hat, the bleached blond hair, the white zinc cream on the face, the stud in the ear. And then there's his brilliantly green eyes, with just a hint of gambler's glint to them. They're the brightest eyes you've ever seen, and look like they could pick out a detail from 200 yards. Like lots of people seeing Warne at close quarters for the first time (you've never played in a match with *him* either), you can't help but be struck by them. Jana Wendt, interviewing him for an Australian publication, noted how his impact was 'aided and abetted by the astonishing green of his eyes . . . There is a depth to them which suggests something that Warne himself denies is there.' They certainly seem to say that one hell of a person lives behind them.

Warne has often said that his life feels like a Hollywood movie, but right now you're the one who feels like you've just walked on to a film set. Lights, cameras, action! 'Facing him is pure theatre,' Nasser Hussain said. 'The blond hair. The flared trousers. The in-your-face chat. The trying-to-read-him. The battle. You are always in the heat of battle with Warne.'

Considering how long he's been playing, it's amazing he's still here. Bowling leg spin puts an enormous strain on the body, and in the early days it put an enormous strain on Warne. He was immensely strong, and spun the ball with extraordinary power. Indeed, he used to impart such powerful side-spin that the ball would swerve in the air before landing – a key component in his success. But after his bowling shoulder required surgery, in 1998, he had to reinvent himself. He cut down on the joint-wrenching googly and hand-snapping flipper (a ball that pitches invitingly short but, imparted with underspin, scuttles through low). Now it's mainly a mix of leg breaks and sliders (balls which float to a fullish length and bounce little).

Not that this has made him much easier to deal with: what he's lost in technical prestigiditation he's made up for with improved know-how. Reflecting on things in 2005, Warne said that, while he was perhaps physically at his peak before his shoulder operation, he didn't really understand how to get wickets or bowl to plans during that period. After 1998 he had as far as possible reduced things to a near-perfect economy of effort. Also, by walking rather than running up to the crease, he is able to bring his upper body smoothly through the same arc time after time, assuring himself of a remarkable accuracy. He bowls very few bad balls. Far fewer than MacGill. Far fewer than anyone. 'I can't remember him bowling more than a handful of long-hops or full tosses,' Hussain added. 'Because of that you were always under pressure. He gave Australia control for fifteen years.'

Warne, a man with an instinctive sense of theatre, doesn't rush in getting ready to bowl his first ball. As with a magician about to pull a rabbit out of a hat, half the trick is in the timing. Just when you think he's ready, he walks halfway down the pitch, bends to wipe his right hand in the dust, and appears to say something to Strauss, though you, the umpire and the stump microphone are just too far away to catch what it is. Then he turns and walks back, his eyes set on the middle distance, his mind deep in thought. No one else has ever made absolutely every ball mean so much.

He reaches the end of his mark. He flips the ball in the air once, twice, turns and walks, passes the ball from his left hand to his right, and, just before he reaches you, says faintly to himself, 'Come on, Shane.' Then there's an enormous surge of energy as he passes you at the crease; his whole weight goes forward, his left arm doing surprisingly little, his right hip swinging powerfully round, his huge right shoulder wheeling over . . . and wheeling over fast, too, as fast as some pacemen, the only difference being that he is taking the pace off the ball with the spin he is putting on it. There's a primal grunt as the ball explodes into flight and his body, his whole being, behaves as though sprung from a trap as it is propelled five or six yards down the pitch.

Now the game really has started.

During his first few balls, each of which kicks off the pitch with remarkable force, and each of which asks a question, you desperately look for clues. From the very start, he's right on the money: immaculate line, searching length. He seems to be turning the ball less than MacGill and also varying his pace more than any other leg-spinner you've seen; some of his balls are very brisk. Because Strauss is a left-hander, Warne is coming round the wicket at him, aiming at the rough footholds and shifting his position within the crease, making it difficult for Strauss to leave the ball and inviting him to play against the spin.

Warne's fifth ball is fired in fast, and had Strauss not jammed his bat down quickly it would have bowled him. The ball squirts out behind square on the leg side and Strauss wants a single, but you're slow to respond and turn him down. He glares at you and Warne smiles, pleased that Strauss has been denied the chance to get off strike. This reminds you of something said in the team talk about not getting stuck on strike for a whole over against Warne. Oh dear, sorry, Straussy.

For the last ball Warne goes wide of the crease and drops his arm to its lowest yet. He generally bowls with a lower arm than many of the great leg-spinners, but this one really is almost a round-arm delivery. The ball lands at least two feet outside off stump, hits some rough, and darts madly across Strauss's front pad, which he's not quite thrust far enough to block the ball. Amazingly, the ball goes on to clip the top of leg stump. Thinking the pad would be defence enough, Strauss's bat is raised out of harm's way, embarrassing testimony to his misjudgement. Warne, who has done this to other left-handers such as Shivnarine Chanderpaul, besides Strauss, is cock-a-hoop. Clearly the whole over has been a set-up. The Australians whoop and leap with joy. While Ian Bell shuffles out to join you, a huge 'Oooh!' goes up from the crowd as the replay screen shows the wonder ball again.

Moments later it's your turn to face the grand inquisitor. It's a new over, so there's a bit of a pause in play, and Warne makes the most of it by giving you the full force of his first intimidatory weapon: The Stare. At first you think he's waiting for something. Then you think he's looking at you.

Finally you realize he's looking not at you, but *through* you, which makes you feel . . . oh, about six inches tall.

These little delays and by-plays are all part of a Warne over, which can vary in length from three and a half to four minutes, depending on which stunts he wants to pull. Thirty seconds is a lot of extra time for you to give full consideration to what has occurred and what might yet occur.

You check the field. A short leg, uncomfortably close; a silly point, also too intimate by half. Two men backward of square for the sweep, another on the off side for cut. Deep midwicket is vacant, inviting you to slog against the spin. Fat chance.

He's coming at you from over the wicket. The first ball comes down fast and straight at you, spinning hard, dips and then kicks up off the pitch. It's the top-spinner. You jump back and get your bat up high and behind it in the nick of time. Bloody hell – your first impressions weren't wrong. He really is quite fast. The second ball is similar, even faster maybe. Again, you go back, jab your bat on it, and the ball drops at your feet, where it skews around madly in the dust. Christ, the bloody thing just doesn't want to stop spinning.

In a trice, he's achieved something important. He's nailed you to the crease. He's bowling a different line to MacGill: middle and leg, whereas MacGill was off stump and outside. You can't go skipping down the pitch to him as you did to MacGill.

Every ball is a mind-bending event, but the next delivery is a genuine surprise. It's the googly. Even before the shoulder op, Warne's googly wasn't that effective, because his wrist action was so obviously different than for the leggie. It's far less well disguised than MacGill's – the tell-tale signs being the higher arm and the slower speed of the ball. He's bowling it just to keep you guessing. You're a new boy and he doesn't want you presuming that his armoury is as limited as some people say it is. Just leggies and sliders? Watch this.

You pick it, but picking it is one thing, playing it another. It pitches on middle and off. You've got to play it, but would rather not. Mindful of keeping the gap between bat and pad as small as possible, you prop forward and at the last minute drop your bat behind the front pad: you don't want to nick a catch to the close fielders breathing down your neck.

The ball strikes your pad beneath the roll . . . Is it leg before? You sense it must be pretty close, and everyone goes up for the appeal, but Warne's appeal isn't that convincing. Maybe he knows it's sliding down leg and wants to keep on the right side of the umpire for when a better shout comes along, when he'll give it the full choir. He's certainly not throwing the toys out of the pram as MacGill had earlier. You've got to hand it to him. Cute. Very cute.

He surveys you, puts his hand to his chin, and rubs it like a pantomime villain thinking up his next dastardly deed. Come on . . . he's pushing you. You look at the umpire as though expecting him to intervene and tell Warne to get back to his mark and bowl, but the umpire's eyes have drifted off to the horizon. Christ, he's pretending this isn't happening. Warne wants to engage you, but the umpire doesn't.

For some reason, he now decides to come at you from round the wicket.

He pads up to the crease on the back of his heels once more, tongue slightly sticking out as though he's musing deeply on what trick he's going to pull next. Over comes his right arm once more. It's the leg break . . . but, whoa!, where is it? You've pushed out your front foot in the hope of kicking the ball away, but you can't get near it, it has pitched so wide and dipped so fast. It lands a good twelve inches outside leg stump before ripping off the turf and only narrowly missing your front glove as you lift your bat over your right shoulder and out of harm's way. That ball turned more than anything MacGill had delivered. Christ, now you know what Mike Gatting must have felt like when Warne bowled him with an extraordinary ball in the first Ashes Test in 1993!

You feel yourself breaking out in a cold sweat, and for some reason recall something Viv Richards once said that had never previously made any sense to you. He said that Chandrasekhar, the great Indian leg-spinner, was the only bowler who had ever made him afraid. It had seemed a crazy thing for Richards, who had run the gauntlet of all the great fast bowlers of his day, to say, but it did not seem so crazy any more.

Warne is about to bowl again. You know you should be thinking about the next ball, not the last, but you don't seem to have the time. Just as he'll sometimes keep you waiting, at other times Warne will simply turn and come right at you, hurrying you for time and denying you the chance to get your thoughts in order.

The problem with him bowling this line is that there's a point when your front pad, front elbow and bat are all getting in the way of you seeing the ball. It's the Blind Spot, a spot Warne has exploited thousands of times over.

All you can think to do is open up your stance slightly, to give yourself a better chance of watching the ball off the pitch if it's going to turn miles again. You know you need to be ready to get forward, but after those first two balls you're reluctant to leave the crease. 'He has the great ability to move you around the crease and pull you into positions you don't want to be in,' said Mark Butcher. 'You've got to get an idea in your head as to how he's trying to get you out.'

Sure enough, the next ball is another leg break down the leg side. Not quite as wide, not spinning quite as much. You can play a shot at it, and consider a pull or a sweep, but you're not feeling all that confident any more. So you just go half-forward, with the face of your bat half-open, not really intending to play a shot but, if you have to, ready to steer the ball towards point. Frankly, you're being pathetically indeterminate. Again, the ball rips back at an implausible angle, strikes you on the roll of your front pad, and flies up over your head. You turn just in time to see it drop to earth, inches behind the stumps. You feel your palms pricking with sweat. And you essay a little stand-up sweep, just to see how it feels.

Last ball of the over to come. Warne is about to bowl it when he stops and, for the first time, decides to speak to you direct. 'Come on, mate, have a go!' he shouts down the pitch. 'Go on – you know you want to!' And you think to yourself, 'Well, I'm buggered if I'm going to have a go just to satisfy you . . .'

Mistake. Big mistake.

As you've told yourself you're not going to be playing a shot, you decide to open up your stance some more to get a better view of these big-spinning leg breaks. After all, if the ball pitches outside leg stump again you're free to go back and cover your stumps and let the ball hit your pads. As you cannot be out leg before, you need play a shot only if you want to. In other words, play Warne French-cricket style, as John Emburey famously did at Edgbaston in 1993, when he frustrated him for hours.

The last ball duly comes down the leg side. But decisively – fatally – Warne has moved a few inches closer to the stumps and rolled his wrist on the ball rather than ripped it. It breaks less than the previous two balls, and is not as wide. No way you're having a go at this one. You go back but, involuntarily, stick your left leg out anyway, thinking you can kick it away. You fail to find your target, and by the time the ball passes through your legs you are already waiting for the clatter of stumps. Good grief – Warne has nutmegged you.

Brilliantly, subtly, Warne gave you three leg breaks in a row, just as MacGill did when he first came on to bowl. But, whereas MacGill just ripped his as much as he could, Warne graded the amount of spin he put on each one, each time slightly less than with the ball before. Warne may do many things in life to excess, but when it comes to his art he knows all about the advantages of restraint.

Nutmegged. When this most undignified fate befell Dipak Patel of New Zealand and Basit Ali of Pakistan people laughed, just as they will laugh at you now. As you head off on the long walk back to the pavilion, to resounding Aussie jeers from the circle of stands, you look towards Bell in the hope of some sort of reassuring gesture, but his eyes are fixed on the horizon. Oh dear, he's too embarrassed to even look at you. But Warne is looking at you from beneath an avalanche of head-pats and back-slaps from happy team-mates, and for the first time you see pity in the eyes of an Australian.

You return to the dressing room, sit in the corner, and, out of opening batsman's habit, check over your body for any cuts and bruises. But there's nothing. You've come to no physical harm whatsoever. But your mind feels like it's been burned. It's like you've just lost a game of chess – a game of chess in which, at best, you were thinking one or two moves ahead, while Warne was anticipating what might happen eight steps down the line. He works people out so fast. But he's not only thinking about you. He's also running a parallel game with the other batsman, while probably also thinking about how to sort out the next batsman to come as well.

Utterly frazzled, you sit for the next twenty minutes with a towel over your head, trying to think of nothing in particular. But it doesn't work. The thought that Warne will be waiting for you in the second innings keeps bursting to the surface.

That's how you played him. Let's look at how the most successful batsmen went about things.

The key to unlocking Warne's mysteries was through something not much commented upon: the line he bowled. Whereas most modern leg-spinners bowled at, or just outside, the line of off stump, Warne aimed at middle and leg, sometimes even outside leg. It was a matter of only a few inches, but it was a crucial distinction. This line made it very hard for the right-handed batsman to play straight or get a full, free swing at the ball, particularly when the ball was drifting sideways into his feet. He was often forced into ungainly manoeuvres – pushed off balance playing round his front pad and against the spin. It was messy and risky.

Of course, if Warne had had a better googly, he might have aimed nearer off stump more often (as MacGill did). But this shortcoming turned out to be a massive strength. 'Warne changed the way people thought about leg spin,' Michael Atherton said. 'From his line, he spins the ball so much that the leg-stump line becomes an attacking line, whereas in the past bowling at leg stump and outside was slightly defensive. He gave you no room to manoeuvre with outside off stump, and forced you to change the way you played.'

Perhaps the first batsman to come up with an answer was Pakistan's Salim Malik. Malik was a brilliant cricketer but a flawed man, whose career would end in the ignominy of a life ban for corruption (a sentence based partly on testimony from Warne). As a batsman, Malik briefly held a mastery over Warne that few matched. The strategy he devised was to take guard on leg stump when Warne was bowling over the wicket and take guard a few inches outside leg stump when he came round the wicket. This kept his eyes in line with the ball and gave him room to play proper, aggressive shots.

Malik eschewed leg-side strokes altogether and looked to play everything through the off – mainly cuts and cover drives. It was an unusual strategy, but proved a brilliant success. In his first Test series against Warne, in Pakistan in 1994, Malik scored 557 runs in three matches without being out to him once. 'I have never seen anyone play the great Australian as well as that,' Mushtaq Ahmed said. 'He played the ball so late that Warney would already have his hands up to claim a wicket, only to see Salim strike the ball . . . Warney had no chance against that kind of talent.' Mark Taylor, Warne's captain in 1994, said that in the end they decided to push point back and allow Malik a single, just to get him off strike.

Three years later, England batsman Nasser Hussain, who had played alongside Malik for Essex, scored a Test double-century against Warne at Edgbaston. 'I spoke to Sal about him and how he targeted the off side,' Hussain said. 'I generally took a leg-stump guard and I tried to hit him through the off side. It helped that I tended to play in-to-out through extra cover. The drift wasn't a problem for me. Then, obviously, if he started bowling further to leg you could sweep him.'

Although he didn't leave his crease, Malik was always positive and he felt that helped him establish a psychological advantage. Any sign of timidity and Warne would have seized on it. Asian batsmen – and Australians in domestic cricket – were generally more positive than players from England, South Africa or New Zealand. The left-handed Brian Lara was also very aggressive and quick on his feet, and scored more Test centuries against Warne than anyone else except Sachin Tendulkar. When once asked where he looked to score his runs against Warne, Lara replied, 'Everywhere.' Warne ranked Lara and Tendulkar as the best batsmen of his time at international level. 'Lara's placement was amazing,' he said. 'He can dominate and turn a game.' But he also knew that Lara took enough risks that the bowler was always in with a chance.

Naturally, sides learned from what they saw other teams do. One of the key elements in England's victory in the 2005 Ashes was that, urged on by their captain, Michael Vaughan, himself a fine player of leg spin, they finally sought to get after Warne. He took forty wickets, but went for more than 3 runs per over and was prevented from controlling the game as he had in the past.

Warne suffered most at the hands of Indian batsmen in India but there were mitigating factors. He usually went there short of full fitness, and wristy strokemakers such as Tendulkar, Rahul Dravid and V.V.S. Laxman made him pay a heavy price. They were able to hit him against the spin through midwicket, even out of the rough and even off middle stump, so that he was manoeuvred away from his usual line and ended up bowling on off stump, where he was also exposed. 'They weren't in awe of him,' Hussain said. 'Warne perhaps bowled too slow, and Laxman just took the ball on the full and used his wrists to get it away.' Warne said that Tendulkar's strength was that he got into position very quickly.

Chris Cairns, the New Zealand all-rounder, who at first struggled against Warne, improved after switching to a leg-stump guard. 'When I see the leg break go up in the air I run down the wicket, making sure I stay inside the line so I can free my arms at the point of contact,' he said. 'If I hit him a couple of times he'll put the men back . . . but I will still keep running down the wicket to hit his leg break over extra cover. If he bowls around the wicket into the rough I'll be more patient but try to play stand-up sweep shots.' Warne reckoned that the best shot ever played against him was when Cairns hit him over square leg on a turning pitch in Hamilton in 2000.

Kevin Pietersen sought to attack Warne if he bowled at him from over the wicket, and he felt that if Warne was forced to go round the wicket he could not be dismissed from there. 'I think about the angles and the degrees of spin and I don't think he can get me this way,' Pietersen wrote in his autobiography. Pietersen would then use his height to reach forward and play the slog sweep through the on side without leaving his crease, which he, like Salim Malik and Jacques Kallis, regarded as a cardinal sin. 'There's no worse way to get out than be stumped.'

But there is no greater testimony to Warne's status as the true champion of his craft than that he successfully countered so many of these assaults. These high-octane duels brought out the best in him. He liked the personal battles, and he liked winning them. His nerve never failed him. He was never beaten. He kept on coming, kept on gambling that eventually he'd come out on top.

He kept on plotting too, many moves ahead. The extent of his planning surprised even those who had been playing alongside him for years. 'The way he thinks about the game and sets batsmen up continues to amaze me,' Ricky Ponting said in 2006.

> He told me how an entire over against Kevin Pietersen was going to unfold at the Oval last year. During the tea break, he said to me, 'I'm going to start around the wicket for the first three balls, bowl them way outside leg stump, and he'll pad up to every one of them.' Then he said, 'I'll go back over the wicket fourth or fifth ball, bowl him a slow, loopy leg-spinner that pitches outside off stump that he'll try to slog-sweep over midwicket, and he'll miss it.' And that's what happened.

Left-handers had a natural advantage against him. They got a much clearer view of the ball than right-handers and didn't have to worry about the Blind Spot so much. They had to play at the ball more often, and it would turn into them from out of the footholds, but as long as they remained watchful things could be simpler. If Warne overpitched, for example, it was a free hit through the covers. One in three of all Test hundreds scored against Warne was by a left-handed batsman. But Warne, typically, had his counter-strategies, and statistically the least successful of all specialist Test batsmen against him – South Africa's Ashwell Prince – was a lefty.

Warne's tactics against a left-hander included using the ball that went straight on to have him caught at slip, or his leg break to win a bat–pad catch. Perhaps his favourite ploy, though, was pulling the batsman out of position with a series of balls outside off stump before getting him to drive at a big leg break and bowling him between bat and pad. Some of his most famous dismissals – against Strauss at Edgbaston in 2005 and against Shivnarine Chanderpaul at Sydney in 1996 for instance – were achieved in this way.

In the end he rarely came off second best. Salim Malik scored few runs against him when Pakistan toured Australia in 1995, while Hussain found life harder when Warne changed tack and started bowling straighter at him. He bowled over after over at Pietersen from round the wicket in Adelaide in 2006 and, though he didn't get him out, slowed Pietersen's scoring to a trickle. Pietersen scored 158 in the innings and Warne's tactics were criticized as negative, but later in the game he went over the wicket and bowled Pietersen round his legs, which proved a turning point in a match which Australia sensationally won from what looked a hopeless position. England's aggression of two years earlier had evaporated in the face of Warne's relentless pressure. 'Every ball was a hand grenade,' Warne said afterwards with obvious satisfaction.

Another episode illustrated just how resourceful he was. Warne's first significant match-winning performance occurred against West Indies, then the best team in the world, in 1992. When the sides next met, in the Caribbean three years later, the West Indian strokemakers were determined to reassert their authority. On the first morning of the series, West Indies collapsed to 6 for 3, but Carl Hooper – a highly gifted batsman who never achieved as much as he should have done – launched a blistering leg-side assault on Warne that Steve Waugh, later one of Warne's Test captains, described as the most courageous counter-attack he ever witnessed. Hooper hit Warne for five fours in two overs and in all scored 60 off 91 balls.

For a while, Warne found Hooper a real handful. The

problem, he realized, was that he couldn't work out when Hooper was going to charge down the pitch at him: Hooper would leave the crease very late and with no apparent warning. But Warne didn't give in. He pored over videotapes of Hooper batting, and after much research he thought he'd cracked his code: he noticed that when Hooper was about to come down the track, he would not glance down at his feet as he would at other times. 'The next time I ran in to bowl, I watched his face and brought my arm over with no intention of letting the ball go,' Warne said. 'His face told me all I needed to know and I never had the problem again.'

'I couldn't name fifteen innings that dominated him,' said Ian Healy, who kept wicket to Warne for seven years.

> His great skill was to move between plans. He knew what they were, and applied them one at a time. He would do it [consider his options] on the spot or in the dressing room. Rarely would he wreck a night working. He didn't overthink. He was a great uncomplicator. He was the only leg-spinner I knew who could so definitely change his plans within one ball. It took others time to shift their line from leg to off, but he could do it immediately and definitely. That was his other great skill, his accuracy.

Steve Waugh agreed that Warne was good at dealing with problems in a straightforward, cool-headed manner. 'In times when his form wasn't what he liked, he would pull out highlights of his career and take comfort in his stellar perform-ances,' Waugh wrote. 'This was often enough to get him back on track. He was a player who didn't need a lot of advice and he knew his game well. He had his own personal checklist that could get things back on track when needed.'

Warne's greatness was formed out of a blend of skill, hard work, intelligence and inextinguishable competitiveness. It was this all-round package that made him superior to other, merely very fine, bowlers. It was worth noting too that, despite his inspiring a generation of Australians, no young leg-spinner had in fifteen years followed him into the national team. His was a devilishly difficult art.

2

Mapping the Mind

NO CRICKETER'S LIFE, on or off the field, has aroused such interest, or been subject to such scrutiny, as Shane Warne's. He lived his whole career in front of television cameras and in front of unrivalled numbers of journalists ready to frame an article out of a single Warne delivery or gesture. He occasionally let himself down, but all in all he handled the attention and expectation that went with his position with remarkable equanimity and grace. He drew people to cricket because he created the sense that, when he was involved, *anything* might happen. He made cricket exciting. He made it cool.

Warne's contribution to cricket, his status in the game, could be debated for a long time. At this point it is too early for a final reckoning, but the fact that he retired with more Test wickets (708) and more Test wins (92) to his name than anyone before him is a fair indicator of his ability and steely-eyed competitiveness, which stood out even in an Australian dressing room famed for its love of success. A sportsman's stock tends to rise the moment he leaves the stage, and in Australia – where Warne's failings had always counted heavily against him – his certainly rose sharply upon news in 2006 that he was retiring from international cricket. 'The Bradman of Bowlers' became the buzz phrase.

At the very least Warne merits a bowl-out with the very

best bowlers the game has seen. He was found wanting in very few areas. Even his struggles in India required qualification, because injuries and fatigue undermined two of his tours there. He was a slightly late developer, but only slightly. By the age of twenty-three he was winning Test matches for his country, and few bowlers – especially spinners, whose craft takes time to master – have done that so young. By the time Warne was twenty-seven, John Woodcock, the distinguished former cricket correspondent of *The Times*, placed him thirteenth in his list of all-time greatest cricketers. And by the age of thirty, he was judged fourth among the greatest cricketers of the twentieth century by *Wisden*; his nearest rival among specialist bowlers was Dennis Lillee, who was bowling fast for Australia when Warne was a child – and who was also, while we are at it, no angel himself. At thirty-five his portrait hung in the Long Room at Lord's.

That Warne could make such an astonishing impact on the game owed much to individual genius but also to a confluence of events. In fact circumstances were perfect for him. Spin bowling was in recession when he arrived on the scene. This made it hard for him to break through, but once he had proved his worth he had the field to himself for several years. He liked that position very much: running from the front and running alone (he never liked other Australian leg-spinners queering his pitch). He got a long way on the element of surprise, there not being many batsmen around with the relevant experience and talent to take him on – and a fair way too by being combative.

But the other crucial factor, which helped prolong his success, was something that no one could have foreseen – that the various scandals in which he became embroiled in the second half of his career actually acted as a creative spur, driving him to even greater heights. The more trouble he got into, the more he seemed to want to make amends – to his family, his friends and the wider public – through his astonishing feats on the field. It led to one of the most brilliant and colourful of sporting lives.

Warne was also a very lucky cricketer. Good fortune played a large part in his story – and at no time more than at the start.

When Warne arrived in Test cricket, on 2 January 1992, in the middle of a home series against India, spin bowling was in such poor health that many doctors wouldn't have hesitated before grabbing a pillow, suffocating the patient, and sending the body for burial in an unmarked grave. It just didn't seem worth bothering with. Fast bowling – explosive pace laced with physical intimidation – had been winning Test matches for so long that it was hard to remember that there could be a Route B.

Few spinners were even capable of finding employment in Tests at the point of Warne's arrival. England were in the early stages of a tour of New Zealand, where Phil Tufnell, a young left-arm spinner of wayward form, erratic temperament and chronic insecurity, would shortly bowl them to victory in the first Test in Christchurch. As Tufnell had done something similar against the mighty West Indies at the Oval a few months earlier, English cricket would greet this event with wild celebrations at the thought that it had finally unearthed a new bowling star. Yet the number of Tests that Tufnell would win over the next ten years roughly equated to the number of fingers he needed to hold his next cigarette.

New Zealand, for their part, were as usual strapped for resources and playing cricket on green seaming pitches that could hardly have been less conducive to wrist spin. Their best spinner was Dipak Patel, who had come to them via Nairobi, where he was born, and Worcestershire, with whom he spent eleven seasons before tiring of waiting for England to pick him and emigrating to Auckland. New Zealand continued picking him until he was almost forty, despite a strike rate of just two wickets per game. As one of their Test batsmen, Ken Rutherford, said, 'If I was a young leg-spinner, I'd be playing tennis.'

West Indies and India were both touring Australia. Since the late 1970s, of course, West Indies had established themselves as the undisputed world champions by packing their side with fast bowlers, and had next to no time for spin. It happened that one of their leading batsmen, Carl Hooper, bowled off spin, so he was given the job of turning his arm over if the quicks failed to do the business or conditions were especially conducive to the turning ball. By the time he played the last of his 102 Tests, in 2002, Hooper had taken 114 wickets at the exorbitant cost of almost 50 apiece. Unusually for them, India fielded just one specialist spinner in Venkatapathy Raju, plus all-rounder Ravi Shastri.

Pakistan, who were playing host to Sri Lanka, were even less enamoured of spin than West Indies. They had just started giving the new ball to Waqar Younis and Wasim Akram, with Imran Khan as back-up, and were in thrall to the lethal reverse swing these players generated. Sri Lanka took with them Don Anurasiri, a left-armer who would play Test cricket for twelve years without doing anything the least bit memorable. Later that year, an off-spinner of unorthodox bent, Muttiah Muralitharan, would help Sri Lanka to only their third win in ten years as a Test nation; within three years he had developed into a seasoned match-winner. Once he had added a 'doosra' to his armoury, Murali started taking wickets at an unrivalled rate, though he would never prove as subtle a strategist as Warne and there was sustained controversy about the legality of his methods.

South Africa were a few months away from returning to Test cricket after the lifting of the anti-apartheid sports boycott, but when they did come back they took the field without a single specialist spinner.

As for Australia, they were in a state close to crisis over spin bowling. For a long time the spinners they'd fielded were of ordinary ability and mostly over the age of thirty. Before Warne was brought in, they went with Peter Taylor, an unexceptional off-spinner, who had done little since taking eight wickets as a left-field selection in a dead rubber game against England five years previously. (Australia's loss of the 1986-87 Ashes series with a match to spare owed much to their inability to field a threatening spinner.) At this point Taylor was ahead of the promising if temperamental Tim May in the pecking order. Taylor could barely have been less like the young larrikin who was about to replace him: he was thirty-five years old, wore his shirts buttoned at the wrists, and looked as though life in a bank would be far too racy for him. He appeared only sporadically in Tests, Australia often preferring to rely on their fast bowlers being given a breather by Allan Border and Greg Matthews, both of whom were primarily chosen for their batting.

And that was it. An array of mediocre left-armers and offies, only one of whom – Raju – was good enough to take his Test wickets at fewer than 37 runs apiece.

As for wrist spin, it barely registered on Test cricket's radar. A few months after this, Mushtaq Ahmed would play his first full series for Pakistan, Anil Kumble would begin to make his mark for India, and England would give a debut to Ian Salisbury. But Salisbury would never make it at the highest level and Mushtaq's breakthrough would not come for another three years – until a tour of Australia, when he exchanged tips with Warne. Warne helped Mushtaq, whose speciality was the googly, improve his leg break and Mushtaq bowled Pakistan to victory in Sydney. But Mushtaq would be a victim of Pakistan's mercurial selection process, and his Test career was not as long as it should have been. Kumble wasn't a conventional leg-spinner at all, concentrating on very brisk googlies and flippers, which helped him prove more durable than any 'leg-spinner' in Test history except Warne himself.

Various theories have been put forward as to why spin went through such a fallow period. With no demands to bowl overs at a respectable rate, captains could slow things down to keep their fast bowlers fresh; this became much harder to do after a minimum of fifteen overs per hour in Tests was imposed in 1991. Some have blamed the demands of 'keeping things tight' in one-day cricket, though this ignores the fact that some of the best leg-spinners in history – Clarrie Grimmett, Bill O'Reilly and Richie Benaud of Australia and India's Subhash Gupte, for example – were among the most accurate bowlers there have been. The wayward leggie was chiefly an English phenomenon. In truth, it was a golden age for fast bowling and a bronze one for spin.

Fifteen months into Warne's Test career, Martin Crowe of New Zealand hailed him as potentially the finest leg-spinner in the world. In one sense it was a big statement, but in another it was a statement of the obvious because Warne scarcely had a mountain of rivals.

Leg spin really had only one champion in recent memory. The great Abdul Qadir – Mushtaq's boyhood hero – had played the last of his sixty-seven Tests for Pakistan at Lahore in December 1990, when Brian Lara, making his debut, had provided him with his 236th and final wicket. At the time, Qadir was one of only eight leg-spinners in history with 100 Test wickets to his name, and one of only four who could boast 200.

History has been unjust to Qadir. After Warne took the world by storm, he was commonly hailed as the saviour of the leg-spinner's art, when in fact Qadir had nobly carried the torch throughout the 1980s. (It wouldn't be the only time the facts were prevented from getting in the way of a good Warne story.) Qadir created a wonderful magic with an elixir of leggies, flippers and googlies delivered from a bounding, bouncing run with such a flurry of arms that it was hard to spot the variations. Qadir's googly was far better than Warne's. He also played the part of sorcerer with relish. At the suggestion of Imran he grew a piratical-looking beard to add to his aura (OK, he thought it might work with the women too) and took to studying the body language and psychology of batsmen. This was quite advanced stuff for its time.

But Qadir had two shortcomings. One was impatience, a common but harmful fault among leggies. The other was that he was always much happier playing in his native land than doing the round of foreign airports, hotels and cricket grounds. He didn't always make Pakistan's tours, and if he did he was liable to get into scrapes. He was sent home early from New Zealand for indiscipline, and on another occasion he thumped a heckler during a Test in Barbados (the police were called, but no charges were pressed). His record reflected his moodiness on the road. While he took 168 wickets at 27 runs apiece in Pakistan, in other countries his return was 68 at 48.

So Qadir's gospel didn't quite circle the globe as it should have done. Opposing teams, most of whom would rather have had their teeth removed without anaesthetic than tour Pakistan, had no trouble making excuses for their failures in his backyard. Third-rate hotels, poor food, dodgy local umpiring . . . you name it, they'd plead it in mitigation. So the beaten batsmen weren't going home with tales of Qadir's wonder. Nor were the missionary effects of satellite television yet being felt. Not a lot of Test cricket in Pakistan in the 1980s was accessible to foreign TV audiences.

Qadir just missed the wave of cricketing celebrity that Warne caught. But if he was bitter, he didn't show it. In retirement he ran a modest cricket academy on a scruffy plot of land next to the Gaddafi Stadium in Lahore and gave interviews — if possible for money — to visiting pilgrim journalists.

One of the few batsmen to apply the lessons he learned from watching Qadir to the challenges posed by Warne was Salim Malik, who played a lot of domestic and international cricket with Qadir and often faced him in the nets. Although Qadir possessed the superior googly, and Warne the better flipper, Malik felt their repertoires were basically similar and that knowledge of Qadir helped him devise his brilliant plan to defeat Warne in their early duels. When David Lloyd coached England on a tour of Australia in 1998–99, he called up Qadir, then playing club cricket in Melbourne, to help prepare his players for Warne.

Leg-spinners were not uncommon in Australia's domestic cricket, which may explain why some Australian batsmen played him positively in state matches. But when Warne first came along in Test cricket, few international batsmen had the knowledge or expertise to deal with the problems he set. Circumstances had handed him a massive head start.

* * *

There was more to it than that, though. The dominance of fast bowling over the previous fifteen years had subjected a whole generation of batsmen to a terrible physical and mental battering. They had been conditioned to one particularly brutal type of cricket, and after so long in the trenches they knew only one way of survival. They had spent all their careers leaping around on the back foot, fending straight balls off their ribs and heads, and cutting and pulling those with any width. Was there another way of playing? They were about to find out that there was, but that they were ill-equipped to do anything about it.

It is hard to exaggerate the fast bowlers' supremacy between the mid-1970s and the early 1990s, when the legislators took severe steps to curb their power by limiting the number of bouncers they could bowl. In hindsight they perhaps went too far, because the real reason for the reign of terror was a freakishly strong generation of fast bowlers, which with time withered of its own accord. There has been nothing like it before or since. West Indies had enough quicks to field two jaw-shattering attacks of their own.

This had a direct effect on run-scoring levels, which sank like so many broken cheekbones. The sheer quality of the bowling was one factor in this; another was the introduction of protective headgear, which was cumbersome and inhibiting. Eventually technology caught up, and strong but lightweight helmets became generally available. But between 1976 and 1990 there were only four instances of a batsman topping 250 in a Test innings. For the most part, runs were eked out in painstaking fashion. The most anyone took off West Indies in a day's Test cricket in the 1980s was 154 – by England opener Graham Gooch, arguably the finest player of fast bowling of the time. By contrast, in later years such a personal tally in a day would become commonplace, except perhaps when Australia were bowling.

Considering the time he spent at the crease, Gooch proved remarkably resilient. He sustained nothing more serious than a couple of cracked hands. Others were less fortunate. Smashed skulls and broken arms, noses and cheekbones became cricket's collateral damage. Later, as Pakistan developed reverse swing, crushed toes were also common sights in hospital X-ray departments.

England and Australia, who tended to play West Indies most, probably had it worst. When West Indies toured Australia in the late 1980s (for the last time before Warne arrived on the scene), the casualties among the home team were particularly severe. Geoff Lawson, who failed to wear a helmet with a grille, had his jaw broken so badly at Perth that one teammate said it looked as though someone had struck him with a large mallet. Lawson was eating food through a straw for the next six weeks. Steve Waugh was also hit on the jaw, less severely, and also had to amend his eating habits for a while. Ian Healy was hit in the groin three times, and Mark Taylor was generally bruised. When the sides next squared up, in the Caribbean in 1991, Craig McDermott – a fast bowler himself, and no great batsman – was struck on the forehead by Courtney Walsh and was never the same at the crease again. David Boon was smashed on the chin and, in a warm-up match, Mark Waugh was clattered on the head.

The overall effect of these incidents was to erode the confidence of the whole Australian side. The physical threat was at the back of everyone's mind. And what was true for the Australians was also the case for others.

Steve Waugh became one of the bravest and most effective batsmen against short-pitched bowling but, as it did with everyone, it took him time to come to terms with the uncompromising nature of the challenge. Of his first Test against West Indies, in Brisbane in 1988, Waugh wrote:

> I felt intimidated the moment I set foot on the ground. These guys had a very real aura about them . . . above all else, [they] were certainly much more impressive physically than I was. I felt like a boy on a man's errand and played accordingly . . . I was mesmerized by [Malcolm Marshall's] explosive run-up, his systematic and beautifully balanced front-on action and his speedy arm . . . He was a martial-arts work in full flow, with a wrist that could eliminate you in one swipe.

Fast bowling was an examination not just of courage, but also of mental resolve. 'These guys had the skill to extinguish all but the strongest resolve,' Waugh added.

> Once they had a player at their mercy, I never saw anyone come back and reverse the trend . . . They had the ability to create a vulnerability in you that you didn't know was there . . . The battle, of course, remained in large part between our ears but with their stellar reputations, the adoring media attention and their relentless assaults on the field, it was exceptionally hard to compartmentalize the issues at hand.

Within ten years, very similar comments could have been made about playing Australia, except that Warne's mind-bending bowling had replaced hostile fast bowling as the principal weapon.

Ashley Mallett, who bowled off spin for Australia with diminishing effect between 1968 and 1980 as pace bowling became ascendant, was well placed to comment on the short-comings of batsmen who, armed with heavy bats and closed minds, struggled to abandon their old defensive mindsets and adjust to the challenges posed by the young Warne. The problem was that for fifteen years batsmen had thought of little else but defence. Anyone caught dancing down the track to Jeff Thomson, Curtly Ambrose or Imran Khan would have been shipped off to the nearest lunatic asylum. That's assuming the nearest hospital didn't claim him first. When Warne came on the scene, aggressive batting had rarely been more out of fashion.

So what tended to happen was that the world's batsmen, presented with this new threat, adopted their default position of staying in the crease and concentrating on survival. While this was perhaps understandable, it represented a catastrophic error of judgement because it played directly into Warne's hands.

'Shane Warne looms as big an ogre for Test teams today as that seemingly invincible barrage of pace from West Indies throughout the 1980s, against which patience was the key,' Mallett wrote in *The Cricketer* in 1998. 'Most deliveries were either at your throat, over your head or aimed with precision at your feet. Against such tactics fast scoring was nigh-on impossible. Survival *was* possible. Against Warne batsmen must take him on.'

Batsmen needed to completely overhaul their mental outlooks if they were to have a chance against Warne, Mallett added.

Negative thoughts are like cancer cells. They eat away at the positives: left unchecked they corrupt, distort and finally destroy. Warne lifts at the sight of a crease-bound batsman: his next victim . . . Fear of failure is such a psychological hurdle that often a batsman becomes so intent on survival that all his natural flair is lost. The odd full toss is tamely blocked and any long-hop is hit hard into the ground – a mis-hit born out of the mind playing cruel tricks; over and again planting the seed of destruction with the thought that no bowler of this stature could possibly bowl a full toss or rank long-hop.

As Mallett observed, it was the teams from the subcontinent – where spin had always played a part in affairs and raw pace rarely had the same impact on unresponsive pitches – who tackled Warne best.

Their method is based on attack. They utilize all the mind's positives, never dwelling on what Warne might do if there is a false stroke. The Pakistanis, Indians and Sri Lankans are aware that to stay at home, to wait and prod against Warne is akin to sitting on a mountain top holding an iron rod aloft at the height of an electrical storm: the fatal strike inevitable.

So, all in all, things really could hardly have been lying more nicely for Australia's young star. Here you are, Warney, here's a bunch of dead-eyed, shell-shocked war veterans. Go on, see if you can pick their pockets without them noticing.

Warne was also fortunate that Australian cricket was on the rise. After numerous humiliations at the hands of Clive Lloyd's West Indians and three series defeats to England between 1981 and 1986 drastic action had been called for – and taken. A long-term policy was devised. Young players of character were identified and encouraged. Allan Border – not an obvious leader of men save for the example he set with his gritty batting – was persuaded to stay as captain and Bob Simpson was appointed as the first full-time coach. A more uncompromising approach to every aspect of the game was pursued. From here on in, Australian cricket would be self-interested, hard-nosed and successful.

Progress was steady, but no more. Nerveless cricket in tight situations delivered victory in the one-day World Cup on the subcontinent in 1987, and the Ashes were regained in overwhelming fashion in England two years later. But one-day cricket is one-day cricket: a lot hangs by fine threads, and not too much could be read into a single good tournament. Five years later, Australia bombed out of the next World Cup, staged on their own soil, when they had at least as strong a group of players as in 1987, if not stronger. And the victory in England had much to do with English cricket being in disarray following the sacking of Mike Gatting as captain and plans for an English rebel tour to apartheid South Africa.

Much work still remained to be done on improving Australian skills and fitness, which was why it took longer to bring down the walls of the great West Indian citadel. After a heavy defeat at home in 1988–89, Australia showed spirit in losing 2–1 in each of their next two meetings with the unofficial world champions (an official world championship wasn't inaugurated until 2001) before they finally got their hands on the Frank Worrell Trophy for the first time in seventeen years in the Caribbean in 1995. This task so dominated Australian thinking that, as we shall see, Australian board officials opted not to suspend Warne and Mark Waugh when they learned – while the team was in transit to the Caribbean – that the pair had received money from an Indian bookmaker. They merely fined them instead.

There is a strong case for saying that the very fact that Australia were forced to push the extra mile to achieve their supreme goal was actually the making of them. Their desperate efforts to gain parity with the best team in the world forced them to raise their standards to even higher levels than they might have otherwise done. They strove to eradicate the smallest flaws within their own games and to root out every last weakness in their opponents.

A crucial element was that, after years of bombardment, they finally came to terms with the unremitting diet of short-pitched bowling. Steve Waugh, who averaged more than 100 in the 1995 series, led the way. He was happy to take blows to the body – indeed, would show off his ice-packed bruises with pride – as long as he clung to the belief that he could survive and eventually chisel out runs. He channelled his energies into remaining mentally composed, whatever the hardships, and in the end he achieved a rarefied state of mind that he described as 'a certain type of loneliness that I found extremely peaceful' and with which he was able to dispose of 'dangerous self-doubting messages'.

Waugh put great store by looking positive and acting positively. 'He told me that the most important aspect to him was body language,' Nasser Hussain wrote in *Wisden* in 2004. 'He liked to almost sprint to the crease to emphasize that he was relishing the battle ahead; he liked to give off an aura of aggression . . . Almost on purpose, [he] maximized the challenge to bring the best out of himself.'

In 1995 Waugh engaged in several face-to-face confrontations with Curtly Ambrose, the steepling leader of the West Indies attack and the bowler who had most tormented him. 'I wasn't going to just stand there and cop physical intimidation,' Waugh recalled. 'It was fightback time . . . We needed to show the Windies it was our turn to dictate proceedings.' By in effect saying, 'You may still bruise my body, but you can no longer hurt my mind,' Waugh's attitude signalled that the years of brutality were over.

If physical courage was one way of showing an unwillingness

to be trampled underfoot, verbal defiance – of the kind Waugh displayed to Ambrose – was another. Sledging had been around for a while but Border used it as a key weapon in his fight to harden the minds of his players and it was a policy endorsed by each of his successors – Mark Taylor, Steve Waugh and Ricky Ponting – even if they were publicly at pains to say that they didn't condone outright abuse. Other nations, eager to match Aussie ruthlessness, followed suit.

It was no coincidence that, as the physical threat from hostile fast bowling subsided, so orchestrated sledging began to flourish. As the scope for breaking bones shrank, so the imperative to find mental chinks in the opposition expanded.

Border's brand of tough cricket reached its apogee in 1993, the year he himself made his last tour of England and Warne made his first. The notion that personal abuse was off limits was confounded by the language adopted by Merv Hughes, Australia's principal fast bowler, whose most colourful tirades were directed at Michael Atherton and Graeme Hick, but Border himself – and Warne – played their part. *Wisden* was scathing in its verdict:

> That he [Border] will be remembered in England with respect rather than affection stemmed from his condoning, not infrequently his participation in, the sledging of opponents and umpires during play, in open violation of the International Cricket Council's code of conduct . . . Border, who usually fielded within earshot of his bowlers, may also have contributed indirectly to the more obvious mis-judgements of lbws and bat–pad catches, estimated by some at more than a dozen in the series, by failing to stamp out the questioning of decisions that sapped the umpires' confidence.

In a more understated fashion, Taylor allowed sledging to continue during his time as captain, while Waugh was a more unashamed advocate, claiming 'mental disintegration', or 'putting doubts in batsmen's minds', as a legitimate tactic – again as long as direct abuse was not involved. But the lie was given to these semantic distinctions when Graeme Smith, of South Africa, outlined in a magazine interview the treatment he had received during his Test debut against Australia in 2002. This mainly involved being sworn at repeatedly by Matthew Hayden and Warne.

Smith said later that he regretted going public with his account on the grounds that, as the argument goes, 'what happens on the field should stay on the field.' And, once he became South Africa captain, Smith became known for targeting opponents with some pretty unpleasant personal attacks of his own. But by then he had learned that playing hard – playing the Australian way – was the way to go. Hussain, who as captain oversaw the start of England's renaissance, was an ardent admirer of Australia's 'no holds barred' approach – further acknowledgement of Waugh's contention that at the highest level of the game, where technically there is little to choose between participants, cricket is largely played in the mind and it is fair to test how mentally strong your opponent is.

Smith was not alone in his debut experience. The Australians viewed any newcomer as someone whose mettle was worth testing, someone whom they might be able to kill off mentally right at the start of his career. Just as a young batsman would have been greeted with a barrage of bouncers by the West Indies, so Australia's opponents were now welcomed with volleys of abuse.

In essence, what happened to Australia between 1986 and 1995 was that they toughened themselves up on the inside and out. They turned themselves into arguably mentally the most resilient cricket team there had ever been and verbally probably the most aggressive too. In doing so, they signalled that the mind had become the game's new battleground. If cricket was a test primarily of physical courage in the 1980s, it became one of mental strength in the 1990s.

This was an area in which Warne would come to excel. For a start, the complex strategies of his bowling presented one of the severest tests of the mental resolve of any batsman. But Warne also developed an uncanny knack for spotting technical or mental chinks in the armour of opponents and playing on them – either through what he did with the ball or through what he said with his mouth. If he sensed a batsman was uncertain he became very vocal and generally tried to make his opponent feel as though he was not worthy of being on the pitch. He also adopted The Stare, as Waugh had done.

As his confidence and reputation grew, so Warne had more to say for himself out in the middle. Although Smith's account showed him being downright abusive, Warne often used quite subtle ways to goad or tease an opponent into a mistake. It wasn't always about animosity. By his later years, Warne was perhaps the most talkative cricketer on the planet. It was partly that he was always scheming, and words were one element in his schemes, but it also had something to do with a desire to be always involved in the game. Waugh might have liked the loneliness of battle, but Warne much preferred verbal skirmishing. He enjoyed the contest all the more for being able to verbally engage with a batsman or umpire. Perhaps the chatter also helped keep at bay those 'dangerous self-doubting messages' that Waugh spoke of. Warne was an amazingly self-confident cricketer, but in truth the self-confidence merely hid those same self-doubting messages from view.

Warne was not just an outrageously gifted spinner of the ball but one of the cleverest cricketers the game has seen. But he was fortunate to join a team that was strong, stable and successful. It provided one of the best environments in which to learn about mind games.

3

The Chosen One

NATURE BLESSES GREAT sportsmen with at least one exceptional gift. It might be a physical attribute such as speed, power, height or suppleness. Or a mental one – discipline, self-belief or motivation. Occasionally, if they're very lucky, they'll be granted two. A select few get several.

Warne was not only a great cricketer, he proved himself an extraordinary cricketer very quickly once he had fully committed himself to the game. In 1993, his first year of uninterrupted Test cricket, he claimed a remarkable 72 wickets. This was a tally that had been bettered by very few bowlers, ever. Yet, as we shall see, a few months earlier he had lacked many of the qualities – not the special ones, just the basics – regarded as necessary in a successful sportsman.

To add to the drama of his rise, Warne was a late convert to cricket. Sport was always a central part of the family culture, with his mother, Brigitte, having been good at running, basketball and tennis until glandular fever hit her at the age of fourteen, while his father, Keith, was a good tennis player. But there was no particular passion for cricket and, although he played cricket at school and in backyard games with his younger brother, Jason, for most of his teens Warne was more enthusiastic about Australian Rules football and tennis. Cricket was largely something he went along with because his mates played it.

Details of earlier generations of Warnes are scant – investigations are hampered by Australia's strict privacy laws – but it was his father's side of the family that had the deeper roots in Australia. His father was born in Australia in the early 1940s; his mother's family arrived from western Germany only towards the end of the decade, when Brigitte was three years old.

Warne rarely talked about his family's origins, if indeed he was fully aware of them. If he lacks curiosity on this subject, it would not be unusual; until recently, the collective desire of Australians to ignore their felon origins – if that is what they were in the case of the Warnes – was strong. The 'convict stain' was not addressed in school textbooks, and there was no easy means of discovering whether ancestors were forcibly transported or emigrated voluntarily from Britain. When the Warnes arrived in Australia, and where they had come from, is unknown. Passenger lists show groups of Warnes arriving by boat throughout the second half of the nineteenth century and the early years of the twentieth century; the height of the traffic was the 1850s and '60s, when the gold rush and an economic boom were in full flow. UK censuses of the same period suggest that Warnes were concentrated in Suffolk, Cornwall, Devon and Hampshire.

One of the few public references Warne made to his possible ancestry came in a television advert he took part in for Sky TV's coverage of the 2005 Ashes. In it, he was portrayed as a convict being hauled in chains on to a transport ship bound for Australia. As he was led up the gangplank, Warne looked back towards land and said, 'I'll be back.'

His mother's family came from Germany as part of a large-scale programme of migration to Australia that followed the Second World War. There was a labour shortage in Australia, while millions of people in Europe had been displaced by

the war, and Australia reached agreements with many govern-
ments, including those in the UK, Holland, Turkey,
Yugoslavia, Italy and Germany, to encourage migrants. By
1950, almost 200,000 people had arrived in Australia – some
through government-assisted passage – and to most of them
their new home must have seemed like a land of milk and
honey, provided they were able to integrate happily with
the local community. There were reports that Germans
who moved to Australia after the First World War suffered
prejudicial treatment, but there seems to have been less of
a problem after 1945. Brigitte's family settled in Victoria,
about 100 miles along the coast west from Melbourne.

Brigitte and Keith married in 1966, and Shane Keith Warne
was born in the inland Melbourne region of Ferntree Gully
on 13 September 1969. While Shane was still young, the
family moved house a few times before settling at Black
Rock, a small, quiet suburb on the shores of Port Phillip
Bay. It was a comfortably middle-class area, which reflected
the family's financially solid background. Keith Warne was
an insurance consultant; the offices of Warne & Webb are
situated among the trees and glass of St Kilda Road, a hand-
some Melbourne street. The family took holidays in
Queensland and around the area where Brigitte's family was
based – at Apollo Bay and at Colac, where one of her sisters
lived on a farm.

Warne's childhood friends remember his parents as being
enviably friendly and easy-going. Keith Warne's great
enthusiasm was cars, and his interest instilled in his eldest
son a life-long passion for flash vehicles. Warne recalled that
he used to earn his pocket-money by putting out the garbage
and washing his father's steady turnover of cars.

The Warne family unit was strong. Jason would act as
Warne's manager for a while, and Warne's parents often

attended his matches, at home and overseas. His mother, who has been described as 'brash, loud and full of fun', was a proud and excited supporter of her son's sporting career from its earliest days, and it would be not unreasonable to assume that it was her close attention that was the starting point of Shane's love of being loved.

Those who knew Warne well said that he always listened to his father's advice, while his mother, although she enjoyed life, possessed quite a puritanical streak: she could be quite strict about appearance and general behaviour. Warne clearly grew up with a strong sense of how to behave; for all his ferocious competitiveness on the field, and some of his private misdemeanours off it, he was usually extremely polite in public, and most people meeting him for the first time would find it hard to dislike him. 'He gets misunderstood and misconstrued so much,' said Kevin Pietersen, who became a close friend. 'People think he's a naughty boy; he's got this image of being an absolute fool who nobody likes. But he's one of the most generous, unselfish, well-mannered people you could meet.' His last press conference as a Test cricketer was typical, Warne ending it by thanking the journalists.

Another thing that it would be reasonable to assume was that fine cuisine was never a strong point in Brigitte's household. Her sons were seemingly so constantly indulged in fast food that even Shane's extensive globetrotting was unable to broaden his taste. Indeed, he steadfastly insisted on sticking to the most basic food at all times, and was never happier than when eating pineapple pizzas or chips.

In fact, his tastes in most things were to change remarkably little. When he was a youth they were playing sport, playing cards, driving fast cars, attending to his appearance, looking at pretty girls, and eating junk food – and that is pretty much how they stayed. And yet the most important constant in his character was that he always wanted to make people like him. This need seemed to hot-wire him to a profound understanding of their natures and, eventually, how they might behave were he to, let's say, bowl a series of balls at them.

For the Warne boys, competitive sport was part of the everyday scene, as it was for many Australians. By his early teens, Shane was showing himself to be good at tennis, Aussie Rules football and swimming, as well as cricket – though nothing out of the ordinary. One of Warne's most vivid childhood memories is of, at the age of thirteen, catching the train into the city with his brother to watch the final day of the Boxing Day Test match against England at the Melbourne Cricket Ground. Australia's last-wicket pair of Allan Border and Jeff Thomson needed 37 runs to win the game and regain the Ashes. The match could have been over in just one ball, but entry was free and the Warne boys went along for the lark. Warne remembers Jason screaming at England's Norman Cowans, fielding on the boundary in front of them, 'You're rubbish, Cowans!' He also went to the MCG to watch Aussie Rules matches.

At fifteen Warne won a sports scholarship to Mentone Grammar School, a modest private school situated a couple of suburbs down the coast from Black Rock. He seems to have taken his scholarship literally: he was at Mentone to study sport, not books. He was never strong or particularly interested in academic work. He first started playing organized cricket at thirteen but his original ambition was to play Aussie Rules. He was signed by St Kilda Saints as a junior player straight from school, and until the club rejected him for a professional contract some eighteen months later, he would certainly have given no thought to pursuing a cricket career.

Teachers and schoolfriends remember Warne as something of a lovable rogue, usually in the thick of the talking and laughing, generally the centre of attention. And generally good at sport.

Initially, it was Warne's batting rather than his bowling that stood out. When he joined St Kilda Cricket Club after leaving school in 1988, and after a brief and unremarkable spell with Brighton CC, Warne came recommended to them as someone 'who looked quite good as a batsman'. He was tried in the club's fourths as a batsman who could bowl a bit. He later moved up to the thirds, still as a batsman, though by then he was showing form as a bowler in the nets and got a few wickets in matches. He bowled some medium pace as well as spin.

It would be a long time before he entered the tunnel of obsession that usually encompasses the all-time sporting greats at an early stage. At twelve years old, Cassius Clay was rising at before five o'clock in the morning to run several miles, and would then spend the afternoon training in the gym. In the year he turned eleven, Tiger Woods entered thirty-three junior tournaments and won them all. At twelve, Björn Borg was playing tennis nine hours a day, seven days a week. At nine, Boris Becker was getting up at 4 a.m. to watch on television Borg play matches in Australia; at fifteen, Becker had left home to go on the road as a junior tennis player, and at seventeen he won Wimbledon. At nine, Don Bradman was for hours hitting a golf ball with a single stump at the back of the family home in Bowral, in rural New South Wales. All were driven in a way Warne was not until he was into his twenties.

And yet it emerged that Warne did possess one exceptional gift that Nature had bestowed on him. That it was a physical attribute is surprising in one sense, because he was not obviously the most athletically gifted person. He was not particularly tall. His legs were stocky, not ideal for running fast, and he carried too much weight, the result of the love of junk food that never died. It was absolutely no surprise, therefore, that his cherished hopes of a career in Aussie Rules failed to materialize. As he himself admitted, 'I did not quite have what it took to make it . . . I lacked pace.' Again, 'I was just too short . . . I wasn't fast enough.'

What Warne had, though, was unusual strength in his hands, wrists and shoulders. In fact the power in his upper body bordered on the freakish. It was probably helped by all the sport he participated in, especially the swimming. But there may have been another contributory factor. When he was eight years old, a boy at school jumped down on him and somehow this caused both of Warne's legs to break. He was briefly in plaster from the waist down, and spent a whole year paddling himself around on a little cart that was like a tiny sunlounger on wheels. This must surely have affected his physique, as Warne conceded. 'It wasn't a lot of fun at the time,' he said, 'but maybe all of that wheeling around gave me the strength in my wrists and shoulders that enable me to give the ball a big rip today.' Warne's habit of walking on the balls of his feet may also have had its origins in this accident.

The biggest problem for young leg-spinners is having the strength to consistently turn the ball. Not for Warne. He could do it from the start, and kept on doing it. Originally inspired by watching leg spin bowled at his first club, East Sandringham, in his early teens, he found that he could spin the ball all the time. He may have been inaccurate at first, but for Warne the gift of being able to give the ball a rip was always there.

This strength was something that struck all the experts

who saw him as a youngster. Shaun Graf, who bowled fast in one-dayers for Australia and captained Warne at St Kilda, said, 'He has got stubby little hands but is very strong in the wrists, forearms and shoulders.' Bob Simpson, the then Australia coach, first watched Warne when he was twenty. 'I was totally impressed by his ability to spin the ball,' he said. 'He had wonderful hands . . . The strength of the boy.' Jack Potter, his first coach at the Australian cricket academy, said, 'It's his shoulders. He's got big shoulders and a big chest.' Rod Marsh, a later head of the academy, and Mark Taylor were impressed by how much Warne made the ball 'hum' through the air. Warne was twenty-one when Peter Sleep first played against him: 'He spun the ball a mile,' Sleep said. 'It was all to do with the strength of the hand, wrist and shoulder.'

Terry Jenner, who would become Warne's closest confidant and mentor, first encountered him at around the same time and remembered 'fabulous hand strength', along with the curious fact that there were no callouses on his spinning fingers. This, it transpired, was because Warne, for some reason, held the ball in a weak grip. While most leg-spinners, perhaps conscious of the revs they want to impart, hold the ball quite tightly, risking the blisters that cut short some careers, Warne just let it rest in his hand. It was an artist's touch.

'He always spun it always,' Jenner told me.

You spin it with your fingers and wrist, and that's where his gift was. He was quite stocky, but that's only an attribute that helped him get shape on the ball. The shoulders and hips are used to transport spin to the other end. You can lose spin by not using your body well, but you can't gain any. As I always say, 'PEP'. Power comes from your shoulders, Energy from your hips, Pivot as a consequence transfers your weight . . . The shoulders right down to your feet – it's a package. I call us coaches 'gift-enhancers'. We don't create anybody; we just help them get the best out of their gift.

Ian Healy, who kept wicket to Warne more than anyone, said, 'If the definition of genius is someone who can do something 5 per cent better than anyone else, then Warne was a genius. Whether it was genetic or pure ability, he had something. He was built for his job. He had very strong shoulders and big forearms. He could do things at twenty-two or twenty-three years of age that no one else could do before they were thirty.'

Nature had blessed Warne with the right physique. What he also possessed was an incredible self-belief. At least, his supporters would have called it self-belief; his critics might have preferred to call it arrogance. Whatever, he just fancied himself.

He was the cocky but personable private school sports jock – irritating and charming in equal measure. He was something different, particularly in conservative cricket circles. When he went to the Australian cricket academy, at the age of twenty, he took everyone aback with his flashy lifestyle. He sported blond hair, and turned up with his own car, much to the envy of the rest of the intake. It was a hotted-up Ford TC Cortina with magnesium alloy wheels, which his father had bought for him. 'He was always different from the rest of us,' Greg Blewett, a contemporary at the academy, said. 'We just weren't sure whether he was for real.'

Potter said Warne was teased a lot for his unconventionality, and this may have spurred him on.

He was a very flashy sort of kid. He was the only one who dyed his hair, and the other kids picked on him. They all called him 'Showbags', which means he was all right on the outside but full of shit on the inside. That was his nickname. The other thing they called him was 'Hollywood'. I think the peer group pressure made him work harder. We had another leg-spinner, who bowled tightly but couldn't spin it much, and Warne would come on and get the wickets. There was always a bit of animosity between the two – a bit like there was later with Stuart MacGill and Warne.

Warne was an amazing talent, but he had an amazing run of luck too. But the secret of his whole success, I think, was that he backed himself. When he scored 99 against New Zealand [his highest Test score], who else would have tried to hit a six to get to his hundred? He only had to push it for one to midwicket. But he was like that. He was so confident. He was like Dennis Lillee. They believed they could win the game for you. And he had that self-belief even back then.

Warne was a young man who loved nothing more than being the centre of attention. And his amazing ability to spin a cricket ball big distances had granted him that. It was a circus trick, a feat of conjuring. And it would make people look at him for ever more. But, as a young man, he had to learn how to put his amazing gift to good use. That was to prove altogether more of a challenge.

Before the prodigy could make his mark, though, he became a project. In its desperation to unearth a match-winning spinner, Australian cricket treated Warne as special from the time he was first seen by former internationals who knew how extraordinary were the things he was doing – even though right up until his Test debut, and beyond, it continued to be Warne's promise rather than his performances that stood out. From a very early stage, he was regarded as the Chosen One.

In little more than two years Warne was elevated from third-XI club cricket in Melbourne to playing his first Test match for Australia, while doing very little of substance on the field. Indeed, he played for his country after appearing in just seven first-class matches.

Of course the policy was justified in the sense that Warne more than lived up to even the brightest predictions, but the preferment bestowed upon him had an impact on how Warne viewed himself and how he conducted himself. No one could be unaffected by being lionized by so many good judges while not doing much on the pitch to warrant it. If Warne behaved as though guaranteed preferential treatment, who could really blame him? He was often indulged, and his ego was regularly fed. Being the cocky high school jock, with the look-at-me hair and look-at-me car, Warne wasn't averse to being viewed as the Chosen One, whether he deserved it or not. And for a long time he cannot have been sure he did deserve it, but was happy to run with the idea to see where it got him.

Australian cricket often reaped the benefits of Warne thinking he could do whatever he put his mind to – this of course was positively an advantage on the field – but the idolatry would eventually drive him to the edge of anyone's control.

There were mitigating factors behind Warne's doing little that was striking during his early days with St Kilda. The matches were played on new pitches every week, so the seamers got most of the wickets, and batsmen tended to play leg spin better (i.e., more positively) than they did at international level, bizarre though that sounds. In fact Warne would rarely do special things for St Kilda, even though he continued to occasionally turn out for the club for the rest of his career. Overall, he averaged little more than a wicket per game. Compare this to the record of another great Australian leg-spinner, Bill O'Reilly, who took 80 wickets at 17.5 each for North Sydney purely in the period before making his Test debut. In subsequent years O'Reilly routinely took his club wickets at under 10 apiece. But in his early years, Warne's teammates at St Kilda saw him as a kid who loved to bowl big leggies but also liked to have a good time. They too were unsure how serious he was about the game.

Even after he failed to make the grade in Aussie Rules, Warne's commitment to cricket was qualified. In 1989 he went to England to play a season of club cricket, but the deal really came about only because he wanted to keep company with a friend, Rick Gough, who had secured a playing contract with Knowle CC in the Bristol area. Partly through Shaun Graf, his captain and coach at St Kilda, who had played some club cricket in the region in the 1970s, Warne managed to acquire a modest arrangement for himself with Bristol Imperial. He led a very ill-disciplined lifestyle, but, perhaps through sheer volume of playing, for the first time showed some genuine consistency in his game, with around 800 runs and 90 wickets in 35 matches, and although he put on a lot of weight (his father barely recognized him when he collected him from the airport) he returned home a much-improved bowler. Graf wasn't impressed with Warne's physical appearance and put him in the third team, but Warne soon got his chance in the firsts – and took it.

Graf was probably the first cricketer of repute to recognize that behind Warne's ordinary statistics lay immense potential. 'There are a lot who can spin the ball on concrete, where they get bounce and turn,' he said.

But when they move on to turf, if they're not accurate, they [the bowlers] tend to get plundered . . . Not Warney. That's how we knew he could bowl. In two years he came on in leaps and bounds. One of his strongest assets is his belief in himself. He bowled to a set line, even then; he'd tell me, I'm going to bowl leg stump, or middle stump, or off stump. Most say, 'I'll keep it more or less on the off, or more or less on the leg.' But he was confident enough right from the beginning to tell me exactly the line he was going to bowl, so that I could set a field.

Graf felt that the St Kilda nets, which were narrower than normal, might have helped Warne acquire his accuracy.

Rodney Hogg, who had had some success bowling fast for Australia when a lot of top players had left to play for Kerry Packer's World Series in the late 1970s, came up against Warne while batting for Waverley – Dandenong. Hogg was thirty-eight and long retired from international cricket; Warne was twenty. After being beaten by three of Warne's big-spinning leg breaks, Hogg went down the pitch, swung, missed – and was stumped by a mile. Looking round, Hogg saw Graf laughing at him from slip. 'I don't know what's so funny,' Graf said. 'This bloke's better than Sleepy.' At that time, Peter Sleep was Australia's first-choice leg-spinner.

Hogg was so impressed that he used his column in a now-defunct newspaper called the *Melbourne Truth* to say that he'd just played against somebody who could easily take 500 Test wickets (this was at a time when no one had reached such a mark). 'The *Truth* was a paper that liked to exaggerate,' Hogg recalled. 'But I thought he was a superstar. I'd faced Abdul Qadir, and I had a lot more trouble with Warne. I thought he was in the same league.' As it happened, Hogg was sacked by the paper within a few days.

Graf began to teach Warne about how to lay a trap, and spring it. With time, of course, Warne would master this art of the jungle, the sniffing of uncertainty, the smelling of fear, and the knowing how to exploit it. 'I was always telling him, "Set him up, set him up, set him up and all of a sudden give him a flipper",' Graf added. 'Against Prahran, Julian Wiener [a former Test player] got a leg break, leg break, leg break and then the flipper. He thought it was short, went down to sweep, and it clean bowled him; he didn't pick it . . . At the time he got Wiener, you knew he was going to be very handy. After Hogg, you knew he was something special.'

Warne's run-up, the engine room of his bowling, was not yet as controlled as it later became. 'It used to be a bit more jerky,' Graf said. 'He purrs up there now like a Rolls-Royce . . . All he does is walk in, with his eyes level. He used to come in with his head a little bit sideways. He's very well balanced at delivery. It helps him to be balanced in his delivery stride, which helps his accuracy.' Jenner described Warne at the outset as having 'a really old-fashioned rock-back action . . . He didn't have a lot of energy, and had just enough follow-through to complete his action. There was no exaggeration in anything he did.'

Word of Warne soon carried along cricket's bush telegraph. Graf said St Kilda talked him up 'pretty hard'. Jim Higgs, a selector for both Victoria – Warne's home state – and Australia, who had played a fair bit of Test cricket alongside Hogg, watched Warne in the St Kilda nets and was quickly won over. Higgs had been a fine leg-spinner himself – Australia's best since Richie Benaud – but he had been dumped once the flash-harry quicks returned from Kerry Packer's circus, so he knew all about discrimination against leggies. Soon after that, possibly through the good offices of

Higgs or Graf, Warne was invited along to net with the Victoria state team. And soon after that he was asked to attend Australia's national academy, based in Adelaide. Higgs, who reckoned Warne had the best leg-spin potential he'd ever seen, had phoned Jack Potter, the then head of the academy, which had only been open a couple of years, had sung Warne's praises, and had persuaded Potter to add Warne to his intake for April 1990.

'Jim Higgs called and said they'd got a blond kid who bowled pretty good leg spin,' Potter recalled.

He hadn't done as well as they had thought he might, and he needed a bit of discipline. Could we fit him in? This was about two weeks after the year's intake had been selected and we were just about to start. Shane had been to England, and apparently his diet was cheese, bread and pies. This was the first time this had happened. Most of our boys had played for the Australian Under-19 team or performed in the state under-19 carnivals. Warne had done neither. He was twenty. The others were mostly eighteen going on nineteen.

The academy's management team sat down with Warne and told him the rules. There was to be no smoking or drinking. Warne was smoking at the time. 'He was a charming kid,' Potter recalled. 'He could win people across with his personality. He said he'd do all we asked.' It is safe to say that he didn't.

Potter, who had bowled occasional leg spin himself for Victoria, took Warne into the indoor nets and asked him to show him what he'd got.

He bowled me this leg break. I just went to take it and it bounced over my shoulder. Indoor nets can bounce a bit, but this one just fizzed and bounced. I just sort of looked at him. He was smiling. So, he bowled three or four of these. I said: 'What else have you got?' He said he'd got a bit of a googly, but it was very obvious.

I told him that if he was going to get good players out he needed to have a ball that went straight on. I told him about Richie Benaud bowling flippers. He went off and practised it with a tennis ball in the corridor of a little pub in Port Adelaide where he was staying. It probably wasn't the best place for Warney, but we didn't have anywhere else at that time. About a week later he came to me and said he wanted to show me some stuff. And he had it. He could bowl the flipper and one that went straight, and he still had his leggie. And I said to him, 'OK. If you can get all this stuff accurate enough, you might make a bit of a bowler!'

The speed with which Warne could grasp advice and thread it into his game would be a feature of his career, but Potter wasn't as impressed with Warne as Hogg had been. Indeed, he didn't really see him as anything out of the ordinary. 'I never ever thought he'd be the champion he turned out to be,' Potter admitted.

We'd had a few leg-spin bowlers at the academy who'd played state cricket, and they weren't that good. The way Warne ripped his leg break, I didn't think he'd have the necessary control. He was a bit overweight and did the bare amount [of work], while a lot of the kids, like Michael Bevan, were just killing themselves to lift the heaviest weights and run the furthest. He did put in, and did lose some weight, but I think he thought, 'Oh yeah, if I'm good enough, I'll make it.'

But, to Potter's astonishment, Warne was to become amazingly accurate over the next few years. In hindsight,

Potter thought this was because he had grasped that if he wasn't controlled his captain would take him off, and he desperately wanted to stay in the game. 'He must have worked hard,' Potter said.

I think one of the reasons he didn't bowl his googly more was that he lacked control with it. He was a bit of a perfectionist. He didn't want to give the batsmen any chance to ease the pressure. What has always amazed me [since the early days] was the way he just took the ball, rotated his shoulders, came in, and bowled it on the spot. You usually can't do that if you spin the ball the way he does. But he holds the ball slightly differently from most leggies, who have two fingers on top of the ball and the thumb on the side. He has his index finger over nearer the thumb. He can spin the ball and not spin the ball with similar actions.

Warne also had to learn how to bowl people out. Blewett remembers Warne bowling in the academy nets to another leg-spinner, Peter Young. Warne was spinning the ball big, but Young just stood at the crease, not even bothering to lift the bat, and watched the ball move harmlessly past his off stump. 'Go on,' he'd shout down to Warne. 'Get me out.'

Potter's involvement was useful to Warne. He helped him develop a flipper and a straight one – the back-spinner or slider – and encouraged him to bring his shoulder into his action, rather than just bowl with his arm, which is what he was doing before he went to Adelaide.

But even more important than all this was that Potter brought together Warne and Jenner. Jenner, then in his mid-forties, had been a leg-spinner himself. He had played nine Tests for Australia in the 1970s, and knew well the byways of his craft. He had started out playing for Western Australia, where pitches offered precious little for wrist spin, and had had to move to Adelaide to further his career. Later, an addiction to gambling on the horses had led him into grave difficulties. After embezzling from a car dealership he worked for, to subsidize his habit, he had been sentenced to six and a half years in prison. He had only just been released, and was still on parole, when he first met Warne. He had been asked along to the academy for two or three evenings a week to coach leg spin and, after eventually overcoming his fear that his young charges wouldn't respect an ex-con, had accepted the invitation.

No doubt because they were similarly unconventional characters who didn't naturally ally themselves to authority, and they were the right ages to form a comfortable father–son bond, he and Warne immediately hit it off. Jenner was quickly convinced that Warne was something special, and with time he convinced Warne of the same thing: that he had a talent that he must not waste. Jenner was anxious that Warne might fail to do himself justice, as he himself had done – and it might easily have happened without Jenner's intervention.

Down the years, Warne captivated many people, but Jenner was perhaps the first person to be truly in thrall to him, and in that sense it was a crucial relationship for Warne, who was to achieve most when he had the unconditional support and love of those around him. Jenner – in an unpaid capacity – remained a trusted adviser and coach for the entire duration of Warne's career. 'I wouldn't be where I was today without Jenner, helping with my action and technique,' Warne said when he retired. 'He's been my doctor. I can pick up the phone and hang up and feel better. Sometimes we don't even talk cricket.'

Jenner's recollections of their first encounter were clear.

My first impression was that he spun the ball more than I'd ever seen a right-arm leg-spinner spin the ball. And it was so effortless. Straightaway I knew this was someone we needed to develop. He had a big leg break and a flipper, but that was all. His leg breaks were quite slow – though as he used more shoulder, and his weight went forward, most things picked up speed. The flipper was quicker, and it was good.

He reckoned he had a googly, but he didn't really. We worked on it. But his fairly weak grip meant that he was missing leverage. His special gift with his wrist allowed him to really get revs on his leg break, but with the googly you have to turn your wrist around, so he had no real control on it. So we spread his fingers on the ball, to give him more leverage, and it worked except he got a massive blister on his finger. So he put it away. He went through stages where he looked to bowl it. At one point I did say to him, 'You do not have to be the best googly bowler. Let Mushtaq Ahmed be the best googly bowler. His leg break doesn't blow wind up yours.' I knew which one I'd prefer to have. And that was basically how he built his career.

The truth is he became the best leg-spin bowler in the world. He didn't have to be the best top-spin bowler, the best googly bowler. He had natural variation on his leg break. What he understood about the googly was, no matter how average it might have been, he still needed to bowl it, so the batsman knew he'd got it. The message I gave him was, 'You're not just bowling it for the batsman on strike, but for the non-striker and the guys sitting in the shed [the pavilion]. And they say, "Gee, was that the googly?" Then just don't bowl it again if you don't feel good about it. But you've already got them guessing.'

Jenner helped Warne technically, of course, and also taught him something of the history of the game and of leg spin, of which he was almost completely ignorant. But arguably his most important contribution was impressing upon his naive and artless pupil the value of deliberately cloaking his craft in mystery, for the benefit of the opposition, and of deliberately talking himself up, for the benefit of his own morale.

Over the years, Jenner would often tell Warne how well he had done and smother him with praise specifically to keep his self-esteem high. Jenner did this because he knew – and Warne came to know – how easily confidence could evaporate when even the slightest things went wrong. Warne became one of sport's great self-promoters, but it was something he had to be taught and Jenner was his teacher. Jenner taught him how to talk himself up, and Warne learned the lesson so well he could stay publicly upbeat after even the most unproductive day. The big haul, he was always convinced, was just around the corner. 'He knows how fragile is this art of ours,' Jenner explained. 'They all do it [talk themselves up] to an extent. Maybe batsmen don't need to do it as much as bowlers. There have been times when I have had to talk him up because he'd outperformed the batsmen but had nothing to show for it. You need the self-belief. We talk about these things.'

Not all Jenner's proposed technical changes were successful, however, and those that were were often quite small things, though they each contributed to the smooth running of the machine.

For some reason Jenner never fathomed, Warne liked to start off with the ball in his left hand, then pass it to his right hand in his delivery stride. Jenner recalled:

I used to say, 'Mate, the grip's more important than that.
Get it into your hand earlier.' He'd just say, 'It'll be all right.
It doesn't feel right . . . What about if I do it like this.' And
he switched it over after one step. And I said, 'I'm happy.'
He did it that day and that was it. He accepted that the grip
was important.

People have said that the reason why he had shoulder
problems was because of his walk-up. That's rubbish.
Mushtaq Ahmed runs up with a bit of a hop. Is he a better
bowler because he has a run-up? Everyone, including me,
tried to get him to run further and faster. We all tried, don't
ask me why, because we were wrong – he's proven that.
It's all about being yourself. We all tried to change him, and
we were wrong. The loose grip I never felt comfortable
with, but when the guy spins it three feet how can you tell
him he's doing it wrong? The same with the googly: tell
him he's wrong because he's not got enough leverage.

Potter had given Warne one influential guide in Jenner,
and Jenner gave him another in Ian Chappell, who had
captained Jenner in seven of his nine Tests. Like Jenner,
Chappell was an unreconstructed character who didn't share
the modern preoccupations with fast bowling and training.
A good cricketer was a good cricketer in his book. He was
loyal to his friends, and had stood by Jenner during his
time in jail. Jenner felt Chappell could inspire Warne and
arranged for the two of them to meet over breakfast one
day. As Jenner had anticipated, Warne responded to
Chappell's plain speaking and wise counsel, and they were
to form a firm friendship. Chappell would be Warne's
sounding board in many difficult situations. One early piece
of advice would resonate with the young Warne, uncertain
as he was of his ability and future. 'Son, the best thing I

can tell you,' Chappell said, 'is know yourself. Do what feels comfortable.'

For a leg-spinner, whose whole craft was so precarious, these were important words, and Warne never forgot them, even though it took him a while to fully appreciate the message. 'I never really got that when I was twenty years old but over time I started to understand,' Warne reflected. 'Ian has probably been the biggest influence on my cricket career. I could listen to his stories for ever. He is a wonderful person, and was a wonderful captain. Of all the people I have spoken to about cricket, he made the most sense. I think I'm very lucky to call him a friend.'

Unfortunately, back in 1990 Warne didn't appreciate just how fortunate he was to have been given a place at the cricket academy.

Within a few months of arriving in Adelaide, in 1990, his love of a jape had got him into serious trouble while the academy was playing a match in Darwin. With the academy in its infancy, its managers were anxious to prove that it merited government funding, and for a long time the full story was hushed up. Warne himself would dismiss the incident as a 'pool prank', but his misdemeanour was graver than that, and showed just how little regard he had for the academy's attempts to instil some discipline in him, his good fortune in being there, and the risks he was running with his cricket career (such as it then was).

The academy team were billeted at the university college in Darwin, and Warne had gone down to the swimming pool wearing only a dressing gown. There, it has been alleged, he went up to three Asian girls who were sunbathing, opened his robe in front of them, and (to put it politely) propositioned them. One of the girls lodged an official complaint and threatened to involve the police.

Once the academy had been informed of the incident, it was debated whether Warne should be suspended, but in the end it was decided to send him and two other boys who were party to the incident straight back to Adelaide by bus. As punishments go, it barely qualified as a slap on the wrist – perhaps an early clue to Warne as to the leniency that Australian cricket extended to its favoured sons.

Craig White, who later played Test cricket for England but had grown up in Australia, had joined Warne on an academy tour of the Caribbean and remembered him as someone who was 'always having a laugh'. White added, 'I don't think many people back then would have said this guy was going to be one of the best bowlers the game has ever seen. He was just a happy-go-lucky guy. He hasn't changed much on that side. I remember him jumping on the carousel while we were waiting for our luggage at an airport somewhere and coming round with the luggage.' Jenner recalled that, when he first met him, Warne 'just loved life, loved his Aussie Rules and loved cricket'.

Warne was soon in trouble again, this time decisively. In October 1990 there was a change of management at the academy, but the departure of Potter did not mean fitness and training became anything less of a priority under Andrew Sincock, the new head coach, and his deputy, Barry Causby. One day during an arduous run in the sand dunes Causby urged Warne to try harder, only for Warne to swear at him. After another crisis meeting among academy officials, Warne was told he would be left out of a forthcoming tour of Sri Lanka.

Warne was left behind in Adelaide to train on his own or with the South Australia state squad. South Australia, who sought to recruit youngsters from the academy, were interested in him staying, but Warne, after speaking to Graf, opted to return to Melbourne, leaving a note at the academy offices to the effect that he was quitting.

It was an early sign that Warne didn't take rejection too well (he would always vehemently deny that he was kicked out of the academy, as was often said) but in fact there was little reason for him to stay on. Most young cricketers remained at the academy for only a year. Warne's time was almost up. He would probably have maintained that no damage had been done, still believing that if he was good enough he would make it. As ever, he was happy to march to the beat of his own drum.

4

Lavish Lines, Lavish Turn

IT HAS TO be seriously doubted whether any other great cricketer has achieved Test selection with less regard for training, diet or general discipline than Shane Warne. And while, with only an incomplete idea as to how to put his gifts to best use, he was still struggling to achieve much on the field, he didn't exactly help the cause others were so keen to fight on his behalf.

Some geniuses may have an infinite capacity for taking pains, but the young Warne wasn't one of them – at least not until the double disappointment of being dropped by Australia and Victoria in the space of four weeks in 1992 finally forced him to reappraise his routine. Until then, self-improvement had never been a dominant feature in his thinking. Not that anyone was really encouraging him to think it should be. Indeed, there seemed to be no shortage of influential people in Australian cricket quite willing to keep faith with him come what may.

This was where Warne, once again, was lucky. Apart from Shaun Graf, Jim Higgs, Jack Potter and Terry Jenner, other important figures sympathetic to leg spin included John Benaud – brother of Richie and, like Higgs, a national selector – and national coach Bob Simpson, who in his playing days had bowled occasional leg spin.

Both Benaud and Simpson were keenly aware of Australia's

rich leg-spin tradition. Australia had produced three of the all-time great leggies in Clarrie Grimmett, Bill O'Reilly and Richie Benaud, and many other respectable exponents of cricket's hardest art. Usually, if there wasn't a leggie around, the Australian selectors would have viewed it as a shortcoming and looked to do something about it. Even though the game's recent obsession with pace had obscured the message, the selectors would have been prepared to take a punt on a young leggie on the nothing-ventured-nothing-gained principle.

But by 1991 they had been on a pretty thin streak for a long time. Since Richie Benaud's last Test, in 1964, they'd gone through a string of aspirants who – apart from Higgs, who had played twenty-two times – had been unable to hold down a regular place in the side: Peter Philpott, Terry Jenner, Kerry O'Keeffe, John Watkins, Peter Sleep, Bob Holland and Trevor Hohns. And, although some key people wished to revive leg spin, the system was ill-equipped to help. It was a few years before the academy, which opened in 1988, employed a leg-spin coach and some talent was squandered. There was a promising youngster called Adrian Tucker, from New South Wales, who might have made the grade with better guidance. By the time Warne arrived, Jenner had been recruited. Again, Warne's timing was impeccable.

Things were so bad that the selectors had asked Hohns to carry on playing even though he was thirty-six, but he declined, opting instead to put his business interests, and his family, first. This meant that the last leg-spinner to turn out for Australia before Warne was Peter Sleep, in January 1990. Sleep's record of 31 wickets at 45 apiece in 14 Tests spread across 11 years tallied with the inside view that he was 'often wildly inaccurate and no thinker'. But until Warne there hadn't always been anyone better. Sleep looked on with envy as Warne was fast-tracked to the top. 'Warne was one of the lucky ones who went straight from the academy to Test cricket,' he said. 'There's not too many people that do that. But the Australian selectors did sometimes do things like that.'

Warne, in fact, was not the biggest punt the selectors had ever taken on a leg-spinner. Watkins was tried after just five first-class matches for New South Wales, though that was a precedent few wanted to shout about. Watkins had been so nervous that he was only entrusted with six overs, never reappeared and soon dropped out of first-class cricket altogether.

The state of Australia's spin bowling was partly a consequence of the obsession with pace and partly due to plain neglect. As John Benaud said, 'I still have nightmares that we could have let our spin bowling development fail so badly.'

The battle to give Warne a chance became an almost ideological struggle between those who believed good spin bowling still had a part to play in the game and those – such as Les Stillman, the coach at Victoria – who felt it was virtually irrelevant. In his playing days, Stillman had been a thrasher who didn't think spinners could bowl. He just hit them back over their heads all the time.

'Despite his obvious talent, Warne struggled to get a game with the Victoria team. Stillman had been carried away by the West Indian theory of four fast bowlers – although in Les's case it was four military mediums,' John Benaud added. 'And obviously the Victoria selectors agreed with Les. So, we had a talent [Warne] consigned to the back blocks of grade cricket by a bunch of selectors/coach with no sympathy at all for one of the great traditions of the Australian game.

Ironically, even though Higgs came from Victoria he couldn't get to first base with the selectors there either.'

Benaud said that, whatever Stillman's view – and he took Victoria to the Sheffield Shield title in 1990-91 largely through the fast bowling of Merv Hughes, Paul Reiffel and Damien Fleming – the three national selectors with a leg-spin bent (himself, Higgs and Simpson) remained determined to do what they could to bring on spin bowling.

There was, however, a limit. In August 1990 they had sent Warne on an academy tour of West Indies, where he did OK, but Victoria did not give him a Shield game until seven matches into the next season. They preferred to play Paul Jackson, an orthodox left-armer, and Peter McIntyre, a leg-spinner, though Stillman wasn't overly fussed about them either. When eventually Warne did play – against Western Australia in February 1991 – he returned figures of 1 for 102 and, in Stillman's assessment, bowled 'some terrible stuff'. Tom Moody gave him his one wicket by skying a catch to long on. In fact it was Warne's appearance as much as his performance that caught the eye: the ear-stud, the long, bleached hair, the excess kilos sitting comfortably round his middle. He was immediately dropped.

Rather questionably, he then returned to England – of his own volition – to play a season for Accrington in the Lancashire League. He'd been whistled up as a last-minute replacement for the injured Shaun Young, and was paid £4,000, plus a car and digs. It wasn't a great deal – Young would have got around twice that money – but Warne would have regarded it as better than getting a real job. He was up against better players than in Bristol, and struggled to find the right length on the soft early season pitches. He finished strongly, but his overall figures of 73 wickets and 329 runs paled in comparison to those of Peter Sleep over at Rishton: 57 wickets and 1,621 runs. Nor had his thirst abated since his last visit to England two years earlier. He could be found most nights at one of his local pubs, the Martholme Grange, where he had a stool reserved for him at the end of the bar.

Meanwhile, John Benaud and Co. had created another opportunity for him. They chose him for a development squad to tour Zimbabwe in September 1991, a tour Benaud was to manage. 'It would have been a very, very brave – crazy brave – bunch of selectors who would have picked a young man for Test cricket straight from grade cricket,' Benaud said. 'A batsman maybe, but not a leg-spin bowler, who'd be soon confronted by the likes of Viv Richards and Richie Richardson.' West Indies were due to return to Australia in late 1992. 'So, totally pissed off with Victoria and determined to get a message out there that we needed a leg-spin bowler to help repair Australia's cricket image, we addressed our selection for an Australia B tour to Zimbabwe and included both Warne and McIntyre. This enraged Stillman, who accused us of trying to choose Victoria's team for him. How astute of him.'

It was on this tour that the quality of Warne's bowling finally made as big an impact as his larrikin nature. When Steve Waugh – who along with Mark Taylor, the captain, and Tom Moody was one of three players with Test experience taken on the tour – returned home to rejoin the New South Wales squad, he was wide-eyed at his first encounter with Warne. 'Man, you should see this sucker from Victoria,' he told the NSW and Australia fast bowler Mike Whitney. 'He's tubby, he's got a mullet, he smokes a shitload of cigarettes, and he likes a drink, but fuck, he can spin a ball.'

Mark Taylor reckoned that even at this early stage Warne's

flipper was a formidable weapon. 'I've never seen anyone bowl a flipper like he did,' he said. 'It was a fantastic delivery between 1991 and 1994. It actually swung in through the air. I can remember him bowling David Houghton with a ball that swung to hit the base of leg stump when Houghton shaped to cut. When that happens, you know something pretty remarkable is going on.'

Warne's success in Zimbabwe – where he took eleven wickets in two matches against representative sides – was the first real evidence that he could become the match-winning force his supporters had hoped. But his progress on the field wasn't matched by any sort of reform off it. A few weeks later, after bowling steadily in three Shield matches for Victoria, he was spotted by an astonished Matthew Hayden acting as Victoria's twelfth man in Brisbane in a match against Queensland, for whom Hayden played. Hayden saw him sitting in front of the changing rooms. 'He had a pie in one hand, with a cigarette wedged between his fingers, and a can of Coke in the other hand,' he recalled. 'Have a go at this bloke,' Hayden said to a teammate. 'He's absolutely no hope.'

Warne was chosen to play for an Australian XI against the West Indians in a four-day match in Hobart that was effectively an audition for the Test team. He confirmed the touring team's vulnerability against leg spin by taking seven wickets, including those of Brian Lara and Carl Hooper, but tellingly, he was singled out by Bob Simpson for a fitness test. Simpson, who had met Warne only once before, put his chubby leg-spinner through a strenuous fielding drill after the rest of the team had left the field, 'just to see how much out of nick he was'. Simpson added, 'He was quite comely in those days . . . He wasn't good [at fielding].'

Still the penny didn't drop. A week later, Warne went along to the MCG to watch the Australia–India Boxing Day Test with some mates, only to bump into Simpson, who was accompanied by Ian McDonald, the Australian team manager. Warne was armed with a beer in one hand and a pie in the other. Nor did he seem at all shamefaced to be caught culinarily in flagrante delicto. 'Just take it easy, son,' McDonald cautioned.

This was less embarrassing for Warne than worrying for Simpson and McDonald, given that Australia's selectors were preparing to give Warne a trial in the Test team. On the last day of the match, McDonald rang Warne at home to tell him he was chosen for the Test in Sydney starting four days later. Off-spinner Peter Taylor had been dropped.

Warne, of course, wasn't ready for this, either as a cricketer or as a person. He was the first player to graduate from the Australian cricket academy to Test cricket, but he wasn't the greatest advert for it. He simply wasn't mature enough. His response to his selection was to tell his family and friends the good news and hold a celebratory party at his parents' house. He drank so much that he was in such poor shape the next morning for a meeting with McDonald at the Australian Cricket Board offices that he had to retreat to the toilet to be sick. Still groggy, Warne then bumbled through his first major press conference; naturally there was a lot of media interest in Australia's wild-card selection. On the first day of the match itself, he was ticked off by Errol Alcott, the Australian team's physiotherapist, for tucking into too many pies during the tea interval.

Warne's lack of fitness told against him. He started well with the ball, his first nineteen overs costing 39, but it was a tough baptism against a team who were expert at playing spin, and on a pitch offering only slow turn India worked their way into a strong position. On the second day things deteriorated. Warne put down a catch off his bowling (Ravi Shastri, 66 runs into a double-century) and went for around 4½ runs per over.

His final figures of 1 for 150 from 45 overs didn't suggest a champion in the making but in the press box the veteran Bill O'Reilly judged that Warne's early spells had shown great promise. O'Reilly – who also expressed some concern at the 'lavish lines' upon which Australia's latest leg-spinner was built – wouldn't live to see Warne live up to his words of encouragement, as he died ten months after this at the age of eighty-six. Kerry O'Keeffe, another leg-spinner turned pundit, scribbled the following assessment in his notebook: 'Overweight, slightly round-arm, no variation, can't bowl.' However, looking back at the end of Warne's Test career, Mark Taylor said that few batsmen ever played Warne better than Shastri in this match. And Shastri himself was impressed. After receiving the man of the match award, he passed Warne and said, 'You know, young man, you'll bowl a lot worse than this and get six-for, or seven-for.'

Warne's eating and drinking, although excessive, were not as extraordinary at the time as they would have been later. In the early 1990s there was still a strong drinking culture in professional cricket circles, certainly in England and Australia; indeed, two days before the match Warne was taken out in Sydney by David Boon and Geoff Marsh to celebrate New Year's Eve, which they did liberally. And during the Adelaide Test, three weeks later, Warne shared midnight feasts of junk food with Merv Hughes, a giant man prone to binge-eating.

But things were changing. Simpson was intent on improving his team's fitness and a few months after this Hughes was dropped from a tour on the grounds of poor physical condition. Hughes would return, briefly, but it was a warning to Warne that he would have to keep an eye on himself.

By Warne's account, it was being dropped by Australia for the final Test of the India series and then by Victoria for their final Shield match of the season that finally stung him into reviewing his lifestyle and admitting to himself that things needed to change – indeed, that he wanted them to.

He had savoured two games of Test cricket. His second appearance had been in Adelaide, where he bowled twenty-three wicketless overs while Australia's quick bowlers maintained their domination over the Indians, before being dropped for Perth, where the surface was unyielding to spin. It was enough to make him realize he wanted more. 'I had had a taste of playing for Australia and realized that was what I wanted to do . . .' he wrote in his autobiography. 'It was time for me to make some sacrifices and become the best cricketer I could. It was up to me, I had a vision and I was focused.'

He must have reviewed what had happened to him over the previous four years since he'd left school. He'd made no real attempt to settle on any long-term employment plan since his dream of becoming an Aussie Rules pro had been dashed. He'd held a couple of small part-time jobs – one was delivering beds on the back of trucks – but they were really no more than fill-ins between his sport.

He may never have previously formulated a plan to make a career out of cricket. When he first went to the academy in Adelaide he was paid only around A$25–30 per week – just enough to cover modest living expenses – but during 1991 three state sides showed an interest in signing him. Apart from South Australia wanting him to stay on in

Adelaide, Steve Waugh – acting on behalf of Mark Taylor, the New South Wales captain – had encouraged him during the B tour to think about moving to Sydney. When this proposal reached the ears of Les Stillman and Simon O'Donnell, the Victoria captain, they told him bluntly to make up his mind – which he did, in their favour. In truth, at that stage Warne was probably too attached to Melbourne to leave, but the competition for his services should have convinced him that he had become a genuine commodity.

Warne might not before have been utterly convinced about what he wanted to do with his life, but cricket had now presented him with a chance to be famous – and that, he realized, was something that he did want.

While Warne knew there were technical ways in which he could improve his bowling, he also knew that the weakest part of his game was his fitness. 'By the end of that [1991–92] season I weighed 95 kilos,' Warne wrote in his autobiography.

When I played footy and ever since I'd left school I'd been 84 or 85 kilos. I had never been fat. But since my first trip to England in 1989 I'd been carrying weight and when I got back from there in 1991 I was huge. Too many pints and too many pies.

There was only one thing to do if I was to play for Australia again, even for Victoria. I needed to make some sacrifices. So every morning my alarm clock would go off at 7 a.m., I'd get up and go for a run then to the gym or to the pool, sometimes all three. I did that six mornings a week for four months – on my own. I had Sundays off. I got my weight down to 82 kilos, losing 13 kilos in about four months. I went off fatty foods, off alcohol, off everything that would stop me from reaching full fitness. All I wanted to do was play for Australia. I kept telling myself that was all I wanted to do and that everything I was going to do would have to work towards me playing for Australia.

Unbeknown to Warne, Australia would actually have stuck by him for longer. Apart from the support for him among the selectors, there was a broader strategy of consistent selection. 'We'd basically decided on a policy – never written – of having sixteen players in our minds who were good enough to play for Australia, and we tried to stay within the perimeter of those sixteen whenever we could,' Simpson said. 'The players themselves were never told that there were only sixteen in the mix, but they knew they were going to be given a fair go and not be in and out like revolving doors.'

Even while Warne was playing his first Test match, the powers that be had decided that he should spend the close season training at the academy rather than be allowed to go back to England to play another season of club cricket, where his lifestyle would probably do him more harm than good. He would not be a fully fledged member of the academy intake, but was detailed to work specifically with Terry Jenner and Rod Marsh, the new head coach, who took personal responsibility for his conduct. He wasn't going to be cut any slack to embarrass everyone as he had during his first stay.

The way Warne told it, he arrived at some sort of Damascene conversion with regard to his fitness. In reality, it seemed he did not begin his new regime until Jenner one day delivered a withering sermon about the need for him to change his lazy habits. It was a dressing-down that had been coming for a while.

Warne had arrived to see Jenner carrying some beers for

them to share but Jenner had told him bluntly they wouldn't be drinking them. '[I told] him how he hadn't made the necessary sacrifices to be playing for Australia,' he said. 'I didn't want him to make the mistakes that I did. There wasn't a decent wrist-spinner under thirty-five good enough to be playing [for Australia]. I wanted him to go home, put his head down and really see how good his best was. He knew that I understood exactly what he was going through.' Jenner told him, too, that a lot of people had put a lot of faith in him.

Warne's first response was to tell Jenner that he wasn't sure he could guarantee that he would change his ways, but in the event he did. 'Our conversation ended with him saying that he couldn't guarantee anything,' Jenner said. 'I had asked him to make a commitment. In the end, he did. He made that commitment by himself, for himself. So, after that second time at the academy, it was for real.'

During his new training regime, Warne paid a visit to Jack Potter, who was impressed by the new figure he saw in front of him. 'He had dropped weight and looked really keen,' Potter said. 'He told me that he had worked very hard, and it was obvious to me that someone had had a word and said, "If you do this, you can make it." He had got some real drive.'

In August 1992 Warne was taken as one of two spinners – along with Greg Matthews – in a thirteen-man squad to tour Sri Lanka, and when the team met in Darwin beforehand for a week's training his spruced-up appearance raised everyone's eyebrows. '[He] turned up trim, hair cropped short with a hint of bleach, plus the now famous earring,' Allan Border, the Australia captain, said. 'He looked a million dollars.' It was the first sign that he was prepared to show the game some respect, although the bleach and the earring (which probably owed much to his Aussie Rules background) were still set to shock cricket's traditionalists.

Simpson was equally impressed. 'He was just a different person, physically and mentally,' he said.

That's when it really all started. The training camp was in the worst possible conditions, hot as hell, and one thing that really struck me was that now that he'd lost a lot of weight he was capable of handling our fielding routines. He was diving all over the place. At one point I noticed blood pouring from his legs, and immediately stopped the whole thing and asked what the hell was going on. And we found that beneath what appeared to be a nice grassy surface was ashes. Every time he dived he was doing damage. But he wasn't going to admit it. Tough boy.

But the manicured image could not altogether hide the fragile confidence and self-esteem lying within. Warne had listened to Jenner's advice about thinking positively, but for all his outward self-assurance he basically conformed to the stereotypical profile of the leg-spinner, whose high-risk game serves to create an insecure personality. His moods fluctuated wildly. He would veer from cocky youngster to frightened novice who told himself he had no right to be anywhere near an international sporting arena.

Warne's late spell to help win the first Test in Colombo against the odds was a small but crucial event. He had been racked with self-doubt after finishing wicketless in the first innings, though in fact Arjuna Ranatunga had played him superbly. He had struggled to sleep and feared that all the training he'd done had been to no avail. He had had to be given a pep talk by fellow spinner Greg Matthews on the night before Sri Lanka's fourth-innings run-chase. 'Don't worry if they bounce twice,' Matthews had said. 'Go out there and spin them as far as you can.' In the event, Border had thrown him the ball more in hope than expectation, with four wickets required and Sri Lanka needing only 36 more for victory. Warne did everything that could have been asked of him. Ripping the ball out of fifth-day footmarks, he had three nervous tail-enders caught close to the bat in the space of thirteen balls to clinch for Australia a 16-run win – a remarkable outcome given that they trailed by 291 on the first innings.

This gave Warne an important boost and encouraged Australia to persevere with him, but he certainly hadn't convinced himself he could cut it in Test cricket. 'Sitting back and watching those experienced guys celebrate, I felt like I'd finally contributed,' he reflected. 'But I didn't feel like I belonged.'

He had yet to convince others too. After missing the next game with a foot injury, he returned for the final Test against Sri Lanka in Moratuwa, but Border gave him only eleven overs in the game and he failed to take a wicket.

The wider significance of the Sri Lanka tour was the remedial work that Warne and Simpson undertook on his bowling. When Warne had been Australia's twelfth man in Perth, during the India series, Simpson had taken him into the nets and persuaded him to try bowling round the wicket; it was another line of attack, one Warne would make famous, but also a refuge when things weren't going well, as it brought the body more into play and was a way of regaining rhythm. But Sri Lanka was the first tour Warne and Simpson had made together, and it presented a golden opportunity for them to spend time talking technique and tactics. This was where Warne's famous leg-stump line was devised, and with it came the crucial accuracy.

'In those days he used to bowl outside off stump and basically spun the ball a mile,' Simpson recalled. 'He didn't have great control and only had the flipper to back it up. That's when we convinced him he had to do a few things with his action and change his line. Bowling outside off stump is just so bad for a leg-spinner. After that, Shane was able to gain accuracy. Also, his drift started to come into play.' Warne's ability to make the ball drift in flight towards leg and then spin sharply towards the off upon pitching would of course become the killer element in his bowling over the next few years.

Simpson also helped Warne get more side-on in delivery, develop more of an aggressive follow-through that further increased the spin and bounce, and work on a top-spinner and slider. His body language also improved. 'Strange as it sounds,' Simpson added, 'Shane didn't really bowl with any expectation in those days. He just used to let the ball go, and that was about it. No real follow-through, no hip drive. And we worked on his ability and understanding of how to get people out.'

Having finally decided to apply himself, Warne soaked up information like a sponge. 'Just to show how quick he was,' Simpson said, 'three weeks after he was shown how to bowl what he called his slider, he was bowling it in a Test match and getting wickets with it. He had a remarkable ability to learn quickly. Sri Lanka was where it dawned on him that he was not going to make it by doing what he used to do. His determination was never lacking. Sometimes he'd stay out late, but in those days he didn't create any worries for me.'

In November 1992 Warne was left out of the first Test of the home series against West Indies – a decision Border said he regretted when Australia narrowly failed to force a win. He was recalled for the second match in his home city of Melbourne, but had to be given another motivational talk ahead of the final day's play, this time from Ian Healy as they walked through the park to the stadium. Healy was shocked at Warne's negativity. Warne, who had taken one tail-end wicket in twenty-four overs in the first innings, had told him, 'I'm worried about being thumped all around the ground in front of my friends and never playing for Australia again.'

As in Colombo, the story that day in Melbourne could easily have been different. But in his ninth over, with West Indies 143 for 1, chasing 359 to win, Warne tried a flipper to Richie Richardson, the West Indies captain and one of the leading batsmen in the game. He reckoned he had tried twenty flippers earlier in the game without landing one right, but this one came out perfectly and completely fooled Richardson. 'It was like someone took the air out of the ball,' Healy recalled. 'I remember thinking, "Too late, Richie," when he didn't get his bat down in time.'

Even then, Warne himself wasn't convinced that the way the ball behaved was all his own work; he thought it might have kept slightly low. But Richardson's demise was sufficient to trigger another West Indian panic against spin. In fifteen more overs, Warne took another six wickets to finish with figures of 7 for 52 – better Test figures than Benaud or O'Reilly ever achieved, and superior to Grimmett's best on home soil. (Grimmett once took 7 for 40 in South Africa.) It was just Warne's fifth Test appearance.

If there was one point of transformation, this was it. 'There was a lot of talk about it being time for Shane Warne to deliver,' Warne recalled years later. 'I'd been smashed all over the park by everyone. That Boxing Day Test made me feel I finally belonged in the side. If I could bowl like that

I knew I could take wickets at international level whoever we were playing . . . [Test] level is not about skill, it's about attitude, and the way you think about it, and having the confidence to deliver.'

Although he did little in the remainder of the series, Warne had done enough to persuade Border of his potential. And he was genuinely an improved bowler. The haul against West Indies was no fluke, as he proved during the next few months. In New Zealand, Border gave him an average of 53 overs per Test, and in six Tests in England an incredible 73 overs per game (Warne's total of 2,639 deliveries created a record for any Ashes series). With the increased responsibilities, his confidence steadily grew. 'Looking back,' he said in 1997 of the flipper to Richardson, 'I can say definitely that that ball was the turning point in my career.'

Mark Taylor believed that the faith Border and Simpson showed in Warne during this period was crucial.

It's easy to pick a spinner in a squad and leave him out of the XI because he can't run in and intimidate batsmen. If there's a new spinner in the side you can bet the batsmen will be after him, and more often than not he'll go for a few runs in his first few Tests. But if you leave him out of the team for too long he will lose confidence and may not be the bowler you expect him to be. That's where leadership and an understanding of spin bowling plays its part.

The evening that the game finished, Warne went out on the town to celebrate with Mark Waugh and Damien Martyn. Martyn was perhaps Warne's closest friend at the academy. In just his second Test appearance, he had played his part with the bat, but his career was soon to go off the rails in a manner that may have served as a warning to his friend.

The three of them hit a bar in South Yarra, where Warne was handed free drinks, and the next morning he was bombarded with attention from the Australian media.

Warne still had a huge amount to learn as a strategist, but he was finally approximating to the bowler the experts thought he might become. Moreover, the ideological battle had been won. Match-winning wrist spin, at least in Australia, was back on the scene.

Jack Potter was right. Warne really did believe that if he was good enough he would make it. To Warne, all the talk about the need for him to lose weight and get fitter were just side issues. He had trained hard for four months because someone he trusted had asked him to show his commitment to playing for Australia. He had shown his determination, and twice in three Tests he had helped his country win.

Warne might have seen the connection between these events and decided that he ought to remain loyal to Simpson's work ethic and stay as fit as he could. But in fact the better he bowled, and the more success he had, the more he seemed to feel justified in going back to eating what he liked and training as he liked. He did not allow his physical condition to deteriorate badly, but nor did he join the craze for gym work that took hold of most international cricket teams in the late 1990s.

Warne's view was that if he was fit for cricket that ought to suffice. This was one of the reasons he sometimes spoke with feeling about how he would have liked to have played for Australia during Ian Chappell's time as captain, because he knew that in those days he would have been cut a bit more slack with regard to his fitness levels and generally how he conducted himself off the field. Chappell drove his players hard and expected 100 per cent commitment, but he understood that not all players came from the same pod. As Ian Healy said, 'He [Warne] wouldn't run round the block for exercise, but he's got no problem bowling thirty overs a day.'

Over the next few years, stories about Warne's love of junk food became legion. Teammates were shocked at how he struggled to find something acceptable to eat on the menus of even modestly upmarket restaurants. Warne was happy with chip butties, pizzas and fizzy drinks – and was known to have tried ordering them into restaurants that didn't provide them.

Nor did he give up smoking, although at one point he was paid a substantial sum by Nicorette to stop for four months – a challenge that ended in embarrassing failure when he was photographed with cigarette in hand a few days before the embargo was due to end. On another occasion, in New Zealand, he got into a row with some fifteen-year-old boys who had taken photographs of him smoking in the dressing room despite it being a no-smoking stadium.

By 1997 Warne's weight was once again a matter of controversy. That year, he unveiled a Madame Tussaud's waxwork of himself in Melbourne only to find that the model, whose dimensions had been taken a year earlier, looked much slimmer than he did. When a journalist asked whether he wished he 'still looked like that', Warne stormed out of the press conference in disgust. At around the same time, Daryll Cullinan dismissed Warne in a one-dayer in Sydney and sent him off with the words 'Go and deflate yourself, you balloon.'

Warne's method of coping with his weight problem was to occasionally go on crash diets to remove several kilos before reverting to his favoured foods. 'For five weeks I will live on fruit and cereal,' he once said. 'But it nearly kills me.'

5
Fame

GREAT SPORTSMEN MAY get cleverer with the passing years, but they are surely most vivid during the first flowering of their genius. How do we like to remember our sporting heroes? George Best? . . . Those goals against Benfica in 1966. Paul Gascoigne? . . . Italia '90. Tiger Woods? . . . Augusta 1997 and that first Major victory by twelve strokes. Boris Becker? The boy in a man's body winning Wimbledon for the first time.

At these times, their gifts are fresh to their owners and fresh to others. They/we are in thrall to the astonishing things they do. Their adversaries are probably slightly less enthusiastic, but even they may look on more in admiration than in anger. After all, they know better than most how difficult are the things that the New Sensation is making look easy. What can they do except shake their heads in wonder and concede he's the better man?

The suddenness of it all is the astonishing thing. One minute we're looking at someone with merely faltering promise; the next, everything they touch is turning to purest gold. They are the most beautifully calibrated sporting machines, but until the last working part had been fashioned and dropped into place they functioned only at well below what proved to be full capacity. In December 1928 Don Bradman couldn't even make Australia's starting XI yet inside twenty months he had set world record scores in Test and first-class cricket. Brian Lara's improvement was similarly exponential: the first time he scored a hundred in a Test, he turned it into 277; his third Test century stopped at a record 375.

Similarly, in his first three years of full-time international cricket Warne was giving displays of spin bowling as brilliant as can ever have been seen. If he wasn't as intelligent a bowler from 1993 to 1995 as he later became, he scarcely needed to be. He had his dipping, swerving leg breaks, his lethal flippers, a competitive spirit to die for, and, crucially, the physical strength to often bowl more than thirty overs a day. The thing that he also had at this time, that he wouldn't have later to quite the same extent, was what Bob Simpson described as 'freakish' control. Contrary to popular myth, there had been accurate leg-spinners in the past, but they were rare enough to prove that theirs was a difficult art. And this was now the 1990s and scoring was on the rise: batsmen had learned from one-day cricket how to work the ball into the gaps.

Not against Warne they didn't. OK, so Warne had the advantage of being an unfamiliar type of bowler, but even opponents better versed in his tricks would have found him formidable.

The effect Warne had on cricket can be best summed up in one word: shock. He had a similar effect on his sport as Cassius Clay had had on boxing when he confounded expectations and beat Sonny Liston for the world title in 1964. They played, and talked, an entirely different game – and their showmanship helped sweep tired convention from their path.

Very few batsmen had the confidence to take Warne on with the aggression that time would show was essential;

In 1993 Warne bowled more balls in an Ashes series than any man in history. Sometimes, as here at the Oval, he got bored of doing it the same way every time

Above: Ian Healy, sitting here on the right of Warne at the start of the 1997 Ashes tour, kept wicket to him in more Tests than anyone else

Left: Warne's weight was a sensitive topic, but he was prepared to make light of it after Australia had won at Old Trafford in 1997

Right: Terry Jenner, always a key adviser, helps Warne try to rediscover his form ahead of the Lord's Test in 1997

Below: The Australians played hard and partied harder: the celebrations begin in England in 1997

Warne is overjoyed to claim another West Indies wicket at the 1999 World Cup, but for much of the tournament he was low on confidence and questioned his future

Alec Stewart was dismissed fourteen times in Test cricket by Warne – more than anyone else. Here he goes at Trent Bridge in 2001

Above: The great comeback: after a slow start, Australia won the 1999 World Cup in style. Warne and the Waugh twins lift the trophy at Lord's

Right: Daughter Brooke and son Jackson with Warne in Cape Town in 2002 for his 100th Test appearance. He flew out his family for the occasion, and marked it with an amazing all-round performance

Above left: Steve Waugh and the baggy green cap, more beloved by some than by others

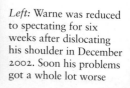

Left: Warne was reduced to spectating for six weeks after dislocating his shoulder in December 2002. Soon his problems got a whole lot worse

Above: The Hampshire
team line up around
their captain for the
2005 season

Right: Having played
for fourteen years
without scoring a
century, Warne walks off
at Southgate after
achieving his second in
two months, July 2005

Warne at the unveiling of the portrait of him that was hung in the Long Room at Lord's in June 2005, ahead of what proved his greatest series

No one played Warne better than West Indies batsman Brian Lara. They were teammates in a Tsunami fund-raiser at the Oval

many were reduced to fumbling impotence. And he could attack or defend at will. Broadly, the strategy was this: he would look to keep things tight in the first innings and then go on the attack in the second, when the pitch might be breaking up and taking spin.

The statistics show that he was doing both to a high level. He was Australia's leading wicket-taker in six successive series — four of which were away from home — and their second highest in the next. His victims included many of the world's leading batsmen, and the manner in which he took their wickets was sometimes scarcely less jaw-dropping than the Gatting ball. At the same time, in these seven series, the proportion of his overs which were maidens was strikingly high (and generally higher than it would be later). In New Zealand in 1993, 46 per cent of his Test overs were not scored off. In England the same year, 41 per cent of them. Then at home to New Zealand the figure was 33 per cent, at home to South Africa 36 per cent, and away to South Africa 36 per cent. In Pakistan, where batsmen tend to be good players of spin, his percentage of maidens dropped to 28, before rising to 33 in the home Tests against England in 1994–95. In these seven series, he was named player of the series on four occasions.

Various ruses were tried to counter him. Having been virtually strokeless at home a few months earlier, New Zealand went to Australia late in 1993 with plans to sweep him out of his groove and in the first Test at Perth they did so. But that was Perth, then a spinner's graveyard. Later in the series, on trickier surfaces, they couldn't keep up the sweeping tactic and Warne destroyed them with ruthless efficiency. In England in 1993, John Emburey played French-cricket style and blocked him for hour after hour at Edgbaston, but it was no way to win a match — and England didn't.

In truth, England were at a loss to know how to play him, as was all too apparent in Brisbane in 1994 when Michael Atherton and Alec Stewart went to the top of the stand to watch Warne through binoculars and try to unravel his variations. Warne took eleven wickets in Brisbane and nine more in Melbourne, where he finished the match with the first hat-trick of his life. His final victim was Devon Malcolm, well caught at short leg by David Boon off a spitting leg break. 'It came out just as I wanted,' Warne said. 'I got lucky.'

Allan Border was scathing about England's timidity and said Australian batsmen would look to be far more positive. But only a few of them were when they came up against Warne in state cricket. Border didn't make much impression on Warne in three state games against Victoria late in his career, and Mark Waugh found batting against Warne much harder than expected in a four-day match for New South Wales at Sydney in 1993. Waugh played brilliantly for 119, and Warne afterwards hailed him as the world's best batsman, but it took Waugh 20 balls to score his first run off Warne, and 65 to hit his first boundary. Far from taking Warne apart, he spent a lot of time using his pads to keep out Warne's outrageous leg breaks, just like everyone else.

Mushtaq Ahmed was among the astonished onlookers as Warne took the cricketing world by storm. He was playing for Somerset in 1993 when the Australians visited Taunton for a warm-up match ahead of the Test series with England. Ian Healy, the Australia wicketkeeper, approached Mushtaq and asked him if he would give their young leg-spinner some advice about his craft. (Warne, at twenty-three, was actually slightly older than Mushtaq.) Mushtaq duly told him to bowl with pace in England, not be shy to use his variations, etc., etc. Not long after, he watched in amazement Warne bowling in the first two Tests of the series. 'I remember sitting watching on TV and laughing at how brilliant he was,' Mushtaq recalled. 'I wondered when I would get to see him again so I could ask *his* advice on how to bowl, and get some tips myself.' (Of course, as already recounted, Warne would indeed pass on tips to Mushtaq in return.)

Warne's match-winning effort against West Indies at the MCG in 1992 had marked the beginning of the end of his Test apprenticeship; from that point, he more often that not bowled like a champion and displayed the self-belief of a champion. There were occasional moments of doubt, such as when Border instructed him to hide some of his tricks in warm-up matches on tour and some batsmen — such as Martin Crowe, Graeme Hick and Hansie Cronje – got after him, but he overcame these mini-crises.

As the man who backed him during his early struggles, Border played a significant part in Warne's development. He might have handled his young star more carefully, however. A pessimist by nature, Border never shed the negative outlook acquired in his arduous early years as captain, and once he realized he had a gilt-edged match-winner in Warne he played his trump card for all it was worth. The massive workload Border placed on Warne – who averaged 62 overs per Test in Border's last five series as captain – must have played a part in his bowling shoulder eventually collapsing, but it was only after Border retired in 1994 that he expressed concern for Warne's welfare. 'He is starting to look jaded and we will have to watch him very closely,' Border said the following year. 'Burnout is a very real threat.'

With each fresh series, Warne took a step forward in realizing that he belonged in Test cricket and knew he could be successful. He believed he could set up and beat even the very best batsmen. It would be years before he would seriously question his ability again. The banishment, or suppression, of doubt seemed near-total.

Until his shoulder collapsed, he used the flipper to devastating effect. Few leg-spinners have ever truly mastered the flipper, but he now deployed it to perhaps greater effect than any bowler in history. It was his deadliest weapon. His removal of Alec Stewart, who had the biggest backlift in the England team, at Brisbane did as much to undermine English confidence in the 1994–95 series as the Gatting ball did in 1993. His flipper was still causing England problems in 1997. 'It just looked like it was going to be a long hop and your eyes would light up,' Nasser Hussain recalled. 'But you had to tell yourself, "Don't do it," because you also knew he didn't bowl them. Just pat it back.'

Within a few years, Warne's strength of mind would be legendary. 'Suppose Shane Warne said to himself, "What if I bowl a bad ball?"' Ashley Mallett asked in 1998 as he tutted at the inability of feeble-minded batsmen to take Warne on. 'Do you think that sort of thinking would allow him to bowl ball after ball with unerring accuracy, bounce and turn? If you think you cannot do it, you won't do it . . . Fear of failure is a real and intimidating negative for people under pressure and unsure of themselves.'

Warne surely became so good at preying on the mental frailties of opponents precisely because at the outset he'd felt the pressure and the doubt himself.

Warne's feats in England in 1993, when he claimed thirty-four wickets in the series, helped send his life helter-skelter. Shortly after the Old Trafford Test in June, Warne proposed to his girlfriend, Simone Callaghan, a promotions girl he had met at a charity golf day in Melbourne the previous year. Warne said later that he was convinced from the start that she was the girl for him, but it must have been hard for her then to be sure that Warne was right for her. He had played just twice for Australia when they met and he was far from a superstar. By the time their engagement ended and their marriage began, in September 1995, he was an automatic choice for any Australia side and was away travelling for most months of the year. During their engagement Simone accompanied him on two tours, but she rarely came along once they were married. She probably didn't know when she met him that Australian cricket teams had a policy – later relaxed – of barring wives or girlfriends from staying in the team hotel.

He was certainly not alone among international cricketers in wanting to marry young, but the statistics were hardly in favour of the relationship lasting. Plenty of modern English and Australian cricketers saw their marriages fail, and given the time they spent away from home it was hardly surprising. When news of Warne's impending marriage reached Jack Edwards, a long-time servant of St Kilda and the Australian board, he was dismayed. He immediately feared it would not last.

Warne's success turned him into a huge star back home. He employed an agent, Austin Robertson, to handle his commercial affairs. Of the sponsorship deals that rolled in, the biggest was £135,000 a year for five years from Nike, who didn't normally interest themselves in cricket. He was paid for a weekly newspaper column. He was also offered £25,000 by a British newspaper to pose in only his jockstrap (he declined). What may have pleased him most, he and Merv Hughes were guests at the Australian Football League grand final at the MCG, where, in front of 100,000 people, they kicked around a ball on the outfield for a while. And of course the relationship with television grew closer as he and Simone appeared on a *60 Minutes* profile of Australia's brightest sports star. The volume of money coming in was such that when Michael Davie, a journalist, sought to interview Shane's father, Keith, Robertson asked whether Davie might not be able to provide 'something for Keith's time'. Davie declined.

Warne was to enjoy fully the trappings of his new-found wealth. Around 1996 he bought his first Ferrari – a 355 Spider – and over the course of the next few years built up a fleet of six cars, which included two Mercedes four-wheel drives and two BMWs.

There's a case for saying that Shane Warne was the first cricketer to cement fame and wealth through television. Cricketers since Gary Sobers had owed much to the small screen for making them recognizable to people who had never seen them in the flesh, but it wasn't really until Warne's era that the sport became a serious business for television and marketeers. His was the first fully professional, media-savvy cricket age.

Eventually, India's Sachin Tendulkar – the biggest star in the country with the most money to shower on its heroes – would enjoy the greatest riches, but Warne hit the big time just before him. These two cricketers in particular came to accept that they were never out of shot of the cameras. Every ball they played, every reaction they gave, was captured for a new kind of posterity. True, comparisons between India, where the population exceeded 1 billion, and Australia, where it had yet to reach 20 million, could only be taken so far, but Tendulkar's game sometimes showed signs of being inhibited by the extraordinary pressures placed on him, while Warne's rarely did. Warne was sensitive to Tendulkar's predicament. 'I admire Sachin for what he has to go through every day,' he once said. 'There are a billion people wanting him to do well and thousands will wait outside the stadium until he walks in to bat, then all charge in. That expectation is one of the hardest things.'

Very few cricketers have ever actively chosen to be famous – Ian Botham perhaps, Kevin Pietersen certainly – but Warne was definitely one of them. He seemed to love the warm glow of celebrity like a cat asleep in front of a fire. Whereas Tendulkar craved anonymity, Warne was generally accommodating when it came to signing autographs, posing for photographs with fans, or giving media interviews.

And Warne loved television. He not only saw it as a vehicle to celebrity and riches but also viewed it as his natural medium. His appearance as a youngster may have struck some as vulgar but his bleached hair, earring, flamboyant gestures and over-the-top celebrations were perfect for TV. This wasn't someone who wanted to blend in with the crowd. His look was very much that of the young, brash Australia as portrayed through TV soap operas like *Neighbours*, a programme that was hugely popular in Britain as well as Australia (where it had become the country's highest-rating programme in 1987) at around the time Warne arrived on the international scene.

'I suppose my look, the way I play – you combine all that sort of stuff and that makes people interested in what I actually do,' he once said. And among those interested in what he did were clothes and sports gear manufacturers, who swiftly beat a path to his door, chequebook in hand, seeking his endorsement of their products. Sporting the accoutrements of youth and a rebel's CV (the trouble at the academy proved to have its uses), he fitted their blueprint. He was made for TV, and TV was to enhance his fame.

The irony was that had Warne's first stab at fame, through Aussie Rules, come to fruition, he would have been far less well known than he was. Aussie Rules is not even played across all of Australia, let alone outside the continent. As it was, as writer Gideon Haigh observed, Warne became the most famous living Australian male. 'Just as no Australian has known the fame of Sir Donald Bradman,' he wrote in 2006, 'no Australian is now more recognizable than Shane Warne.'

By the early 1990s, television in Australia had recently undergone an important revolution. Satellite had enabled the national ABC network and commercial broadcasters to spread their reach beyond the cities into the rural areas of the country; and between 1986 and 1994 every state in Australia increased its channels from two to five. This may have been small beer compared to the dozens of channels available to Americans, but for many Australians television was suddenly able to play a much more important part in their lives.

Sport was one of the big winners in this process. By Warne's time, and by the time the national cricket team was becoming the best in the world, virtually the entire Australian population was able to receive coverage of Test matches for the first time. Australia's overseas matches were also in the process of becoming available via satellite. Indeed, television was soon an integral part of the event. When Australia played India in a one-day match in Sri Lanka in 1994, play was delayed by fifteen minutes until a satellite link with India could be established.

When Darren Lehmann first played for Australia, in 1997, he was immediately struck by the celebrity status enjoyed by the team. They rubbed shoulders with actors, rock stars and politicians, some of whom would visit them in the dressing room during matches. One evening his new teammates took him to a nightspot in Sydney, where they were feted.

'They were just excited to have us socializing at their club,' Lehmann recalled. 'The manager came down asking us if everything was OK. The place was teeming with beautiful people, we weren't paying a cent, and everyone wanted to know us . . . You do live in a kind of bubble, and you really need to be on your game as a person to not get consumed by it.'

Lehmann said that in Melbourne and Sydney the players often ran into TV stars – especially if they were in the company of Warne, 'who knows them all . . . Warney is our most famous player, and all the celebrities gravitate towards him.' Warne regularly received fan mail up to knee height. 'It's not all free and easygoing for Warney as it is for the rest of us,' Lehmann added. 'It may sound like he gets special treatment, but he doesn't. He is still very much a team man . . . but it's a little strange in "Shane's World".'

Television provided Warne – who very rarely read books – with many of the reference points in his life. When he wanted to promote his charity, the Shane Warne Foundation, which aims to help seriously ill and underprivileged children, one of the means he chose was to make a walk-on appearance on *Neighbours*. When his marriage broke down, he gave his most frank interview not to one of the newspapers for whom he wrote columns – ghosted, naturally – but to Jana Wendt, whose reputation had been forged as a television personality.

And when Warne announced his retirement from Australian cricket, in December 2006, he turned it into a major television event, with his retirement press conference, which lasted forty-five minutes, being broadcast live on Australian television. A tribute programme was screened the evening before his final Test appearance, and the day after the game was scheduled to finish he gave an interview to chat-show host Michael Parkinson which was shown more than once in Australia over the following days. The timing of his announcement could not have been better, coming as it did five days before a Boxing Day Test match against England in his home city of Melbourne, and Warne needing one more victim to become the first bowler in Test history to claim 700 Test wickets. Perhaps unsurprisingly, Channel Nine's average audience for Boxing Day was 2.1 million – its highest ever for a day's Test cricket in Australia.

When Warne likened his turbulent career to a soap opera, as he often did, it was an entirely accurate description, because the characters in soap operas tend to go through an implausible number of good times, bad times and reinventions, but it perhaps wasn't as sage an observation as it might have appeared. Unlike teammates Steve Waugh and Mike Whitney, who liked to leave the team hotels and explore the foreign countries they visited, Warne was happy staying in his room, where channel surfing would have been high on his list of activities. He probably likened his life to a soap opera because it was the most obvious comparison he could think of. Serial dramas like *Neighbours* and *Happy Days* were Warne's cultural reference points. Damien Fleming remembers rooming with Warne and waking to find him crying at the end of *Notting Hill*.

During the 2006 Adelaide Test, he nicknamed Ian Bell – whom Warne fancied as a 'bunny' – the Shermanator, after a nerdy red-haired kid in the 1999 teen film *American Pie*. Bell, who at twenty-four was considerably closer to the film's target audience than Warne, thirty-seven, immediately got the reference. In Australia too Warne usually spent the evenings of Test matches in his hotel, eating room service and watching TV, and *American Pie* had been shown on Australian TV in Adelaide three nights earlier. But the crucial point was that he was very happy for his life to be like a soap opera. He sought, and found, fame.

He often saw things in terms of their impact as television events. For example, he said that if Australia's remarkable comeback win at Colombo in 1992 had been shown on television in Australia, 'it would be remembered as one of the great matches of all time.'

Like any TV star, Warne was highly image-conscious. He always thought twice before allowing photographers to take pictures of him without his shirt on, in case the images showed him looking unflatteringly overweight. For magazine interviews, he came up with his own suggestions as to the clothes he might be photographed wearing. He underwent hair replacement therapy, and around the time of his retirement there was press speculation that he had had his teeth bleached. And he claimed that, in order to lose weight so that he would look better on television when he announced his retirement from one-day internationals, he had taken a diuretic which caused him to fail a drugs test ahead of the 2003 World Cup. Whether you believed this explanation or not (and the Australian Cricket Board decided they did and gave him a reduced ban as a result), it was an entirely plausible argument. But more of that later.

Warne's willingness to embrace the camera was unusual. Even in an age of television omnipotence, it is remarkable how many professional sportsmen have got through their careers without showing any fondness for the medium. Though they performed daily in front of the cameras, they remained in a perpetual state of shy detachment from their wider audience. That was plain from how tongue-tied and inarticulate they were when fulfilling their contractual obligation to give post-match TV interviews. They would much rather not have been there.

The true performer not only lifted his performance for big games, but displayed genuine enjoyment in the theatre of the occasion. In the era before blanket TV coverage, Fred Trueman, Keith Miller and Denis Compton were all great cricketers and genuine entertainers, who loved pleasing the crowds. More recently, and with television now largely determining the scheduling of the game, England's Darren Gough plainly enjoyed the limelight, as does Pietersen. But there was never anyone who strutted cricket's boards with quite such obvious relish as Warne, who saw spectators as an integral part of the performance. 'When I go out to play, yes it is for Australia, yes it is for my country, but it is also for the 100,000 fans,' he said. 'I like to think of myself as an entertainer, who will go out there and try and put on a show . . . You look at the whole. I'd like to think I've made cricket more enjoyable, more fun. For the people who've turned up, I like to think I've given them entertainment.' It's no coincidence that Gough, Pietersen and Warne are all close friends.

When Warne was fielding on the boundary's edge, he loved to engage with the crowds. He would sign autographs between deliveries, exchange friendly banter and generally play-act for their amusement. 'Show us your mystery ball, Warney!' they'd shout. And Warne would peek down his trousers.

Unsurprisingly, Warne immediately shone when he did some commentary stints during one of his lay-offs: his interpretation of the cricket was predictably first-rate, but he was also personable and knew how to tell a good story. In front of a microphone, he was completely unfazed.

Warne loved nothing more than an audience. This lay at the heart of the extraordinary extent to which he was a big-match player. Test match cricket is self-evidently the toughest form of the game, yet Warne's record in Test cricket outstripped his statistics in state and county cricket, which themselves outstripped his record in club or grade cricket. The harder the pickings, the more he thrived. His record in big one-day tournaments, including World Cups, was second to none, and his bowling average in Ashes matches was two runs lower than in other Tests. He gained a terrific buzz from playing to a crowd and to cameras. In such arenas, everything worked to his advantage because, while he delighted in the challenge, many of his opponents were intimidated by the added pressure. He capitalized on that.

Warne was well aware of the part TV played in his rise. He insisted many times that the ball with which he bowled Mike Gatting at Old Trafford in the first Test of the 1993 tour of England – his first delivery in an Ashes Test – was a glorious fluke, and that he had sent down other deliveries that were just as good, but he came to accept that that ball was the most famous he ever bowled. And its fame was largely due to its impact as a visual event. Television caught it all. The swerved flight down the leg side, the vicious bite off the turf that turned the ball eighteen inches to clip the top of the off stump, and Gatting's rooted-to-the-spot astonishment were all testament to the extraordinariness of what happened. As with Gordon Banks's save from Pelé's header in the 1970 Mexico World Cup (which was instantly hailed as the greatest save in football history), television had captured a moment of sporting genius so perfectly that it guaranteed it immortality.

Having bowled many other wonderful deliveries, Warne was entitled to argue the case for perspective. He was actually as pleased with the first ball of his very next over, a big-spinning leg break that had Robin Smith caught at slip. Indeed, it was only when he saw a TV replay of the Gatting ball in the dressing room at the next interval that Warne realized quite how amazing it had been. (Duly inspired, in his first over after the interval he bowled two terrific deliveries to Graham Gooch, both of which Warne thought better than the Gatting ball, before having Gooch caught off a full toss.) But years later he was sceptical of its status. He much preferred getting a batsman out with a trap that he had spent several overs laying than with a one-off wonder ball. In his autobiography, he wrote, 'As for [the Gatting ball] being the "ball of the century", as it has been described, I don't think that can be for anybody to say. So much of cricket's rich history has gone unfilmed.' But in the modern world, if it wasn't on film, it hadn't happened.

Having been seen (on television) by so many astonished people, that one delivery certainly had a bigger impact on Warne's life than any other (though the Richardson ball in Melbourne was probably more significant for his career). As he himself said, during the rest of that tour of England hundreds of people were to ask him about the Gatting ball – and hundreds more have asked him about it since. 'That ball sort of changed my whole life . . .' he said. 'Suddenly people wanted to know who I hung out with, where I hung out . . . what I was actually doing.' And he didn't find it easy handling the overnight fame. 'It was hard,' he added. 'It was bloody difficult getting followed around all the time. [You'd] leave your hotel room and there'd be four photographers following you and jumping in a car and you'd go down the pub or you'd do whatever, and they're waiting out the front. That was hard.'

Had he been playing in an earlier era, things might have been very different. For instance, it wasn't until Kerry Packer wrought a revolution in television coverage of cricket, in the late 1970s, that anyone had thought of positioning cameras at both ends of the ground, so that viewers weren't forced to spend half the overs, in Packer's words, 'watching the batsman's bum'. Had cameras been functioning only from the Stretford Road end of the Old Trafford ground, much of the magic of the Gatting ball would have been hidden. Indeed, BBC Radio's *Test Match Special* commentary team was situated at that end, and Jonathan Agnew, who was commentating at the time and had not seen Warne bowl before, initially struggled to account for what had happened – until he too had had the benefit of television's bird's-eye view. 'At first the ball looked as though it was going to pitch on leg, then it began to drift,' Agnew told me. 'It dipped and went so fast – that was the killer. My commentary did not sound at all definitive, but then that was how it was. It was a case of "Bloody hell, what's happened here?"'

Many of Packer's innovations were eventually taken up by the likes of BBC Television, which had the rights to the 1993 Tests (though, as the BBC is a non-commercial organization, it did not insert advertisements between overs – a device that would open the door to cricket's huge marketing potential). Before Packer, the BBC – which had been showing Test cricket in England since 1938 – had made do with no more than six cameras in total, and Australia's ABC was no more comprehensive in its coverage. But once Packer had bought up so many of the world's leading players for his breakaway World Series Cricket, he immediately doubled the number of cameras on his grounds, and this practice was continued when he subsequently secured the rights to show official Test cricket in Australia on his Channel Nine station (in exchange for abandoning his rival product). He also introduced other technological devices that were to transform cricket coverage around the world, such as slow-motion replays, stump microphones, stump cameras, and side-on cameras to determine run-outs and stumpings.

The 1982 Boxing Day Test match in Melbourne between

Australia and England – which Warne attended as a thirteen-year-old – was the first occasion when a giant television screen was used inside a cricket ground for the benefit of spectators. By the time Warne was playing, such screens were becoming common around the world.

All these changes served to bring viewers closer to the action, and for a proper appreciation of the subtleties of the spin bowler's art this was crucial. Television was able to reveal the full extent of the psychological drama as Warne laid his traps and snared his victims. Thanks to television, it became clear that, in his way, Warne held every bit as much terror for the batsman as a rampaging fast bowler. Television didn't turn Warne into a spin-bowling wizard, but it certainly burnished his reputation. As Tony Greig, one of Channel Nine's commentators, said, 'We don't hold back at all. If someone's good, boy, we unashamedly make 'em the best in the world.'

Warne actually helped trigger a refinement in television technology: the super slow-mo camera, which captured more images per second (75 of them to be precise) and allowed an even more detailed examination of precisely how he (and other spinners) gripped their different deliveries and how many revs they were putting on the ball. The super slow-mo, originally called Spin Vision, was introduced for Australia's tour of the Caribbean in 1995 and Warne's eagerly anticipated duels with Brian Lara.

This special camera was to have a harmful effect on some spinners – Pakistan's Saqlain Mushtaq was a case in point – because it laid bare the secrets of their craft, but Warne was relatively unaffected, because he was not really a 'mystery' bowler. Good batsmen could pick his googly anyway, and many of the problems he posed were down to the subtle degrees of spin he put on his leg breaks – and no amount of video homework could help opponents with that. He did have two deliveries, the slider and the flipper, which went straight on when the batsman might be expecting turn, but his flipper was less effective after his shoulder problems in any case. Indeed, Stuart MacGill claimed that the super slow-mo actually helped himself and Warne to better understand the mechanics of what they were doing.

Thanks to TV, Warne's fame reached South Africa – where the Australians toured in early 1994 – even before he had set foot in the place. There was enormous interest in the whole squad, because it was Australia's first visit since South Africa's return to the international sporting community following the collapse of apartheid, but Warne was easily the chief attraction.

'Wherever we went we were feted like rock stars, receiving free meals at restaurants, drink cards at bars and instant recognition,' Steve Waugh wrote. 'Being such a showman and an outrageous talent, Warney had the status of an Elvis Presley. The public couldn't get enough of him, particularly as the South African team were quite conservative on the field and many of the players avid churchgoers off it. Warney was a superstar with all the trimmings, and our team of assigned bodyguards took special care in supervising his safety after cricket hours.'

On another occasion Waugh said, 'On tour he would often spend a lot of time to himself, listening to music. This was his sanctuary away from the burning spotlight. Often he would have room-service pizza, watch movies, or study and analyse the day's play . . . It was difficult for Shane at times with his enormous profile. He had to keep in check all those people who wanted to be around him. There were times I felt sorry for the lack of privacy he was afforded.'

There was another thing to bear in mind. Channel Nine actually played an important, if unofficial, role in the administration of Australian cricket. Packer quite deliberately signed leading Australian players – Warne included – on commentating contracts in order to supplement their incomes, which he was keenly aware were low by the standards of some other sports. When a pay dispute between players and the board threatened to result in strike action during the 1997–98 season, it was executives at Channel Nine – fearful of their product being removed from the screen – who were instrumental in brokering a deal.

Warne's admiration for Richie Benaud was bound up in Benaud's status as a TV icon. The two of them were inextricably linked in the minds of many cricket followers because of their common craft, but their relationship was probably not as close as was popularly supposed, even though each clearly held the other in high regard. After all, Benaud was almost forty years Warne's senior. But Warne would have listened to the warm words of Terry Jenner and Ian Chappell about Benaud's standing as a great leg-spinner and inspirational captain, and known that here was the man he should measure himself against.

Warne would have been crazy not to pick Benaud's brains. Benaud knew all about the mechanics of bowling and had been commentating for around a quarter of a century before Warne arrived on the scene. He was granted one of the best seats in the house in the commentary box, with access to replays, and in his prime he was a superb analyst. Warne said that Benaud was reluctant to volunteer advice, but if Warne asked him for his view on how he was bowling – which he did 'every now and then' – his assistance was guaranteed. Overall, Warne said, Benaud provided him with 'enormous help'.

Benaud remembered them first meeting on the golf course shortly after Warne's Test debut in 1992. Warne had asked him then if he had any advice. 'I told him the same thing Bill O'Reilly told me,' Benaud said. 'Find a leg break that you can turn as far as you can and then keep putting it on the same spot.' For years, Benaud praised Warne as the best young leg-spinner he had seen, though Warne rather outstripped that description before Benaud gave up using it – which was probably around the time Warne overtook Benaud's career haul of 248 wickets, at Old Trafford in 1997, and displaced him as statistically the most successful leg-spinner in Test history.

Benaud had no reason to begrudge Warne his many triumphs, because they allowed him to bask in reflected glory. How many young viewers listening to Benaud's TV commentary in Australia or England would have known that he was once a great leg-spinner himself had it not been for Warne? Would such a huge occasion as the deciding contest between England and Australia at the Oval in 2005 have been interrupted for the crowd to pay tribute to Benaud's last commentary stint in England had Warne's career not kept Benaud in business as a leg-spin guru?

Warne clearly revered Benaud's achievements. He once said that when he was bowling he would sometimes look up at the scoreboard, see his own figures, and say to himself, 'Benaud would have done better.' Whether this would actually have been the case is less certain. Jack Potter had the privilege to study both at closer quarters than most. He batted against Benaud in state cricket when Benaud was at his peak, and worked with the young Warne in the nets. 'The only other leggie with Warne's accuracy was Benaud,'

Potter said. 'But you could sort of sit on Benaud, though you wouldn't get a lot of runs. But you couldn't sit on Warne, because he would drift and spin the ball past the bat, because he really tweaked it.'

6

Invisible

W ANTING TO BE famous and coming to terms with that
fame were not quite the same thing, as Warne was
to discover. He had been fast-tracked by Australian cricket
into the Test arena, and had then fast-tracked himself, through
his phenomenal performances, to stardom. For a young man
who had previously led a narrow, comfortable, middle-class
existence in suburban Melbourne, celebrity, once found, was
bound to have a seismic impact. No one could really teach
him how to react; he would have to find out for himself.
Mistakes were inevitable.

What made things especially demanding was that he was
required to do his growing up in public. Many of his teammates were spared this ordeal. The likes of Justin Langer,
Matthew Hayden and Damien Martyn played for Australia
in a few games and were then dropped. When they eventually
came back into the side, several years later, they had had
the chance to take stock and were much stronger and wiser
about what playing cricket at the highest level meant. They
not only did well, but generally knew how to handle themselves (even if all three took their cricket rather seriously).
Warne was afforded no such luxury. After the Boxing Day
Test of 1992, he was a certainty for selection provided he
was fit, and in the event he didn't miss a Test until 1996,
when he underwent surgery on his main spinning finger. If

observers thought Warne's euphoric cavortings in front of spectators after Australian victories were the behaviour of an immature young man, then they were spot on. They were.

It may be significant that the three Australian players of his generation who pretty much remained permanent fixtures in the side from early on – Warne, Mark Waugh and Ricky Ponting – all got into various sorts of trouble, whether it was taking money from bookies, excessive drinking, or gambling. This trio, close mates in the mid-1990s, were the team's risk-takers. They played their cricket with a gambler's eye and a flamboyance bordering on arrogance. It was young man's cricket.

Warne never really grew up, because the public persona he was trapped in made it very difficult to. Off the field this was a disaster for him, but on the field it was a great asset. He was cricket's Peter Pan. Forever young, but also – fortunately for him – forever competitive. Yearning always to be young, he never grew cynical about his cricket.

The big trick for Warne was to grasp where celebrity ended and the cricket began. It was all about a longer C-word than Warne or Merv Hughes would ever have used: compartmentalization. Some sportsmen, such as Tiger Woods, Michael Owen and Sachin Tendulkar, have managed this very well by leading determinedly private lives when not involved in their sport, though some sportsmen have shown that it is possible to embrace celebrity without it affecting one's performance on the pitch. Whatever the route taken, it is necessary to learn to keep each aspect separate and to remain in control. 'I don't like to say that I'm a man with two faces,' Jose Mourinho once said, 'but Jose Mourinho the manager and the man are very different. It's important to separate them, and I do that very easily.'

In many ways, Warne compartmentalized very well. He

admitted that he had made mistakes early in his career, but he rectified these. 'When you're young and impressionable, you can get caught up in your own press,' he told *Alpha* magazine in January 2007. 'I went through a period in the mid-1990s when I was too trusting. Over time, you learn to get the right people around you.' He learned not to take his worries with him onto the pitch. He enjoyed his greatest Test series, in the Ashes series of 2005, when his personal life was in turmoil, which must have taken enormous mental strength.

He had an excellent disciplinary record. In fifteen years as a Test cricketer, he was only once punished under the International Cricket Conference's code of conduct for an on-field offence, in 1994. (He was once censured by the Australian board for writing that an egg could be fried on Graeme Smith's face in 2 seconds.) Although he was a master at 'working' an umpire, and was among Australia's sledgers-in-chief, he knew exactly where to draw the line. He became expert at pushing umpires to the limit but not beyond – although towards the end of his career it was hard not to draw the conclusion that umpires were reluctant to throw the book at a living legend and ought to have been tougher with him. But if so, that was officialdom's fault, not Warne's.

In this respect, Warne's tactics were typically Australian. 'The very act of pushing a boundary or challenging an edge contains an acknowledgement of the existence of limit,' Gideon Haigh wrote of the Australian cricketer's psyche. 'Ruthlessness is not an absolute; it involves a comparison with a known standard, and that standard in Australia is still an Anglo [English] one. And while our sport has been less inhibited, more cut-throat, we tend to bend rules rather than break them. Maradona's "Hand of God" goal in the 1986

World Cup, an instance of admitted cheating justified by national pride, would not have made him a hero in this country.'

But away from the pitch, things were different. Cricket had clearly defined laws and codes which governed what its participants could and could not do on the field. Warne knew he must abide by these, and was willing to do so. They formed the professional parameters within which he operated; they framed his work. But in life the rules of engagement were far less clear. In life, circumstances were more fluid, and this made it harder to recognize what was morally acceptable and what was not. Warne was far from alone in this. Sportsmen are notoriously bad at real life. Jennifer Beller, a researcher at the University of Idaho Center for Ethics, studied the moral development of 35,000 athletes and non-athletes, and concluded that the average adult athlete was self-centred, insular and had the moral reasoning of a thirteen-year-old. 'For years, people said sport builds character,' she declared. 'Our research shows it negatively impacts character. Sport has failed to develop traits such as honesty and responsibility.'

It was worth noting that almost all the controversies for which Warne is remembered took place off the field – the prank on the academy tour, taking money from a bookmaker, the failed drugs test, the extramarital affairs.

I asked Rod Bransgrove, the chairman of Hampshire County Cricket Club, who knew Warne well in his later career, why he thought Warne found it hard to resist off-field temptations that he must have known were wrong. 'I honestly believe Shane thinks that when he's away from the cricket he's invisible, or he can make himself invisible,' Bransgrove said. 'When he's leading his life off the field, he doesn't seem to understand that people still know who he is. It is surprising for someone who understands his celebrity so well in so many ways.'

It was as though in his own mind Warne had compartmentalized his two personas – superstar cricketer and private man – so thoroughly that they had absolutely no connection. But of course they had.

In one way Warne effortlessly adapted to the big time, in another he seemed to have little idea how to conduct himself in public. Perhaps he was trying too hard to convince himself, his teammates and his huge TV audience that he was indeed the real deal. Self-doubt was out, self-belief in.

As someone who regarded himself as a television performer, Warne seemed compelled to give full expression to his theatrical side, and television was certainly expecting ever-more flamboyant shows of emotion from sportsmen of all types.

The huge pressure of performing in front of large audiences for large sums of money had had a lot to do with a general decline in the behaviour of young professional sportsmen during the early 1980s. It was a predictable phenomenon: the more they were paid, the more attention was lavished on them, the more childishly they carried on, the more they despised authority. It was the first flush of reality television . . . John McEnroe railing at tennis umpires, Alex Higgins headbutting a snooker official, Eric Cantona leaping into the crowd to kick a spectator, Javed Miandad shaping to hit Dennis Lillee with his bat, Mike Tyson biting Evander Holyfield's ear: sport was not short of its heat-of-the-moment idiocies. Compared to many, Warne's behaviour was mild. It was just rather racy for cricket.

It was noticeable that Warne's most extreme outbursts were mainly connected to celebrations. They were what cricketers call the 'send-off': a few caustic words directed at a beaten opponent before he trudges back to the pavilion; an insult added to an injury. In other words, they weren't planned, but occurred in moments of euphoria. They were purely instinctive things. As Warne himself once said, 'We play at a very high level of arousal, on the edge of fury.'

It was only with experience that Warne learned that it was unnecessary to sledge opponents when he'd already won the battle. It was far more useful to bait or goad a batsman into a misjudgement. At this early stage he was still a relatively unsophisticated strategist. As Patrick Smith wrote in the Melbourne *Age* when Warne sent off South Africa's Paul Adams with mock laughter during a Test in Port Elizabeth in 1997, 'Under pressure he turns into a boor. The pleasant young man of television interviews is readily interchangeable with an immature hothead.'

Even as a relative newcomer Warne usually had a fair bit to say for himself, and could be quite canny. In the New Year Test at Sydney in 1994, he gave South African opener Gary Kirsten, who was playing his first series, a tirade of abuse as Kirsten enjoyed repeated good fortune. 'Warney led the way and tore into me the most,' Kirsten recalled many years later.

He was still at a particularly talkative stage of his career . . . but I also had the impression, sometimes, that the rest of the team looked to Shane to take the lead when a member of the opposition needed a bit of a blast . . . Unlike fast bowlers, Shane saved his best efforts for when you were standing next to him at the non-striker's end . . . I recall him telling me that I was wasting both my time and his – that I didn't belong on the same field as him – and also that I might want to consider a career change if I wanted to make a living . . . When they try to work on your mind as well as just your emotions they become much more effective. The very best sledging has a technical edge to it, and when that is backed up by bowlers as good as Glenn McGrath and Shane Warne it really does affect you.

But Warne's verbals didn't really work in Sydney. He got his man in the end, but Kirsten survived long enough to top-score the innings with 67.

Of course, the Australian side that Warne had joined delivered an unusually hard brand of cricket. Allan Border was in no frame of mind to apologize for the way his team played, and Warne must have been encouraged to mimic the foul-mouthed abuse aimed at opponents by Merv Hughes, the most vocal of Border's bowlers. Healy and the close fielders would have lent their support. It is not to excuse what Warne did to say that the standard had been set by others.

But he certainly didn't need any second invitation. On his first tours of England and South Africa, he gave verbal send-offs to Matthew Maynard at the Oval and to the mild-mannered Andrew Hudson in Johannesburg that Hughes might have been proud of. And in Australia in 1993 he had found in Daryll Cullinan an opponent ready to engage in enough squabbling to keep an entire kindergarten occupied. Cullinan brought things on himself. He hadn't been in the South African team long before he was standing at slip and dishing out verbals to batsmen who probably didn't know who he was. The Australians, who took the view that you had to earn the right to have an opinion, took exception, and Warne delighted in giving Cullinan the full treatment, especially when he took his wicket four times in six weeks. He gave him a pretty juicy send-off too at Sydney. But whereas with Hughes the oaths were just part of the fast bowler's furniture, they sat far less easily with Warne, whose image was altogether softer. Warne's cricket was about intelligence and guile, and, although he had something of a reputation as a rebel, most onlookers wouldn't have associated this with his contorted face spitting out vitriol.

If publicly challenged, Warne generally claimed to be unrepentant about his aggression. It wasn't an issue on which the Australian team were prepared to negotiate: broadly, their attitude during Border's later years as captain was to be as aggressive as they could within the guidelines set down by officialdom. If officialdom was weak and allowed them to get away with more, then they would. Warne would brush away the criticism by saying that there would always be people who chose to dislike him, just as others would choose to like him, as though he was powerless to stop the process.

But what Warne, among others, discovered to his consternation was that television, the very thing that had helped create his iconic status, also served to show that his feet were very much made of clay. In earlier times, television might have failed to capture the quick-fire word or gesture of hostility. Not now. Very little escaped the multitude of cameras focused on the pitch. Slow-motion replays and stump microphones exposed flashpoints in all their inglorious detail.

And it wasn't just some TV commentators shaking their heads that players had to contend with either, because in 1991 the ICC had introduced match referees, plus a code of conduct, in an effort to police the game more strictly. The referees sat in the stands in front of TV monitors, ready to note down any indiscretion. As Warne naively pointed out in one of his books, there were moments when the risk of being caught on camera or microphone having a go at an opponent could be minimized (such as between overs, when the television companies left the cricket to show money-spinning adverts), but in the heat of battle such tricks were usually forgotten. This exposure of the ugly conduct that went on out in the middle of a cricket ground marked the final demythologizing of the game.

One of the reasons Warne's feud with Cullinan became so celebrated was because TV captured every episode and encouraged everyone, including newspaper journalists, to dissect it. That it had begun in Australia had contributed to South African crowds giving the Australians a hard time when they visited their country a few months later, despite their general enthusiasm for the tour and excitement at Warne's presence.

South African crowds have always loved to hate Australian cricketers, just as English crowds do. Warne, as Australia's most dangerous and colourful player, and Hughes, who looked like a cartoon villain with his handlebar moustache, huge torso and spindly legs, became special targets. It was a sort of mark of respect – though when the Australians were being pelted with fruit when fielding near the boundaries and subjected to nuisance calls in their hotel rooms they certainly wouldn't have seen it that way. For several years Warne struggled to find a measured response to the rowdier elements of foreign crowds. When Australia won, he was apt to gloat, dancing around the players' balcony and giving the finger to the crowd. The behaviour of some spectators was unforgivable, but Warne could be an embarrassment too, and his antics were guaranteed to scramble squadrons of Australian newspaper columnists into flights of indignation. But sport is littered with cases of young men making fools of themselves as they hurtle along the precarious path of fame and fortune.

The most notorious on-field incident in Warne's entire Test career was the send-off he gave Andrew Hudson after bowling him round his legs in Johannesburg in 1994. It wasn't so much what he said as what he did, which was to rush towards the South African opener while screaming primally in full earshot of the umpires, 'Fuck off! Fuck off out of here!' Had Ian Healy not dashed over and restrained him, Warne might have physically attacked his opponent. 'Rarely on a cricket field has physical violence seemed so close,' *Wisden* reported.

There were extenuating circumstances: for some reason, Border had decided not to call on Warne until the forty-fourth over of the innings, which was a very late juncture for him, and the taunts of the South African crowds had got to many of the Australian players. But the chief factor was the strain Warne was experiencing after eighteen months of near-continuous international cricket and Elvis Presley-style attention.

The incident caused an outcry. It was inevitable that Warne would be punished under the ICC's code of conduct, although match referee Donald Carr, a former England captain of the amateur days, applied his powers feebly (as many referees did) by fining him just AUS$400 (about £170), which merely served further to incense critics back in Australia watching on television. To make matters worse, Hughes had been caught swearing at another South African player, Gary Kirsten, and had been seen brandishing a bat at a spectator who had spat at him. Carr had also fined him a footling AUS$400. David Hookes, the former Test batsman, demanded that both players be called home, while other influential voices in the media said that Warne and Hughes had made them ashamed to be Australian.

Generally, when its team was winning, the Australian

Cricket Board was disinclined to come down hard on the misbehaviour of its players. Occasionally it would make noises about them needing to moderate their aggression, but this rarely resulted in change. Border had been treated with kid gloves for several years. In this sense, the lenient action taken against Warne after his first misdemeanour at the academy was typical, as was the ACB's handling of the Warne–Mark Waugh bookie scandal.

But in this instance, such was the outcry in Australia that the ACB issued fines of its own — AUS$4,000 on Warne and AUS$8,000 on Hughes, whose third disciplinary offence this was in fifteen Tests.

These swingeing punishments upset the entire tour party, who felt the treatment the team was being subjected to in South Africa hadn't been taken into account, and left Warne deeply shocked. It was the first really serious setback of his career, and it forced him to confront what had happened to him in the previous eighteen months – what a big star he had become, how it had changed him and the responsibilities it placed on him as a role model to thousands of youngsters.

Perhaps because he associated self-analysis with the self-doubt that had tormented him in his early months as a Test cricketer, Warne was generally reluctant to examine himself too deeply in case the scrutiny eroded his self-belief, but in this case he apologized profusely and reflected at some length on why he had let down himself, and his country, so badly.

One of the first things he did was study the television pictures. 'The film of that incident is pretty awful and the guy in the footage is not the real me,' Warne said. 'I look an angry man. It's like I'm back playing football.'

He gave an interview to Patrick Keane of Australian Associated Press, in which he admitted he was having trouble coping with his success. 'I've got a really short fuse at the moment and I feel myself snapping . . . The continual ride over the last eighteen months has got to me and I'm just burning up. I feel angry all the time.' He said that his team-mates knew he had not been himself going into that day's play, a claim their autobiographies would bear out. He later described himself as 'a time-bomb waiting to explode'. He also reflected, 'Some of the success I'd enjoyed might have made me big-headed for a while.' On another occasion, he said, 'The problem with some people is that when they have success, they begin to believe their own publicity. It happened to me. You get aloof.'

Warne was also to endure another painful trial-by-TV several years later, although in this instance he was entirely innocent. He was widely accused of having uttered a disparaging remark about a teammate, Scott Muller, that was picked up by an effects microphone. Muller was making his second (and, as it turned out, last) Test appearance, against Pakistan in Hobart in November 1999, and during an undistinguished game he fluffed a throw in from the outfield to Warne, who was bowling. The microphone caught someone saying, 'This bloke can't bowl and he can't throw.' The remark didn't become public until after the game, but once it did there was a general assumption that it must have come from Warne, who had been standing alone near a microphone at the bowler's end. It was only after exhaustive investigation that it was established that Warne had merely sworn as Muller's throw came in, and that the microphone that picked up the remark was actually situated on the boundary near a Channel Nine cameraman, Joe Provitera.

Even so, the story took time to die. Some suspected that Provitera was taking the rap for Warne because Warne had a contract with Channel Nine, and a running joke took hold in Australia that any problem in any walk of life could be blamed on Joe the Cameraman. Warne, reasonably enough, was upset that his word wasn't readily accepted, but by the time the incident happened, people had come to learn that his public denials couldn't always be taken at face value.

In his first book, *My Own Story*, written in 1997, Warne spoke of the tremendous pressure that television placed on sportsmen by putting them before an audience of millions.

> At times it feels like the cameras and the public are watching your every move. People constantly criticize Mark Taylor because he chews gum so much on the field or Steve Waugh because he doesn't smile enough. At times I feel trapped by all this. It is no wonder some of us occasionally blow our tops in tense situations on the field. It's a wonder it does not happen more often . . . One step out of line and we're in trouble. Sometimes you feel like you have no escape, that everything you do is watched, analysed and often criticized. It's part of the game and in the end we have to learn to deal with it the best way we can.
>
> What some people forget is that we are different off the field. To put it simply, I'm a bit like Jeckle [*sic*] and Hyde. Off the field I'm laidback, on the field I'm super competitive and aggressive and sometimes go too far. But I'm an emotional cricketer and who wants robots?

Maybe this explained why he tended to get into scrapes off the field. Being obliged to live so much of his life in front of cameras, and behave well in front of them, he perhaps felt that he was entitled to be not held to account for what happened when they weren't there.

One of Warne's most notorious misjudgements was the acceptance of money from an Indian bookmaker, referred to only as 'John', in Sri Lanka in 1994. John gave Warne

US$5,000 (about £3,300), and then sought from him information about team selection and pitch and weather conditions, which Warne provided. It is a well-documented episode, but its part in Warne's story has been largely misunderstood.

It was an incident that shed fresh light on Warne's true character: the depth of his gambling so early in his international career, his attitude to money, his poor judgement in matters away from the cricket field, and his difficulties in providing accurate, consistent explanations. In some people's eyes, Warne's inaccuracies hinted at darker secrets. If they were right, the secrets remain untold to this day, despite several inquiries into corruption in cricket in which he did not even get a namecheck.

In personal terms, it proved a hugely costly error. It brought Warne no end of criticism, cost him money in lost endorsements and contributed to the Australian board deciding against ever appointing him Australia's official captain. This in turn affected his confidence: it was no co-incidence that he then struggled with his cricket.

Yet, equally, Warne showed great courage in publicly stating that Salim Malik, the Pakistan captain and a high-profile figure in the game, had attempted to bribe him to deliberately underperform. (Malik was probably acting in the knowledge – not yet made public – that Warne had already taken money from John.) To accuse a fellow competitor of such a heinous offence rarely wins points in sport and when it later emerged that Warne had himself taken money from a bookie the backlash was all the stronger. Yet, in the end, Warne and the other Australians who submitted evidence against Malik were vindicated when he was handed a life ban by the Pakistan Cricket Board in 2000.

Warne was unquestionably wrong, and greedy, to take the

bookmaker's money – offered supposedly without strings while he was playing in a one-day tournament in Colombo – and yet on the balance of probability the real disgrace of the Shane Warne–Mark Waugh 'bookie scandal' was not Warne's foolishness, or even Waugh's deeper involvement with the mysterious John, but the Australian board's cover-up.

The board's decisions to hide from public knowledge both John's payments to Warne and Waugh and the fines the board imposed on the two players (AUS$8,000 in the case of Warne, AUS$10,000 in the case of Waugh – almost exactly the sums they had received from John) when once it learned what had happened in 1995, were among the most disastrous errors of administration ever committed by a cricketing authority.

The board later justified its actions by saying it did not want the public jumping to the wrong conclusion (that Warne and Waugh's testimony against Malik was no longer valid because of John's payments to them), yet the immediate consequence was that Warne and Waugh remained available to play in a Test series in the Caribbean that held huge significance for Australian cricket. It was a golden chance for Australia to finally displace West Indies as the best team in the world – a chance they duly took. Whether they would have managed it without Warne and Waugh must be doubted.

If the board's actions helped the national team, they certainly did no favours to the two cricketers in the long term. Had Warne been exposed at the time, he might have learned to grow up and be more publicly accountable for his actions. He might have been forgiven and allowed to become Australia's captain. As it was, the cover-up can have only heightened Warne's sense of leading a protected and privileged existence.

Stern action might also have acted as a warning to cricketers in other countries – such as Hansie Cronje, the South Africa captain, who might have thought twice before continuing the clandestine relationships with bookmakers that would eventually lead to his ruin.

Instead, when the story eventually came out in the Australian press in 1998, four years after the original event, the outcry was all the greater, and the recriminations were all the more bitter. Warne immediately flew to Adelaide to join Mark Waugh in reading out statements to the media about how they had been 'naive and stupid' to take 'John's' money. Warne was shocked at the passions the issue aroused. Some critics likened his actions to those of players like Salim Malik, who faced grave allegations of corruption; others wanted him and Waugh sacked from the team. Even Melbourne's newspapers turned against him. The *Age* sacked him as a columnist while the *Herald Sun* said that he should never be allowed a leadership role in Australian cricket. Warne, who was now captaining Victoria, found himself using his captain's press conferences to defend himself at a time when he was desperately trying to believe again in his bowling. The context in which Warne and Waugh took the money was lost, because in the intervening four years match-fixing – in which corrupt bookmakers paid money to players to influence the course of matches to the advantage of the bookies – had gone from an unknown phenomenon to a widespread and serious threat to the game. In fact it was not until the month after Warne met John that the first public suspicions of malpractice were voiced when India were deducted points by match referee Raman Subba Row for allegedly not making an effort to win a one-dayer against West Indies in Kanpur. (The ICC later rescinded the decision, saying that Subba Row had exceeded his authority.) Soon

Pakistan were engulfed by corruption allegations, and by 1998 the atmosphere was febrile. It wasn't the time to be admitting to friendships with shady characters.

For a start, Warne and Waugh looked like hypocrites for levelling accusations against Salim Malik when they had already taken money from a bookmaker themselves. They were considered to have behaved in an un-Australian manner, which is about as serious a charge as could be laid, for they had 'sold' their country and lost sight of the honour of representing their nation on a sports field. These were the grander charges. In Warne's case there was probably also an element of 'tall-poppy syndrome' at work: he had enjoyed almost six years of uninterrupted success, and for many the scandal provided an essential and overdue counterweight. Again, this wouldn't have applied had the facts come out when the Australian board first learned of them in February 1995.

It did not help that the processes of match-fixing were not fully understood by many people. Corrupt bookmakers were not necessarily interested in fixing the outcomes of matches; this was hard to do, because it required the co-operation of several players. The bookies set markets, and took wagers, for 'side bets' such as how particular players might perform, or how many wides and no-balls there would be in an innings. These bets could be achieved by bribing just one player. Captains were particularly desirable targets, and the biggest names to receive life bans for corruption were all Test captains: Cronje, Salim Malik, and India's Mohammad Azharuddin. All manner of illegal betting activity was termed 'match-fixing', whether it was actually the match result that was being fixed or not. Providing information was also lumped under this emotive umbrella.

Whatever popular sentiment said, there was a distinction

between what Warne was found guilty of – receiving US$5,000 from a bookmaker and then giving his opinion about how pitches might play, the weather, and the probable balance of the Australia team – and agreeing to personally underperform in matches or to persuade others to do so. This was a distinction which Warne was anxious to emphasize, but it was lost on a lot of his critics.

But Warne did not help himself. In 1998 the climate was such that he commonly denied knowing that John was a bookie, whereas in 1999 he testified on oath to a Pakistani inquiry into match-fixing and betting allegations, held in Melbourne, that John had described himself to him as 'a bookmaker'. Warne told the court that John, who was staying in the same hotel as the Australian team in Colombo and whom he had met the previous evening in a casino, had asked him to come to see him in his room. John's opening words, according to Warne's account, were, 'It was an honour to meet you last night. I'm a bookmaker from India. I bet on the cricket. I've won lots of money on Australia.' John had seen Warne lose money at the casino, and he now offered him an envelope stuffed with American dollars, as a token of appreciation. Warne initially refused it but when John persisted – saying he would be offended if he refused and that there were no strings attached – Warne finally took the cash.

But there were strings attached. A few months later, John rang Warne in Australia to ask about weather and pitch conditions and team selection. And only a few weeks after the Colombo tournament Australia were playing in Pakistan when Warne and Waugh were separately approached by Malik and asked if they and some teammates would under-perform in certain situations in return for US$200,000 (about £135,000). These were staggering proposals – few known cricketing bribes, either accepted or merely offered, matched such a sum – while Malik's openness suggested he was confident his targets would accept. He must have been talking to John. But both Warne and Waugh turned him down.

Warne has been criticized for not grasping that Malik and John were acting in unison, yet at the time of the Pakistan tour Warne had not had contact with John since receiving the money; nor was he expecting any. Waugh, on the other hand, had had a much closer relationship with John. He had received more money from him than Warne in an arrangement described as a 'business deal'. He had introduced John to Warne at the casino. Waugh took more phone calls from John to answer questions about pitch and weather conditions (he refused to talk about strategy and selection), and these started during the one-day matches in Sri Lanka. When, several years later, Australian journalists got wind of the story, they heard from team sources about Waugh's involvement, but not Warne's. 'Technically,' Warne would say, 'I did give information for money, but not in the way portrayed.' Waugh couldn't say the same.

But Warne's testimony wavered on other issues. He told the Melbourne court that he had reported Malik's approach the next day to his captain, Mark Taylor, and to Bob Simpson, the coach, but this was contradicted by the accounts of other Australian players (not themselves entirely consistent). Tim May, whom Malik wanted to bowl badly along with Warne, recalled in an interview that Simpson and Col Egar, the team manager, learned of the offered bribes only when Mark Waugh walked in after Australia had lost a one-day match Malik had wanted them to lose deliberately and joked, 'Ah, would've been better off taking the bribes, guys.' May added, 'And the manager and coach were there – "What? What are you talking about?" And so that's where it all sort of came from.' That one-day game was actually almost three weeks after the Test in which Warne was approached – three weeks in which Warne and May had said nothing to the management.

But the context to this whole affair must not be forgotten. At the time he met John, in September 1994, Warne was just twenty-four years old and still riding the first wave of his fame. He'd been on the road as an international cricketer for almost exactly two years – since his Test career had spluttered into life in this very same city of Colombo – and in that short time he had become one of the most recognizable sports stars on the planet. He was earning serious amounts of money, but probably hadn't yet adjusted to how best to spend it. He was used to being pestered by autograph-hunters and admirers who wanted their photographs taken with him, who sought to engage him in conversation for a few minutes, or wanted to give him tokens of their appreciation. He could easily have taken John pushing money into his hand as just another aspect of this worship.

Warne, like many Australians, had always loved to gamble. As a child, he had often watched his parents play various card games, and he had taken up cards at school. As he became more affluent, his visits to casinos became more frequent. Nor was he alone in this. A lot of international cricketers would play the tables, and the casino in Colombo was a popular haunt with several visiting teams in a city where rival attractions were perhaps limited. Similarly, card games were also popular among cricketers all over the world: they were standard time-killers in the dressing room on rainy days. Asked about his gambling habits in 1998, Warne said he played blackjack and roulette, and bet on Aussie Rules, 'but never on cricket when I was involved'. Asked in 2006 whether he would like to be a professional poker player, he said, 'If I'd got A$20–30 million (about £8–12 million), I wouldn't mind giving it a go, but I haven't.' The night he met John he had lost US$5,000 on roulette, so when they met again the next evening and John offered to make up his losses it must have been hard to turn down. Warne took the money to the casino later that day, exchanged it for what turned out to be US$5,000 of chips – he said he hadn't previously counted it – and promptly lost the lot. Easy come, easy go.

Warne wasn't the only one to be stunned by Malik's offers. Tim May found it hard to believe the offers had really been made. Neither Simpson nor Egar bothered to mention the offers in their tour reports. All this despite the fact that during overseas tours in 1992 and 1993 two Australians, Dean Jones and Allan Border, had been approached by Asian players suggesting that there were ways they could earn extra money. Both these incidents were spoken about among the tour parties, yet who had done anything about them? When the story came out in 1998, Warne admitted he had been 'naive and stupid' not to have realized that John's money was designed as a recruitment fee. But should he have really known better?

The context to this affair should not have been forgotten, but it was. When Rob O'Regan QC produced his report into allegations of match-fixing in Australian cricket, he argued persuasively that the fines imposed on Warne and Waugh were insufficient punishment. But he had fallen into the common trap of viewing matters from the perspective of 1998 rather than 1994. 'In my opinion this punishment was inadequate,' he said.

It did not reflect the seriousness of what they had done . . .
I do not think it is possible to explain their conduct away
as the result merely of naivety and stupidity. They must have

known that it is wrong to accept money from, and supply information to, a bookmaker whom they also knew as someone who betted on cricket. Otherwise they would have reported the incident to team management long before they were found out . . . In behaving as they did they failed lamentably to set the sort of example one might expect from senior players and role models for many young cricketers. A more appropriate penalty would, I think, have been suspension for a significant time.

But back in 1994 Warne and Waugh were not 'senior players', as O'Regan claimed. Warne, at that point, had been playing regularly for Australia for just two years, Waugh for less than four. Six teammates in Sri Lanka were more experienced. Warne certainly had justification in claiming he had been naive and foolish. Unfortunately, because of the way the Australian board handled the matter, he wasn't destined to grow up in a hurry.

7

Australia versus England

FOR INTERNATIONAL SPORTSMEN such as Warne, playing in a team environment, nationalism is a key element in the competitive process. They play for personal and collective pride, and of course they play for financial gain, but they also play for the honour of their country.

This is particularly true in Australia, where sport is one of the principal means for the nation to express itself on the international stage. 'We're stuck down here at the bottom end of the planet, so when we do battle on the sporting fields of the world, it gives us a thrill,' said Geoff Lawson, the former Australia fast bowler. 'Sport represents what we are.' Whether they like it or not, or can carry it off or not, Australian sportsmen who compete internationally are burdened with the status of quasi-ambassadors.

Cricket especially has helped define Australia's relationship with England, which, as the 'mother country', has always been an important point of reference whenever Australians look beyond their own shores to the wider world. It is probably one reason why Australia has dominated the contests for the Ashes. 'The margin of superiority is slight, but it is consistent,' David Stone, a philosopher, has written, 'and therefore calls for explanation . . . My own belief is that it is due to a difference in attitude towards the opponent: the Australians hate the Poms, the Poms only despise the

Australians.' Cricket writer Gideon Haigh concurs: 'Sport is, in some respects, the most dynamic, demotic and enduring dimension of Australia's relations with the country that gave it birth.'

Sporting excellence has also been one way of compensating for the nation's philistinism. 'Australians are practical people who like hard and fast standards by which to measure success,' John McDonald wrote in the *Sydney Morning Herald* after Australia regained the Ashes in December 2006.

> If you swim faster than everyone else, you're the world's best. If we beat all the other cricket teams, we're the world champions . . .
>
> We are not so confident when it comes to comparing novels, paintings or musical compositions, which require more complex forms of evaluations. Although we have made heroic attempts to turn culture into sport by awarding so many art prizes and book prizes, we cannot deny that in these areas the Poms have the edge. Perhaps this provides a justification for Australian philistinism: let's leave the arts to the Poms, the Frogs and the rest, and get on with the serious business of sport.

It must be doubted whether Warne saw sport or cricket in these broad terms. He was proud of being Australian, of course. According to Terry Jenner, one of the reasons Warne had continued for so long was an absolute passion for playing for Australia. 'He's a very proud Australian who has played through all kinds of pain and injury,' he said. David Lloyd said one of his clearest memories of being England coach was of Warne fielding during the Old Trafford Test in 1997 and shouting across the field to his teammates, 'Come on, Australia, this is what it's all about!' Lloyd said that it was rare to hear a player speak so clearly, and he suspected that

Warne had chosen his moment well, when the crowd had fallen quiet.

But Warne was never one for overt shows of patriotism. His loyalties were chiefly to the teams he represented – St Kilda, Victoria, Australia – and to his colleagues in the dressing room. He wasn't particularly stimulated by notions of Australia nationalism, as were many of his colleagues in the Test team. Melbourne, his state, was much closer to his heart. When he played his last Test series, it was noticeable that he gave a more vibrant performance, and bid a fonder farewell to the crowd, in his final match in Melbourne rather than at Sydney, which was actually the scene of his last-ever Test.

He is actually quite parochial. He has never aspired to live anywhere other than Melbourne and Southampton, where he lived when representing Hampshire; both are coastal cities. And in his sport he seemed to have no need of a wider perspective; the love of the contest was enough motivation for him. This was not so surprising – he had, after all, stumbled into cricket, Australia's one true national game, more or less by default. His original choice, Aussie Rules, was a game that didn't stretch much beyond the boundaries of a few Australian states. There was no reason why Warne's early notions of sport should have taken on an international dimension at all.

Also, what happened in the late 1990s was that Warne, faithful to his own strong sense of self that Ian Chappell had inculcated in him, began to grow apart from Australia. During this period, he began to shows signs of emotionally detaching himself from his country following the response there to a string of controversies, starting with the bookie scandal in 1998. Later there would be the sex scandals and the drugs ban. It was not that Australians doubted he was a champion cricketer; it was how he chose to conduct himself in other areas that concerned them. And Australians do have a very strong sense of morality – something that is reflected in their media.

Warne found the censoriousness hard to take. Unable to live up to impossibly high standards, he felt he was being treated unreasonably, and, although he had no choice but to live with it, he found it hard to forgive what amounted to Australia's only qualified approval of him. Like many sportsmen, he wanted to be judged solely on his performances, but that was hardly practicable. Whether he liked it or not (and it seemed that he did not) there were responsibilities that came with his position.

When he retired, he spoke of his relief that his behaviour would in future not attract quite the same degree of scrutiny from the media as it had. 'There's always going to be attention on what I'm doing and it's nice to have that sort of interest,' he said, 'but hopefully it won't be to the same intensity – the same judgemental, moralistic sort of stuff . . . Hopefully it [retirement] will keep people off my front lawn and from following me around in cars. Maybe I can get my gear off and dance on top of a bar now if I want to.'

At some point, I would suggest, Warne started seeing himself as something distinct from his nation, even if emotionally he remained tied to Melbourne as home, his beloved St Kilda Aussie Rules football club, and Australian cricket as the vehicle which gave him everything – fame, glory, money.

He was an egocentric character who liked being famous, and these were not traits to endear him to the average Australian, who has never lost his instinct for taking the shears to a tall poppy. When Warne admitted to mistakes – such as being naive and stupid in the case of the bookie scandal – the Australian press took it as an open invitation to ridicule him. 'Sometimes in Australia they look for the negatives, the bad things,' he once said. 'Over in England it's a bit more positive.'

Even in the kindest interpretations of the bookie scandal, Warne was guilty of using his position as a well-known cricketer to line his pockets, and this was not edifying to those Australians – and they are the majority – who like their heroes gritty and honest. In this respect Warne did not compare favourably to the greatest god in the Australian sporting pantheon, Sir Donald Bradman, who had been a child of an economic depression and was noted for his work ethic and abstinence. There was too much self indulgence in Warne's story for most people's liking. His parents had been comfortably off, and he had grown up in an age of pampering the like of which Bradman and his contemporaries could not have dreamed of. Warne had at various times eaten too much, drunk too much, smoked too much and, in some people's eyes, earned too much. He generally favoured combining sport with having a good time.

Warne may have arrived on the scene at the right time in cricketing terms but as far as the wider social scene was concerned his larrikin activities were out of step with the times. Australia had always been a deeply conservative country, but in the late 1990s it was embracing political correctness with vigour. Social mores were changing rapidly. Women were taking huge strides in their struggle for equal opportunity; some had begun sitting on the boards of major corporations. In the past, Warne might have got away with an occasional sexual indiscretion, but now he was offending a more prominent and vocal female constituency.

Peter Roebuck, a former English cricketer who spent much of his time in Australia from the mid-1990s writing on the game as journalist and author, was well placed to assess the strange phenomenon of Warne becoming more admired in England than in his own land. Australians, he argued, were not inclined to pry into the private lives of their celebrities, but in the case of Warne they had no choice because his misdemeanours were exposed by British tabloid newspapers and transmitted back to Australia.

'Warne's personal excesses have been forced down people's throats in a way that is uncommon in these parts,' Roebuck said.

Australia doesn't have the same tabloid influence or pressures as exist in England. Personal lives don't get mentioned often in the newspapers here.

For a cricketer to be a target at all is unusual. It is mostly footballers. I don't think Warne's excesses would have been particularly pursued in Australia for several reasons. First, we have mainly state newspapers here, so there isn't the same competition. There's a tabloid maybe in each state, but there aren't two. There isn't that tremendous tussle to get the story. Second, the guys are by definition state champions. You don't knock your own blokes.

Thirdly, there has been that divide between off-field and on-field activities. Aussie Rules players get exposed a little more now, but usually when someone makes a complaint. It won't be as a result of an investigation by an Australian paper. When Ricky Ponting was said to have a drink problem, the only thing to come out was him being rude to people in Calcutta [in 1998]. Pictures of him with a black eye [after an altercation in a nightclub] only appeared because the photographer happened to be at the same nightclub at the same time. It was not pursued.

But once it was out in the public domain, it was slightly

different. Shane Warne was a very big figure. He was the greatest cricketer of the day and certainly a person who craved attention . . . It was going to be mentioned. And whereas in England someone's the story one day, someone else the day after, here the same story goes on for months.

So when Warne became the subject of negative stories, as he did many times over in Australia from 1998 onwards, he naturally didn't like it.

Nor did it help that some sections of the Australian public turned against him so swiftly. While the success of the Australia cricket team was the source of enormous national pride, the players themselves were never held in especially fond regard – a symptom, perhaps, of a deeply conservative Australian public not feeling entirely at ease with the ruthless gamesmanship the team employed under Border, Taylor, Waugh and Ponting. Warne, of course, was at the cutting edge of this process, treading a fine line in brinkmanship.

'Australians are desperate to be well thought of,' Roebuck added.

They are assertive as opposed to confident. It's an uncertain country, desperate to get noticed, and therefore bangs away. It hasn't got that inner confidence of a sophisticated and ancient civilization. It is noisy and direct, a conservative country in the guise of a rebellious country. There are more rules and regulations and layers of government here than in England. It's a balance between anything goes and rules and regulations. Australian cricketers don't walk, but they accept the umpire's decision. In any code of sport, they accept the umpire's decision, but up to that point they can do almost anything. There's a phrase here, 'Cop it sweet.' You've got to cop it sweet. Authority spoke, the decision's been taken. Australia is not as anti-authoritarian as it thinks it is.

Odd though it might sound, the Australians like sportsmanship. The Australian cricket team is not well loved in Australia: Australia is loved. When people support the Australian cricket team, they are actually supporting Australia. The individual players are not necessarily particularly popular, though one or two touch a chord.

I think in England Warne is regarded as a bluff good fellow, rather a wild card, a jack the lad. I think in Australia – where he's better known, and he's better understood because he's been here so much longer – I don't think he's regarded as especially honest, nor especially naive, and I think people would see him as quite manipulative in his handlings of people, and team situations, and not especially to be relied upon in various areas. But the larrikin element in Australia will still cheer him, and he's played to that. He loves that side.

Australians would contend they know him better and therefore are less optimistic about his character. The English rejoice in him because he's gone there for two or three years and they can see his good points, which stand out – his sense of team, his ability, his generosity in certain areas, and the fact that young players look up to him.

Given Australia's conservatism, it was really no wonder that Warne was never made captain of the national side. He had the tactical awareness, without a doubt, and was vice-captain to Steve Waugh in 1999 and 2000, but the post was not just about playing cricket and winning matches. It required a person of diplomacy, good sense and moderation. The captain, once embarked upon a term of office, did not lose the job through the ups and downs in personal or collective form that tended to unseat leaders of other Test teams. Australian captains tended to remain captain until they retired. Kim Hughes famously resigned the captaincy in tears in 1984, when the pressure got too much, and handed over to Allan Border, but Hughes didn't last much longer as a player, and his credibility took a long time to recover from the shame of the retreat.

'The captaincy position is a very senior, important position in the nation,' Roebuck said.

Cricket is the national game, and it has been a unifying force. This is a colossal country. Perth is further away from Sydney than Moscow is from London. So cricketers have mattered. The Australian captain matters much more in Australia than the England captain does in England, or even the England soccer captain in England. He is one of the major national figures in a country that can't point towards Shakespeare or Dickens.

It's not a temporary thing. You don't resign, you stay until you retire. Warne was not appointed because he was too much of a risk. You couldn't appoint him for six or eighteen months and see how it worked out. You would be stuck with him. And with Warne who knew what story would come out next? Could we have an Australia captain of whom that could be said? Not in local opinion.

Mark Taylor, who captained Australia between 1994 and 1999, agreed that the Australian captaincy carries a special status. 'The job has an importance that goes beyond cricket,' he said.

In my time, I got rung up about who I was going to support at the next general election. I got put on the front pages of the newspapers about the republican debate, even though I'd made no comment. But it was expected that I would have a view.

At the end of the day, you just happen to have a gift at sport. To suggest that the country's cricket captain is some sort of guru who can lead the country to greatness, or bring world politics under control . . . I'm not sure you can put that on a sportsman, but there does seem to be that assumption.

In fact some Australian captains didn't mind sticking their toe in the political waters. In retirement, Ian Chappell became a vociferous supporter of better treatment of Australia's immigrant communities.

Certain standards of behaviour were required. 'I would say that once you reach a certain level of achievement in an international sport like cricket there do come expectations of responsibility and that's probably right,' Taylor added. 'But being paid a lot of money, and understanding what you should and shouldn't do off the field don't necessarily go hand in hand. Shane Warne has had more pressure put on him than any other cricketer in Australia. He has actually transcended the Australia captain. Even people in the United States know who Shane Warne is. They wouldn't know who Ricky Ponting was.'

It was as Taylor's successor that Warne had his best chance of taking over. The transition actually came in two stages, because Taylor stepped down as one-day captain in 1997 while continuing to lead the Test side for another eighteen months. Steve Waugh, who was four years older and had been playing at international level seven years longer than Warne, thus had a head start by being given charge of the one-day side, with Warne appointed as his deputy. But when Taylor finally retired the decision wasn't quite cut and dried because Warne's one-day results as Waugh's stand-in were clearly superior (he had led the team to ten wins in eleven games). However, by then Warne had only just started playing again after shoulder surgery, and the Australian selectors would not have been sure that he was capable of getting back to his best as a bowler. There was also the freshly minted problem of the match-fixing scandal. All in all, Waugh was the safer, if less imaginative, choice of captain, but Taylor believed that Warne's credentials were given serious consideration before the selectors made their predictable decision:

> I think the players responded to Warne. He had an excellent knowledge of the game, as I think you have to to be a good spinner. You need to know about field placings and the psyche of people around you. He knew batsmen very well. That would have made him a very good captain.
>
> Unfortunately for him, he was probably around in the wrong era to be Australia captain. If less onus had been put on what happened off the field, I think Warne could easily have been captain. As it was, I think serious consideration was given to him. The uncertainty for Steve was that he was about the same age as me. I retired at thirty-four and he was thirty-three. The concern for the selectors was whether he would stay around for four or five years. As it turned out, he did. He played until he was thirty-eight.

Warne certainly had his supporters, though. Ian Chappell was one. He wouldn't have overly worried about diplomatic considerations and was excited at Warne's aggressive style when he led Victoria. Warne reminded him of Richie Benaud, one of the finest captains of all.

Disappointed though Warne would have been to be passed over, Waugh's accession proved hugely beneficial both to Australian cricket and, eventually, to Warne himself.

Each national captain comes into the job intent on making his own mark, and Waugh's aim was to build on Taylor's adventurous policy of being willing to lose in order to win and ruthlessly seeking to win every game from ball one. Taylor commanded a talented enough group that they won many more games than they lost, but towards the end of his reign they had sometimes been beaten through complacency. There was a notorious defeat by England at the Oval in 1997, when Australia were chasing only 124 in the fourth innings; the champagne was already on ice and some members of the team, including Warne, were playing cards when the openers went out to bat. There was to be no such slackness under Waugh.

The danger for Australia was that such an all-star team as Waugh led might prove less than the sum of its parts. Waugh sought to counter this by introducing measures which subjugated the self to the whole and enforced the notion of the Australian team as a venerable institution more precious than any one player. He linked the team with very public displays of national pride. He took his players to visit the battlefields of Gallipoli, where so many Australians had lost their lives in the First World War, and was instrumental in a flag-flying ceremony taking place before the Brisbane Test of 2002 as a mark of respect to those Australians killed in the Bali bombings. Above all, he reinforced the concept of the baggy green Australian cap – which was awarded to every new player – as a treasured symbol of loyalty to the team.

Each player was to feel specially privileged to be representing his country, so the practice was introduced of each player being issued with a shirt number which accorded with his place in the chronological list of Australian Test cricketers (Warne's number was 350). But the message was never lost: the Australian team was more precious than any player. It was an admirable philosophy excellently articulated, and purely in terms of results it was an overwhelming success. Under Waugh, Australia won forty-one Tests and lost only nine.

However, it was perhaps harder for Warne than anyone else to adapt to this new regime. He was easily the team's biggest star, and could hardly stop being the most famous player overnight. A team without stars was a nice concept, but it was hardly practicable for the one true superstar – who was, for various reasons, making headlines on an almost daily basis.

Although it was never suggested that Warne objected to the Waugh philosophy, he did not appear to subscribe to it as wholeheartedly as some. For example, it became a tradition that every Australian player would wear his beloved baggy green cap during the team's first session in the field in every Test, after which they could swap it for something less traditional if they wished. Several Australian players were so devoted to their baggy greens that they wore them throughout the game. Waugh himself did so, taking the same battered hat to all his 168 Tests, as did Justin Langer, who retired from Test cricket at the same time as Warne and proudly brought his tatty cap to show off at the post-match press conference. 'It has been the vehicle for me to learn how to handle success, failure and criticism, and how to fight back from adversity,' Langer said. 'I have learned about mateship, about leadership. I have hopefully forged a strong character. It is all because of the baggy green cap.' Glenn McGrath also spoke reverentially of the honour, pride and tradition that went with wearing the baggy green.

Warne, however, always switched after the first session to a favoured floppy white sunhat, which he wore most of the time when not bowling. If he was identified with one single piece of headwear during his Test career, it was the floppy white, not the baggy green. Even at his farewell Test appearance, he, unlike Langer, passed up on an opportunity to show a sentimental attachment to the baggy green, walking on to the outfield for the post-match presentations wearing a sponsor's cap.

This was perhaps one indication of Warne's semi-detached attitude towards his homeland. Another was his reluctance to drape himself in the Australian flag. When Australia celebrated their whitewash over England in Warne's final series, Mike Hussey, Brett Lee, Michael Clarke and Andrew Symonds all wrapped national flags round their necks, but not Warne. When Waugh retired from Test cricket, he was carried from the field by his players with an Australian flag draped around his shoulders. It was the perfect emblem of the never-say-die Australian cricketer that the country loved to glorify above all others: the hero who had fought against the odds and come out on top. Waugh was an obviously gritty cricketer to whom things didn't come easily, and sometimes only pride (possibly national, though it could have been personal) seemed to keep him going. This wasn't the case with the more gifted, more effortless-looking Warne.

This is not to suggest that Warne did not shed every last ounce of sweat in the team cause. He often did. But he couldn't help but be his own man. His fame set him apart from his teammates. The individual way in which he operated – usually as the team's sole spinner, a sort of one-man army – set him apart. But his bitter-sweet relationship with the Australian public also isolated him.

The boundaries of loyalty were always a bit fuzzy with this son of an Australian father and a German mother. Warne was sociable with the opposition in a way few cricketers were – famously the first man into their dressing room at the end of a game to share a beer and deconstruct the match.

Perhaps he also wanted to keep his ear open for any helpful clues for future battles, it is true, but there was always a sense with Warne that the love of the contest came before love of his country.

In 2005 Warne even appeared to toy with emigrating to England. On the face of it this was strange, as he might have been expected to fear the English tabloids more than any Australian newspaper. But such was the attention he endured in Australia, where there were fewer star personalities for the media to concentrate on, that the idea of living in England became the more palatable prospect. Life in England represented life out of the limelight, for himself and his family.

Surveys have suggested that 90 per cent of Australians have no issue about their 1 million expatriates in general, but they are definitely more ambivalent about their celebrities treading the path to Europe or the United States. Robert Hughes, the art critic and author, was accused by Australians of disloyalty for settling overseas, as was novelist Peter Carey when he left for New York. Following her move to England, feminist writer Germaine Greer was in the habit of passing withering critiques on her former home. Australian prime minister John Howard once wished her a hearty good riddance, saying, 'If she wants to stay in another country, good luck to her.' Ian Thorpe, who kept Warne company near the top of the list of leading Australian sportsmen of the day and had endured rumours about his sexuality for years, moved to Los Angeles shortly before announcing his retirement from competitive swimming, and annoyed his countrymen by turning up on the American sitcom *Friends*, having not once deigned to appear on *Neighbours*.

Louis Nowra, an Australian playwright and novelist, argued in 2005 that Warne's willingness to play for Hampshire was a sign that his troubled relationship with the country that spawned him was collapsing. He accused Warne of undermining the unity of the Australian team that Waugh had so carefully nurtured:

> On the surface, Warne's decision makes sense but if others follow his lead it would undermine our cricket team . . . The success of Australian cricket in the past decade has been built around the notion of the team coming first, not individuals. Close bonding between players has been a crucial factor in this present group being called one of the great teams of any era . . . He's saying that he's still indispensable to our team but under-appreciated in his home country and, boy, are we going to miss him when he moves to England. It's the equivalent of the boy who is so outraged at being given out in a game of backyard cricket that he heads off home with the only cricket bat.

Nor were Australians happy when in 2006 Warne announced that he was retiring from playing for Australia, Victoria and St Kilda but intended to play two more seasons of county cricket in England. They were even more horrified when Steve Waugh speculated in his next newspaper column that Warne might one day coach the England team.

Australians were immensely proud of Warne as one of their greatest sporting heroes. But they were also acutely aware that he had the power to embarrass them. Things were never easy.

The trouble with sportsmen is that they are predominantly young, predominantly athletic, and predominantly flooded with large quantities of testosterone. The trouble with crick-eters is that they are away from home an awful lot of the time playing matches. Their sport is almost unique in taking them away on tour for several months on end.

The curse of being on the road is the curse of the night. Cricket is sometimes played in the evenings but more usually in the day; either way, there are plenty of nights when there are precious few things to do save going to bars or nightclubs. Bars and clubs have fans, and some of them are female. That is the curse of the night.

Some sportsmen didn't have to venture out of their hotels to find members of the opposite sex. Boris Becker, a major tennis star while still in his teens, found girls of similar age camped on his doorstep. 'All those girls, hysterical, crazy, already waiting for hours for him outside hotels,' Gunter Bosch, his coach, said with a shake of the head. 'Is it fair to do this to a child? How can he find out what's real and what's sham? The girls are simply offering themselves – all he has to do is take.'

Becker, who found the blind devotion of his fans quite disturbing, soon grew tired of the situation. 'It was right for me at twenty, it was fun,' he said. 'Then I woke up one day and it was boring.' But not all sportsmen were so easily sated. George Best likened pulling girls to a sport, and wanted to be the best at it. He gave it a pretty good go. Wilt Chamberlain, a basketball superstar, claimed 20,000 conquests and, not unreasonably, devoted a chapter of his autobiography to the subject.

Warne wasn't in Chamberlain's league, but in mid-1999 – four years into his marriage – there appeared the first of what would prove to be many allegations of him playing away from home. These scandals suggested that the Australian Cricket Board had been correct not to choose Warne as captain; they would have dogged him and his team, and the media would have made life almost intolerable for all concerned.

History shows that sportsmen are not good at choosing

women for their discretion, and Warne appeared to be no exception as several of his conquests sold their stories to English tabloid newspapers. As was the case when cross-examined about his dealings with John and Salim Malik, Warne generally proved a poor witness in his own defence when publicly speaking about such matters in damage-limitation interviews with Australian television channels and magazines. Some of these performances were among his most unconvincing on TV, but, interestingly, he felt compelled to turn out anyway. Television was always the final jury.

Warne's attitude towards the selling of these kiss-and-tell stories was perversely puritanical:

> There are people out there who see me [as a means] of making a quid, which is as low as you can go . . . When you spend an intimate time with somebody you don't expect it to appear in the front pages of the newspapers . . . Maybe I'm just gullible and a bit naive in that way, but I can't understand how anyone would do that for a quick buck . . . That whole subject makes me very angry . . . Unfortunately I've put myself in too many of those situations over the years.

Warne's chief excuse was that he was away from home a lot of the time and that temptations presented themselves which, out of solitariness, he had succumbed to. 'I'm not trying to make excuses – [but] it's very hard being on the road,' he told Jana Wendt.

> It's very lonely. I mean you can sit with your mates with the cricket stuff, you know, as much as you like, but at the end of the day there are opportunities because of the person you are and the 'celebrity' – I hate that word – when you want to just go out for a beer like any normal person does.

There are opportunities there . . . whether they just want to make money out of you, whether there's a set-up . . . meal ticket, whatever they want. And when you're lonely and you're away for six months, things sometimes just happen and then you regret it afterwards and you think, 'You idiot.'

I've slept with a couple of people and made some poor choices and put things in jeopardy with what I was happy with, and that's my own fault. I've got no one else to blame.

He had a point. Warne was away from home an inordinate amount. He first toured with Australia in 1992, when he spent five weeks in Sri Lanka. After that, he was an automatic selection for every series. In 1993 he spent six weeks in New Zealand and sixteen weeks in England. In 1994 it was nine weeks in South Africa and the United Arab Emirates, and another nine weeks in Sri Lanka and Pakistan. In 1995 – the year he and Simone got married – he was in the West Indies for ten weeks. In 1996 he spent six weeks in Asia for the World Cup, but missed a short tour of India following hand surgery. In 1997 he spent nine weeks in South Africa and fifteen weeks in England. When time travelling around Australia is taken into account for domestic international matches, Warne was certainly living out of hotels more nights than he was at home. He was on the other side of the world both when his first child, Brooke, was born in 1997, and when his second, Jackson, was born two years later.

The problem was, Warne wasn't always able to cite loneliness as his defence. In 2000, when he spent the English season playing for Hampshire, he brought Simone and his two young children with him to live in Southampton. Yet within a few weeks he stood accused of harassing a young woman for sex with obscene phone messages. The case of Donna Wright, whom Warne had met at a nightclub in

Leicester, was a disaster for him and his image. She said she rebuffed his advances, but he had continued to pursue her. It was alleged that he left sexually explicit messages on her phone while performing a sex act.

The episode did lasting damage to his reputation, particularly in Australia and particularly with women. Warne was being accused not only of infidelity, but also of harassment, and he made a thin defence during a TV interview with Channel Nine. But there was no apology, and he seemed chiefly hurt that the matter had become public at all. 'I thought it was a private matter,' he said. 'I didn't think it was going to become public, and now that it has become public I suppose it's a mistake. If it had stayed private it wasn't a mistake . . . Hopefully I won't be talking on the phone with any people again about this sort of stuff just in case it becomes public.'

Warne hoped the story was dead and buried, on the grounds that 'your private life is your private life', but the Australian Cricket Board begged to differ. As in the case of the Andrew Hudson incident, it was sensitive to domestic opinion, and in a country as politically correct as Australia there was no chance of Warne escaping censure. Malcolm Speed, the then chief executive of the ACB, met Warne in London and told him that the majority of the board's fourteen directors wanted him stripped of the Australian vice-captaincy. Within a few weeks, that happened, although interestingly the selection panel – made up of former players Trevor Hohns, Allan Border, Geoff Marsh and Andrew Hilditch – were in favour of Warne keeping the job. Warne, the master strategist, would never captain Australia again.

Warne said that his wife, Simone, was 'disappointed' at the Donna Wright story, but he claimed that their marriage was strong enough to cope.

The more fame dragged Warne away from the person he

had been, the more he seemed to dislike his own company, and this probably had as much as anything to do with him seeking company on nights away from home. Sandy Gordon, the psychologist to the Australia team, remembered Warne once telling him that he didn't have any friends, before adding, 'I don't know who I am or where I'm from.' Some of Warne's behaviour certainly wasn't rational. When you looked at what it cost him – a chance to captain Australia, his marriage, and sponsorships – it can only be described as a kind of madness.

Warne certainly wasn't proud of some of the things he had done. Once asked what the public thought of him, he replied, 'Arrogant, rude, obnoxious, bighead.' When she interviewed him in 2006, Jana Wendt noted that he used the words 'dumb', 'dummy' and 'stupid' about himself many times. 'There is something gnawing at his sense of self when it comes to the subject of intelligence,' she concluded. 'I suppose a person credited with peerless tactical skills and uncanny psychological insight on the cricket field is likely to be perplexed at accusations of stupidity.'

8

Confidence

BENEATH THE INTIMIDATING exterior of his match-winning feats and ferocious competitiveness, Warne remained deeply sensitive to criticism and prone to soul-searching. Like all great sportsmen, he became very good at hiding the self-doubt – as he had to if, in the heat of battle, with the eyes of the world upon him, he wanted to prosper. He was good at disguising how tired he was, how sore his body. He possessed tremendous mental resilience, yet those who knew him well knew of the uncertainty that could grip him.

Warne's own description of his condition, in a TV interview with Channel Nine, was beautifully neat. 'Leg-spin bowlers require two things,' he said. 'One is love, the other courage. We need love because what we do is difficult; and it takes courage because sometimes we get smashed out of the park.' It was a rather subtle way of admitting that even he sometimes felt insecure, and a rather modest way of saying how brave he needed to be.

The toughest times of his career were the periods when he felt least loved, whether by his captain, the selectors, or the public at large. There were probably times when he didn't even like himself – the way he was behaving, or the way he was bowling. Even Warne, the greatest spin bowler that has ever lived, needed confidence to do his job well.

Of course, what he would have liked was everyone's unconditional support, but he came to realize that he couldn't have that. There were always conditions attached, and in the case of the Australian public so many of them that the relationship became severely strained. Despite the abuse he sometimes took from the English crowds, Warne seemed to feel more loved in England than at home.

The biggest crisis of Warne's career came in 1998–99, when he was trying to recover from major surgery to his bowling shoulder at the very time when he was dogged by scandals. That his bowling had been torn to shreds in India on his last assignment before the operation did not help his morale. This was a period when nothing seemed to go right for him on or off the field, and the strain was such that he seriously considered retirement. Even one of the few positive things to happen, the birth of his second child, brought him distress, because he was on the other side of the world when it happened. For years he had led a charmed life; now, all of a sudden, the great cricketing genius felt unloved and flawed.

The shoulder operation put him out of action for six months, and he endured some sleepless nights fretting over whether he would make a full recovery. 'Self-doubt crept in . . . There was a risk that I would never be the same bowler again,' he said in his autobiography. 'At times I was upbeat but at others I was down in the dumps. I didn't always find it easy to sleep, sometimes because the shoulder caused me some pain, but mostly through worrying whether I would be able to produce the big leg break and the full range of tricks afterwards.'

If ever there was a time when Warne understood how fragile was his craft, this was it. It took almost a year for the old vigour and vitality to return to his game. It must have been a harrowing time. Eventually, of course, he came through to enjoy many more days of glory, but he did not respond well when it seemed his career was ebbing away.

He found it hard to hide his disappointment when he was dropped from the Test team, and distractingly spoke to his captain and teammates about retiring while they were in the midst of a World Cup campaign. Steve Waugh told him to wait until he got home to think about his future, but Warne seemed too agitated for that. He wanted reassurance, a reaffirmation of love, right there and then. But in sport there could be no guarantees. In a team game, the only way to be sure of your place is to play really well, and there was a period when Warne was no longer doing that.

It was inevitable that Warne's body would eventually break under the burden. 'Things were going to happen,' recalled Mark Taylor, the Australia captain at that time.

> We tend to think spin bowling is an easy craft. It doesn't look as energetic as bowling fast, taking two or three steps for thirty overs a day, but it's every bit as energetic. In those two or three steps everything happens . . . the ripping of the shoulder, the ripping of the wrist, the ripping of the fingers. All that energy goes into the ball 180 times a day, plus warm-ups, plus practice. Eventually, like every fast bowler, you're going to get niggles and strains, and with Warney it was the finger and shoulder. It was the sign of a great bowler that he was able to come back from those sorts of injuries.

Warne usually felt the strain towards the end of long, sustained periods of cricket. His right shoulder always needed regular massaging, but it was the third finger of his bowling hand − the finger which, in his own words, 'straightened with a snap to give the ball a decent flick' – which was the first area to cause real problems. It started feeling sore during three major series inside seven months in 1994–95. It began to affect his follow-through and the way he bowled the flipper. He got through the next Australian season only with difficulty, receiving cortisone injections straight into the knuckle of the finger. But there was no respite, as no sooner had the domestic programme finished than the 1996 World Cup took place on the subcontinent. There the finger deteriorated further; by the eve of the quarter-final, Warne was alarmed to see veins popping out through the knuckle. He got through the rest of the tournament – helping Australia to get to the final but unable to prevent Sri Lanka pulling off a shock win – before consulting specialists about the state of both his finger and his shoulder.

He opted to have surgery on the finger. It was a risk, and there were dire predictions that his career might be over, but he couldn't carry on as he was; something had to be done. This was the first big injury he had had, and his game – and confidence – needed rebuilding with care. He started back unpromisingly for St Kilda and Victoria; the old turn and dip weren't there. But Jenner worked with him in the nets, getting him to push the ball through with more momentum, and things began to come together again. However, he had to get used to the fact that the finger had been desensitized by the operation and never felt quite as it used to.

Warne was merely accurate in his first Test match back, against West Indies in Brisbane in November 1996, but in the second game, in Sydney, he produced a sensational delivery that spun almost a yard out of the rough to bowl Shivnarine Chanderpaul, turning the match Australia's way – and convincing Warne that the old magic was still there. 'It was probably the furthest I had ever turned a ball to get a wicket,' he said many years later. 'I knew I was back.' In all, he took twenty-two wickets in five matches against West Indies. Three months later, in Johannesburg, he bowled Jacques Kallis round his legs with another ripper.

The Chanderpaul ball and the Kallis ball were like milestones on the road back to the top. The trouble was, Warne was so dependable, and so hungry to be in the fray, that it was very hard to prevent him from being saddled with a huge workload. Taylor conceded how easy it was for him to just keep Warne bowling from one end for hour after hour.

'I tried to think to myself, "Well he's not quite got the zip he had ten minutes ago, I should give him a break,"' Taylor recalled.

But it was very hard to get the ball out of his hand. He always believed he could get a wicket, and at the absolute worst he was keeping the pressure on. He very rarely gave away cheap runs. And he was one of those bowlers, even when he was bowling below his best, you felt something might happen. There'd be a bit of a bat–pad, or a close lbw shout, or one would pass the outside edge. You always thought he wasn't that far from a wicket, so there was always a temptation to leave him on, and that's probably why he has bowled longer spells than maybe he should have at times.

There were a few times when I said, 'Warney, I've got to give you a break – have twenty minutes off.' He would look at me a bit grumpily, as if to say, 'But I just about had him.' But he would come back later and say he felt better. It was a chance for him to get into a different mindset, a chance to get away from the competitiveness of me-against-him.

But Warne had to nurse himself in practice, and gremlins started to affect the smooth running of the great machinery. He struggled badly in the first Test in England in 1997, when Nasser Hussain (who scored a double-century) and Graham Thorpe put on 288 together to set up an emphatic victory for their side. Warne, uneasy with anything but leg breaks, bowled thirty-five overs for one wicket. Jenner's assessment was that Warne's follow-through still wasn't right and that this was causing him to spin the ball less, which in turn was eating into his confidence.

With some remedial work they got him back on track later in the series, but early in 1998 another sustained period of cricket led to his shoulder flaring up. Warne had been hungry for work: he had set himself to take the thirty-six wickets he needed for his 300 in Test cricket in the six home matches against New Zealand and South Africa, and had got there with one match to spare, but he was averaging nearly sixty overs per match. It was an unmanageable burden.

Ian Healy, who was then keeping wicket to Warne, believed the shoulder developed problems because it was compensating for what the spinning finger was not able to do. Sore and weary, Warne was stood down from a one-day series in New Zealand, but nevertheless within three weeks he was leaving for a demanding tour of India. Australia should never have taken him: it was too much too soon. But he was simply too valuable to them, and on Indian pitches he would have been expected to do well. Against Indian batsmen, he was needed.

It was the most chastening experience of his career, and the start of a hellish sixteen months. For the first time since he had reached the top, he was outclassed. India's batsmen – brilliant players of spin at any time – realized that he wasn't bowling the ball as fast or turning it as far as of old, and they took unprecedented liberties. Navjot Singh Sidhu simply ran down the pitch at him and smashed him over the top.

'There weren't many periods when he was tired and not full of beans, but that Indian tour was one,' Healy recalled.

It was the end of our summer, so no wonder he wasn't bowling very well. The drift wasn't there, he wasn't even spinning the ball out of the rough, and Sachin Tendulkar was using his feet really well. It's often said the line to the Indians should be wide of off stump, because they'll play leg-side shots off middle stump, but there was no way if Warne was fresh that he would have got hurt that much. They played him brilliantly and patiently, and made him work.

Other things played into India's hands. Australia were without Glenn McGrath and Jason Gillespie – both injured – and their pace attack was weak. Their batting also failed to fire against India's spinners, which meant that Warne never had a total to bowl at.

In a warm-up match against Bombay, with Tendulkar in the opposition, Warne bowled sixteen wicketless overs for 111. As usual, he was keeping some of his tricks up his sleeve for the Test series, but Tendulkar put down a sizeable marker with an unbeaten double-century. In the second innings of the first Test, Warne – often seen bent over, hands on knees through fatigue – was torn to shreds by Sidhu, Tendulkar and Mohammad Azharuddin, Sidhu taking 14 from one over, Azharuddin 18 from another; they were the two most expensive overs he had ever bowled in Test cricket. In the second Test, in Calcutta, he returned figures of 0 for 147, which remained statistically the worst of his career. In the third and final match, in Bangalore, with India having already won the series, he at least claimed five wickets, but they cost him 186. By this point his groin was also hurting, and Taylor suggested he return home. But Warne chose to stay for the one-dayers, and in six matches against India he claimed just three wickets. When he spoke about the need for courage, this tour must have been what he meant.

He was under the surgeon's knife within days of returning home. Two operations, three months apart, repaired damage around the shoulder socket and improved mobility in the joint. He spent six weeks with the arm in a sling and six months overall in rehabilitation, during which he had to exercise four times a day. It must have been a daunting programme and a massive test of his commitment, and it is easy to imagine how his fears would have multiplied during these long hard months in the shadows. After all, Richie Benaud's career had been ended by shoulder problems. Nor had training ever really been Warne's thing. Slightly disturbingly too, Australia had filled his place in the team with a big-spinning leg-break bowler from Sydney, Stuart MacGill, who was doing well in Warne's absence.

Worse was to come. He had only recently resumed playing for Victoria, and was still not sure whether he still had his full repertoire at his disposal, when news broke of the bookie scandal.

It was several months before he could get the match-fixing story out of his hair. Even during the 1999 World Cup in England there were reports – false as it turned out – that a fresh match-fixing story was about to break which involved Warne. He later conceded that the match-fixing scandal had been an untimely distraction and had set him back mentally.

Warne returned to Test cricket for the last match of the Ashes series in Sydney in January 1999. He wasn't at anything like his best, and it showed. The trademark drift through the air was absent. 'To me, the drift was a sign of how well he was bowling,' said Taylor, whose final Test match this was. 'It meant to me he was getting something extra on the ball, he was getting his body into it. At Sydney, he was coming back from injury and got a couple of wickets, but there wasn't the energy on the ball that he'd had prior to that. He may have come back too soon, but he'd got to come back some time, and when you've had an injury there's a mental side to overcome as well as a physical one.'

On a helpful pitch, he was comprehensively outbowled by MacGill, whose twelve wickets gave him twenty-seven for the series. Warne admitted to nerves, saying it felt as though he was starting out again. Looking back, Jenner was convinced that Warne's competitive instincts had got the better of him and he had come back too soon – although, as Taylor said, there were physical and mental hurdles that had to be cleared some time.

The following month, Warne and MacGill were both taken to the West Indies for what transpired to be an enthralling Test series. Unfortunately, it wasn't destined to go down as one of Warne's career highlights. Indeed, at the time, he feared it marked the beginning of the end for him personally when Waugh, in his first Test series as captain, and Geoff Marsh, the coach, chose to drop the team's most celebrated player – and vice-captain – for the decisive game in Antigua. MacGill had outbowled him all tour, and was turning the ball far bigger distances. Warne was relying on leg breaks and sliders, lacking the self-belief to deploy the googly and flipper, and generally trying to get batsmen out too quickly: he'd forgotten how to be patient. Finishing wicketless in the first Test, which Australia won, and not playing in the last, which they took to leave the series drawn at 2–2, Warne, for perhaps the only time in his life, failed to have any real impact on a series. More to the point, he had taken just four wickets in four Tests since his comeback. Was he yesterday's man?

Waugh's decision was arguably the right one in the sense that Australia won in Antigua, but probably wrong because of the deleterious effect it had on Warne and, briefly, on Warne's relationship with his captain. For a cricketer who had more than 300 wickets to his name, and was not yet thirty years old, it was a huge slap in the face.

It didn't help that Warne was up against the most brilliant batsman in the world in full crisis-management mode. Brian Lara was under fire after West Indies were dismissed for a paltry 51 in the first Test, and when he went out to toss up with Steve Waugh in Jamaica – the crowd booing him all the way to the middle – he had said to Waugh, 'This is the last time I'm gonna have to put up with this shit.' But, rather like Warne himself, Lara was a greater danger the higher the stakes. 'Lara is a good player against average bowling sides and a great one against formidable attacks, but when harassed into a corner by his own brinkmanship or if he's targeted, he elevates himself into a genius,' was Waugh's verdict.

Leg-spinners are supposed to find left-handers harder to bowl to than right-handers, and Warne and MacGill certainly found Lara and Jimmy Adams a handful in Jamaica, where they batted through the second day together, Lara scoring 213. Lara then played an even more brilliant match-winning innings in Barbados, where an unbeaten 153 carried West Indies to a target of 308 with one wicket to spare. In an attempt to thwart Lara's boundary-hitting, Waugh placed seven men on the rope for Warne – a tactic for which he was criticized by Ian Chappell, who felt Waugh wasn't supporting his bowler properly. But one of the main features of Lara's play was his extraordinary precision, and it was in full evidence here.

In any case, the problem wasn't Waugh's captaincy but Warne's bowling. Before play on the third morning in Barbados, Warne had a training session with Jenner in which they worked on his shoulder rotation, but they didn't come up with a solution. 'I think that was the only time we had a session where we didn't get an outcome,' Jenner recalled. Ian Healy, who was keeping wicket, agreed that the problems were primarily Warne's. 'Lara played well, but Warney didn't spin it,' he said. 'He was bowling into Lara's rough but it didn't spin, so Lara started to walk out and work him on both sides of the wicket.'

Even though he played throughout the one-day series that concluded the tour, Warne took his demotion from the Test team badly. He convinced himself that the decision was permanent and meant he would never play Test cricket again. It was a gross overreaction. Jenner had to reassure him: 'I said to him, "You weren't dropped, mate, you just weren't ready to play." He lost his confidence . . . I think he probably figured that, because of his shoulder, he wasn't coming back.'

Retreating into himself, Warne wasn't particularly helpful to his new captain. 'What he sometimes couldn't do was tune into the mood of the side,' Waugh wrote in his autobiography about Warne's behaviour in the Caribbean. 'Often he stayed indoors, avoiding the public, due to his enormous popularity, and he didn't eat anything you'd find served at a restaurant, so he didn't spend a lot of time with the guys socially. All this meant that I was left a little unaware of how the team was functioning off the field.' Jenner agreed that Warne had got things wrong. 'In retrospect, he may have handled it a little differently, but he was so disappointed and frustrated,' he said. 'Previously he'd always been able to come back from injury and bowl as if he was brand new. It seemed to me that physically he'd recovered but mentally he hadn't regained confidence.'

The early weeks of the 1999 World Cup caused Warne more distress, pushing him to the brink of despair. The English crowds, perhaps sensing that he was vulnerable, enjoyed baiting him. The Indians treated his bowling with little respect at the Oval, where one of his overs cost 21, and Waugh wrote in his diary, 'I can understand, after what happened today, why some people are suggesting that Shane's merely a very good bowler now, but not the great bowler he used to be. I can sense that some teams are treating him like that, too.' His name was also popping up in the British tabloids: one story concerned him being caught smoking; another, more damagingly, alleged he had been having an affair for two years with a porn star, Kelly Handley. With his wife heavily pregnant back home in Australia, this was bad timing. In Australia's next match, at Lord's, Neil Johnson of Zimbabwe drove him for four fours in an over.

The next day, Warne shocked his teammates by saying that he was planning to quit the game. They weren't sure if he meant with immediate effect, or after the tournament, and his histrionic behaviour didn't go down well with some of them. Waugh could certainly have done without this personal crisis as he planned Australia's route through the final ten days of the tournament. 'I had to cope with a distracted and somewhat distant vice-captain who was apparently on the verge of retirement,' he wrote in his autobiography. 'Psychologically he was at an all-time low.' As the team went on a walk through Hyde Park that morning, Waugh and Warne had a frank discussion about Warne's situation.

I sensed a man in desperate need of support and cheering up. His head was in a pickle, a fact that had been further confirmed by Sandy Gordon [the team's psychologist] when he informed me that Shane was causing some friction behind the scenes over the captaincy. He was lonely, hurt, annoyed and frustrated, and quite frankly sick of the media attention. He just wanted to be Shane Nobody for a day to get his bearings back.

Back at the hotel, Waugh put the word around that Warne needed looking after, and he himself tried to involve him more in discussions and team tactics. 'However, ultimately he had to give more to the cause and only he could muster that,' Waugh added. 'Knowing Shane well, I believed he would lift in the definitive games because of who he was: a champion competitor who loves everything being on the line and the result being dependent on him. Shane needs constant support, encouragement and reassurance that he is the man . . . He loves to be loved.' Jenner said, 'He needed that reassurance, because he'd just been dropped . . . He's a human being, with ambitions, like the rest of us, not a freak.'

Three days later, Warne bowled in much-improved fashion in a group match against South Africa in Leeds. Four days after that, he turned in one of the greatest performances of his career to pull out of the fire a World Cup semi-final – again against South Africa – that had looked irretrievably lost for his side when Waugh threw him the ball in a state (the captain himself confessed) close to desperation. Australia had made a modest score of 213, and South African openers Gary Kirsten and the dangerous, aggressive Herschelle Gibbs had posted 48 in twelve overs. 'It was strange to think', Warne remarked pointedly, 'that my argument about being the man to perform when it mattered had cut no ice in the West Indies two months earlier.'

Warne's confidence was on the mend, and he now relished the opportunity to try to change the game. It was, as he said later, 'do or die'. 'Something had to happen,' he said. 'We could feel the World Cup slipping away.'

'I decided to bowl the most lavish leg break in my armoury to Gibbs,' he said.

It seemed to follow a similar trajectory to the Gatting ball six years earlier, dipping in to his legs in the flight, biting off the pitch and fizzing past his bat to take off stump. This gave me great confidence. I knew I was back to my best, the extra time healing and strengthening my shoulder during the World Cup had worked and it enabled me to rip my leg break again. That single delivery restored all of the confidence that was slipping away in the previous weeks . . . Whenever I really tried to rip the leggie I was apprehensive, but after that ball the situation of the match changed and away we went.

In his next over, Warne dismissed Gary Kirsten, who had abandoned his cautious game and tried to hit out. Kirsten admitted later that he had been panicked by Warne's ball to Gibbs: 'Deliveries like that cause batsmen to do strange things, and I made a bad judgement call . . . I decided to try and take him on, to attack him to prevent him from dominating.' In Warne's next over Hansie Cronje fell, although Cronje was unlucky, as he appeared to be caught off boot, not bat. Warne later claimed a fourth wicket with the last ball of his final over as he tried, in his words, 'to drag the rest of the team with me, get them on the same bus I was on, inspire them and win the game'. In fact the game was eventually tied, with Australia going through to the final on net run rate. Without Warne's efforts, they would have been sunk.

This was the second time Warne had turned a World Cup semi-final on its head, because in 1996 he had taken four of the eight wickets West Indies lost for 37 to lose by just 5 runs in Jaipur. Mark Taylor, his grateful captain, had described that as the most unbelievable match he'd ever played in. But without doubt this performance against South Africa not only won a big game, it revitalized Warne's self-belief, and with it his career. Ricky Ponting said in 2006 that he thought that had Australia lost that Edgbaston semi-final Warne would have certainly quit one-day international cricket. Warne might have played on, but had he merely bowled ordinarily at Edgbaston that day, and Australia not gone on to win the World Cup, his self-belief would not have been anything like as strong; as it was he subsequently took another four wickets, and another man of the match award, in the final against Pakistan. Waugh called it one of the greatest-ever bowling spells in one-day cricket.

With these two games, Warne swept himself back into the hearts of his teammates, and his countrymen, many of whom had stayed up all night to catch the denouement of the epic semi-final. Understandably, Warne (who denied that relations between himself and Waugh had ever been strained) spoke fondly of the team bonding that went on after the final victory at Lord's. Understandably, he talked a little more to friends about his thoughts of retirement — but there was no way he was going to quit after bowling so well. Some colleagues weren't happy at having to listen to him publicly talk about his own situation when the team had pulled off such a stunning triumph, but he could be forgiven a little self-absorption after all he'd been through.

Warne was back. And, little did anyone know it, he was about to get a whole lot better.

9

The Creative Spur

THE HERSCHELLE GIBBS ball — which came, as it proved, at almost precisely the mid-point of Warne's fifteen-year international career — was a crucial event not only because it hauled Warne out of his cycle of despair. It also changed his outlook. It taught him something about himself that in the long run was to prove invaluable.

What the Gibbs ball taught him was that bowling unplayable deliveries, indeed greatness itself, was largely a state of mind. If he believed in something, it could happen. He had the weapons at his disposal; he simply had to summon them at the right moment. Or, if he couldn't summon them, he would make it look as though he might. One way or another, he could make things happen. He could will them.

This was the point of Warne's reinvention from technical maestro to theatrical magician.

The change was partly born out of necessity. Warne didn't know how long his body would allow him to go on, how much more it could take. Six months of rehab, and six months driving his mind and body back into shape, had made him realize how precarious was his sporting existence. Not knowing how much of a future he had made him play for the moment — and brilliantly so. Deep down, he rarely had full confidence in every one of his tricks, but that was deep down, and he was damned if he was going to let the opposition glimpse the doubts. From now on he was going to give his game everything, sell himself to the hilt.

To an extent, he was driven by fear – fear of the end, fear of failure: the two fears he had lived with during the second half of 1998 and the first half of 1999. He would live on his wits, and an inextinguishable competitiveness. Batsmen found him more bullying, more interrogative. So did umpires. In his first Sheffield Shield game for Victoria after the shoulder op, he was fined his entire match fee for slamming the umpiring in a post-match press conference. Not the smartest move, and as his confidence returned, so his relations with the men in white coats grew gentler and more seductive. Like many seasoned cricketers, he learned to control his anger as he moved through his thirties.

There was an urgency to all that he did. His bowling was not impatient, as it had been when he was striving in vain to regain his old touch, but there was a desire, a need, to get things done faster. He didn't know whether he could put his fingers or shoulder through the long days of attrition as he had in the past, and such days became less frequent. It helped that Australia's attack was stronger now than it had ever been since Warne's emergence, and it laid waste to all opponents. While Warne took care of the spin – with MacGill as his understudy – the fast bowling was in the hands of the impressive trio of Glenn McGrath, Jason Gillespie and the new sensation Brett Lee, who was in many ways another Warne – blond, photogenic and personable. All Lee lacked was the scandals.

Perhaps Lee would have been a better bowler with them, because they didn't seem to do any harm to Warne's game. Living on the creative edge seemed to draw Warne more readily into misadventures, but, bizarrely, the more trouble he was in off the field, the better he played. Some foolish behaviour may have ruined his prospects of captaining Australia, and jeopardized his marriage, but it also created within him the desire to compensate everyone for the disappointments he inflicted upon them – to appease judgemental, moralistic Australia and make everything all right again. Perhaps lurking somewhere within him was a judgemental, moralistic Shane Warne that needed satisfying too. As he said frequently in later years, he knew he had behaved stupidly at times, but he just couldn't stop himself. Perhaps if his mistakes had diminished his cricket he might have thought harder about what he did.

As it was, the off-field controversies became Warne's great creative spur, driving him to ever higher levels of achievement. This was the final magical element in the chemistry of his amazing game.

And so Warne, who had set out wanting to be famous, now set himself to rushing around playing fireman to his celebrity – to creating two dazzling back-page headlines for every front-page sorry-Simone, sorry-folks clanger. Playing brilliant cricket was designed to be the alkali to the acid of the bad news days, the plea from the heart for everyone out there – teammates, public and media – not to disapprove of him, but to love him. 'The one thing I'm proud of in my life is, no matter what has happened, I've still been able to front up, play my cricket, and still do a pretty good job,' he once said.

Warne's career can be divided into two phases: before the shoulder operation and after. Before the operation he was technically better. His repertoire was at its widest, and his tricks at their most brilliant. In those years, he bowled the leg break and flipper to more devastating effect than anyone has ever bowled those deliveries. He was his sport's great freak. Afterwards he was more intelligent and more subtle, and used his most outrageous tricks sparingly, as weapons of surprise. When the surprise worked, he was as thrilled that his restraint had paid off as that he could still rip the ball a long way; whenever he bowled a batsman round his legs, as he did India's Mannava Prasad in December 1999, his celebrations were wild. 'The best I ever bowled', he once reflected, 'was between 1993 and 1998 before the shoulder operation, just spinning the leg break as far as I could. But I didn't really understand how to get wickets or bowl to plans.' He loved to lay, and spring, a trap. He liked being clever. He did this in his early days for sure – often with the leggie, leggie, leggie, flipper routine – but he got cannier with age.

Warne described his change of methods thus in 2000:

I am generally able to bowl without any pain . . . my shoulder now is almost as good as new. Like the engine in a car, I had to run it in gently at the start but now, more than two years on, I feel I can bowl with absolute confidence. People have said that I don't rip the ball as viciously as I did in my early days. I disagree. The fact that I no longer bowl huge leg breaks every time is not the same as losing the weapon. There are times when I impart big spin on the ball, such as the delivery that removed Herschelle Gibbs in the World Cup semi-final. These days, I don't employ that ripper as a stock ball. I believe I bowl with more variety now, and the strategy includes regulating the amount of turn on each leg break. I think I've become a smarter bowler. Maybe I outsmart myself now, who knows? I use the big one as a shock ball; it's my wicket-taking ball. But it does not always need to deviate a foot or eighteen inches to take the edge.

And the results spoke for themselves. In 71 Tests up to mid-1999, it took Warne on average 64.8 balls to claim each wicket; in 74 Tests afterwards, this figure plunged to 51.6.

Cleverer though he undoubtedly was, Warne's greatest weapon after 1999 was probably his reputation. He had more than 300 Test wickets to his name – more than any other leg-spinner in the record books. He had a history and every one of his opponents knew it. After all, pretty much his whole career had been on TV; they would have seen his many triumphs. In April 2000 Warne was voted one of *Wisden*'s five cricketers of the twentieth century. It was an astonishing tribute. He was the only one of the five still playing, his closest contemporary being Viv Richards, who had retired from Test cricket in 1991. He had been anointed as a living legend. This must have given him a huge psychological advantage over his opponents. 'I love bowling to batsmen I haven't played [before],' he once said. 'I feel I'm ahead before we start, because they may have seen something I've done before. I suppose there is an aura when they face me, which is to my advantage.'

It helped that the media weren't great on perspective. The television companies that screened the big matches weren't in the business of knocking the product (remember Greig's 'If someone's good, boy, we unashamedly make 'em the best'), and the written media were quite happy portraying Warne as hero on the back pages and villain on the front. There wasn't much in between. The fact that Warne had had a bad twelve months was quickly forgotten after his World Cup heroics: he was once again the man with the special powers. What precisely they were was less clear. Coaches would have told their charges to play the ball, not the reputation, but for most people that was easier said than done. Only the very best were capable of detaching themselves from the Warne hype. 'I don't really play Shane Warne as Shane Warne,' Kevin Pietersen said. 'I play a cricket ball. It's the cricket ball that gets you out. That's the most important thing. Keep things as simple as you can.'

The last thing Warne wanted was batsmen keeping things simple. He wanted their minds to be a maelstrom of fears. How much is he going to turn it? Is it going to turn at all? What is the pitch doing? Am I scoring fast enough? Am I indeed good enough to be out here, batting against this giant of the game?

It was an outrageous mix of intelligence, skill and bluff, as Warne conceded in an Australian magazine interview in January 2007.

> I'm smarter with my bowling and that comes through experience . . . I try to get inside the batsman's head and create something that is not really there. I want them to think there are more things happening with the pitch than there actually are. It might be the way I drop a ball into the rough when I first bowl, so they think it's turning a long way. It's a stare here or there, a little smile, rubbing the hands together – you are creating something. Your body language is saying you are on top. One of my strengths is I can sum up a batsman's weaknesses quickly and plan the best way to get him out.

They say the true test of a man is how he comes through adversity, and Warne definitely came through his year of adversity a more resilient character. He once said that the main things needed to play for a long time were mental toughness, inner strength and luck, and he possessed the mental toughness and inner strength to believe he could not only survive at the top, but thrive. Greatness was a state of mind – specifically, strength of mind – and, after conquering his fears at the World Cup, Warne came to realize that, though his body might not be unbreakable, his mind was indestructible. He could do anything. He knew he had the ability to make batsmen fumble and whole teams crumble.

He backed himself in a mental battle with any batsman in the world, and spent his time reinforcing this to himself in lots of little ways. During the World Cup, he had written a newspaper article saying that the game would be better off without Arjuna Ranatunga, the combative captain of Sri Lanka, who delighted in getting under the skin of the Australians, and he had been fined for his remarks. When the two next met on the field, in a Test match in Kandy three months later – a game in which Warne took over the captaincy mid-match after Steve Waugh was injured – Warne dismissed Ranatunga with his fourth ball. The next time he faced Sachin Tendulkar in a Test match, in Adelaide, in December 1999, he had him caught at bat–pad for 61, which, given the scores Tendulkar had racked up against him in India, was a triumph. To Warne, the fact that the decision was debatable was neither here nor there: he had managed to convince the umpire, and that was enough for him.

The more time went on, the more trouble Warne went to to burnish his reputation. He used the media to talk himself up and keep the myth of his greatness alive and well. Having done a lot of his growing up in the public spotlight, he was naturally quite candid at press conferences, occasionally using them to articulate the self-doubts he was feeling. After his divorce in 2005, he often publicly stated his hopes of a reconciliation with Simone.

The openness of Warne's nature was one of the most remarkable facets of his personality. It helped make him a good leader, particularly of younger players, who could learn so much from him. For a sportsman who traded in deception, he was strikingly happy to share the secrets of what he did. Towards the end of his career, he conducted a number of masterclasses for TV companies, to be screened during the interval in games. In them, he went through his range of deliveries, explaining what they did and how he did it. On the morning of a Test match in Colombo, he gave a short coaching session to two young Sri Lankan spinners, and of course he had rather embarrassingly helped Mushtaq Ahmed befuddle Australia on their own soil. But knowing how Warne did what he did was not the same as playing it. And what did for batsmen, as Warne learned with time, was not one particular ball but a sequence of deliveries designed to unpick a mind and a technique. Warne's openness was the ultimate tribute to his belief in his craft. 'This is how I do it . . . See? No, you missed it . . . Have another go.'

But, like his bowling, Warne's use of the media wasn't always quite what it seemed. Over time, he came to see interviews as opportunities to promote himself and plant doubts in the minds of opponents. Because he was capable of talking so well, and was so obviously comfortable with the platform that a press conference or a TV interview provided, his messages were often taken at face value. But for Warne, who had no interest in reading and so set little store by the value of the printed word, the truth was to some extent negotiable. If Warne said such-and-such a batsman was frightened to play him, he was. To him, it was one man's assertion against another. Even if reporters suspected he was using them as accomplices in his mind games with the opposition, they were usually grateful for a colourful line and happy to go along. Warne's comments were all part of the show. For the press, the next step was to get the reactions of his adversaries to his claims. It was never dull writing about Warne.

The fact Warne said that Kevin Pietersen would be his 600th Test wicket, and Ian Bell his 700th, and that neither prediction proved accurate was not important. He was daring to suggest he could – would – get them out.

Warne backed himself, and wasn't afraid to say so. Indeed, he loved making it clear that no batsman was too good for him. Of course, as was perfectly obvious, Warne *was* too good for most. There were just a handful who were his equals – Tendulkar, Lara and Pietersen perhaps – and it was interesting that Warne was careful to show them due defer- ence, one master acknowledging another. Warne read the game with utter clarity, which was what made him a good captain and promised to make him such an excellent commentator after he finished playing. He knew exactly who could play him and who couldn't, and wasn't afraid to make his opinions public – which must have been infuriating for those who, after long hours of practice and study, thought they were getting better against him, but just couldn't earn recognition from the great man himself. Ian Bell was very much like this in his second series against Australia in 2006– 07: definitely better than he had been, winning a few little battles, but unable to command Warne's respect.

For most people, this would have been a dangerous game to play, but Warne was good enough to get away with it. Very few sportsmen in any field are prepared to risk being dismissed as an arrogant big-head; those that do are probably, like Warne, calling things as they see them but also delib- erately trying to get their adrenalin flowing. Muhammad Ali, John McEnroe, Andre Agassi and David Campese were all known for displaying assumptions of superiority. Warne wasn't the only Australian cricketer to talk up himself or his team – Steve Waugh did it, and so did Dennis Lillee and Glenn McGrath. But Waugh was captain and speaking for a collective; Lillee and McGrath were fast bowlers who could back up their words with a spicy bouncer or two. Warne had no such luxury. 'That's what makes Shane so gutsy,' Ian Healy said. 'It's easier for fast bowlers to do it. A spin bowler can't bounce someone out. Yet Warne put himself up to be knocked over a hundred times, but rarely did it happen. His was a supreme skill, the most helpless craft you can perform. You try and do it. How helpless does it feel?'

Warne also stamped on anything that hinted at how his bowling might best be neutralized. The Indians had demonstrated perfectly well that the way to deal with him was to attack, yet time and again Warne would say he relished batsmen coming at him. This was nonsense, yet it was amazing how many batsmen were never bold enough to go after him. Batsmen in domestic state cricket, like the South Australian pair Darren Lehmann and Greg Blewett, prospered by being positive, and Lara and Pietersen also amply demonstrated the benefits of aggression. When Duncan Fletcher said his England side had played Warne well in the Brisbane Test in 2006, Warne dismissed his claim as 'rubbish', even though it was obvious to most observers that, despite his team's defeat, Fletcher had a point.

The danger with Warne was that you could play him well one day, but the next he'd come back with a fresh plan and would have your goose cooked before you knew it. 'He has to have one up on you,' Nasser Hussain said. Pietersen concurred: 'As a batter, you can't win the war.' Daryll Cullinan's big mistake was that he couldn't resist getting into a war of words with the Australians. But he was not in a position of much strength: Warne had already dismissed him nine times when South Africa toured Australia in 1997, and it emerged in the media that Cullinan had received psychological counselling to help him deal with his problems with the bowler. It didn't stop Cullinan calling Warne a 'balloon' the next time they met, in a misguided attempt to boost his fragile self-esteem. It was hardly surprising, then, that in the following game Warne made reference to Cullinan's session on the couch – before dismissing him for an eight-ball duck. Cullinan accused Warne of 'overstepping the mark', but he would have been well advised to have kept his mouth shut.

'It was intriguing to watch such a competent player as Cullinan crumble because of another man's mere presence,' Steve Waugh said. 'His footwork dissolved along with his desire to be combative, while his body language signalled complete submission. In contrast, Shane launched into action, increasing the tempo with assertive gestures, verbal interrogation and extra intensity, and bowling with a controlled rage that enabled him to impart extra revolutions on the ball.'

Of course Warne's greatest bluff was the mystery ball. Always wanting to keep batsmen guessing – as Jenner had told him to – he promoted the idea that he was always looking to add to his arsenal, and he routinely dropped hints that he was either working on some new trick or other or had greatly improved an old one, such as the googly or the flipper, which lost some of its power after the shoulder operation.

Ahead of his second Ashes series, in Australia in 1994, he said he had developed a new delivery – one that 'goes along the pitch and comes back to me and spins up in the air'. Warne's claim was greeted with a widespread scepticism that was neatly summed up by *Mail on Sunday* reporter Peter Hayter: 'This secret new delivery starts off going down the leg side, stops in mid-air, whistles the tune of Advance Australia Fair, reverses back to the bowler, then shakes the hand of every member of the fielding side before homing in on and uprooting all three stumps.' Warne repeatedly talked about having developed a new delivery, but in truth, as Bob Simpson observed, there were no new deliveries: it was all high-class kidology.

Perhaps precisely because he knew from personal experience all about the fragility and fearfulness of the cricketer's condition, Warne developed a knack for smelling out weakness and fear in opponents. He understood that all cricketers were at times afflicted by insecurity; some just hid it better than others, and Warne hid it perhaps best of all.

He developed a great gift for empathizing with his opponent. A bowler who can understand what makes a batsman tick goes a long way towards grasping how to bowl at him. In Warne's case, studying a batsman's methods and mindset lay at the heart of his strategies. Having had little interest in academic study, he could never have gone to university, but what Rodney Hogg once famously said of Mike Brearley might also have been said of Warne: he had a degree in people.

Every time Warne prepared to bowl the ball, he asked himself one fundamental question: What sort of shot do I want the batsman playing? Once he had answered that, he knew what plan to adopt, and he tried not to worry about the possible consequences. 'He is a great reader of batsmen and can analyse them quicker than anyone else,' Mushtaq Ahmed said. 'He always believes he can set batsmen up and get them out, but is never overconfident about his ability.' Mark Butcher also felt the power of Warne's mind at work: 'He will sometimes spend three or four overs setting you up for the *coup de grâce* and you've got to get an idea in your head as to how he's trying to get you out.'

The same was true when Warne was batting. He seemed

able to get inside the bowler's head and second-guess where he was going to put the ball. In his last two series against England he scored nearly 450 runs. 'It was as if he was putting himself inside the mind of the bowler and predicting what he might do,' Duncan Fletcher said of Warne in 2005. 'This is when a bowler then has to think like a batsman and counteract that.'

With a ball in his hand, Warne instinctively knew when a batsman was feeling defensive or vulnerable. He preyed on their caution. A typical time when he looked to strike was in the final overs before an interval or at the end of the day. He played these opportunities for all they were worth, theatrically drawing out each ball, making fine adjustments to his field anything to prolong the torture. And he conjured up many of his greatest wickets in just such nerve-jangling curtain-closers: Basit Ali with the final ball of the day in Sydney in 1995; Shivnarine Chanderpaul two balls before lunch at the SCG in 1996; and Andrew Strauss with the final ball of the day at Edgbaston in 2005. Each of these wickets was taken with a big-spinning leg break delivered from round the wicket.

As we have seen, in his early days a lot of Warne's verbal sallies at batsmen came in moments of euphoria: the wicket had been taken, the damage done. But after the shoulder injury, if he felt a few well-directed words could help him disturb the enemy's mind, then he was happy to send them into battle along with whatever type of delivery he could bring to his command. Two illustrations book-ended his comeback year. In January 1999 he turned on its head a one-day match that England were winning with ease by talking out Nasser Hussain, who was going well on 58. Hussain had just hit a four over the top and Warne invited him to do it again: 'Great stuff, Nass, that's the way to do it.' Predictably, Hussain tried a repeat and was stumped, triggering a collapse that led to Australia sneaking home by 10 runs. Similarly, Ian Chappell tells a story that dates from December 1999, when Warne was bowling to Sourav Ganguly in a Test match in Adelaide. Ganguly was letting ball after ball go by. 'Hey, mate,' Warne shouted down the pitch, 'this crowd didn't pay that money to watch you let balls go. They're here to see this fella [the non-striker Sachin Tendulkar] play shots.' Eventually Ganguly was out stumped off Warne, attempting a big hit over the top.

Warne was an absolute natural at talking himself up, talking the opposition down, and talking batsmen out of their senses. After the World Cup of 1999, he never stopped believing that anything was possible, however thin things might look. 'I probably go over the top occasionally with the appealing and those type of things,' he said in 2006, 'but that's me expressing myself, that's me trying to do anything we possibly can to win the game. At times I have probably pushed the line.'

Warne's greater determination to play mind games placed even more onus on batsmen to be mentally strong in the face of all that he was likely to send at them. Coping with Warne became the ultimate test: a test of technique obviously, but also a huge test of temperament. In the end, he was probably examining a batsman's mind more thoroughly and more ruthlessly than any bowler had ever done. It must have been an uncomfortable experience. How many followed the route of Daryll Cullinan in seeking the help of psychologists can only be guessed at, but the chances were that there were quite a few.

The role of psychologists in cricket was almost non-existent when Warne first played for Australia. The notion of an international cricketer consulting anyone with a view to strengthening the mental side of his game would have been treated with derision in many quarters. The generally acknowledged starting point for the involvement of psychologists in professional sport was 1976, when the United States team first took a specialist with them to the Olympic Games, but it was only in the mid-1980s that things really took off. Dr Rudi Webster had assisted the West Indies team, but found it difficult to persuade his players to spend any time training their minds for the battles ahead. Lower down the scale, by the mid-1990s psychology classes were being taught at the Australian academy. But the whole subject was liable to be greeted with behind-the-hands sniggering. No one wanted to admit to mental weakness. All this had played into Warne's hands in the early days.

It wasn't until 1997 – just after they had lost their fifth successive series to Australia and their fourth in a row involving Warne – that a psychologist, Dr Steve Bull, was brought in to help prepare the England team. There was much to be done. In the build-up to the previous Ashes series in Australia, England players had watched videos of their opponents doing well, seemingly unaware that they were in danger of reinforcing in their own minds how good the opposition were. But initially Bull's role was only a modest one: David Lloyd, the coach who brought him in, recalled that it really went no further than 'engendering togetherness' among a group of players who had yet to be centrally contracted to the national team. However, there was no doubt that the role of psychologists in helping to prepare players grew dramatically after that.

'I've maintained for many years that all sports at the top level are more mental than they used to be simply because standards have improved so much and the margins are so much smaller,' Bull said. 'Everyone has got better in all departments. So the role that the mental side plays as a differentiator is more significant than it was years ago – to the extent that if one of two evenly matched teams has an off day the other side can capitalize to the point where it might look like there's a huge gulf between them.'

Bull agreed that spin bowling was an area in which strength of mind (either the bowler's or the batsman's) could play an inordinately large part:

You can liken spin bowling to a chess match in the sense that someone like Warne builds plans, lures a batsman into a certain situation, and then strikes with a killer move. Warne has been very, very good at this.

What I would say about Warne is four things all wrapped up into one, which makes him the package that he is, each of them irrespective of his natural talent as a cricketer. One, he is fiercely competitive, and that is a mental thing. Two, the body language he displays is brilliant. I remember a comment from him once, along the lines of 'When you turn up for a day's play, the spectators and opposition shouldn't be able to tell from your body language whether you're in a winning position or a losing one. It should be consistent whatever the state of the game.' He was brilliant at giving off that image of supreme self-belief and confidence.

Three, he is clearly an intelligent cricketer. We talk to our younger cricketers [in England] about the importance of being thinking cricketers, and he's clearly a thinking cricketer, and I think we went through a phase in English cricket where our players weren't as independent thinkers as we would have wanted them to be.

Four, he clearly absolutely loves what he does. He seems

Relations between Warne and Australia coach John Buchanan, seated to the right of him at Lord's in July 2005, were not always easy

Warne took more Test wickets under Ricky Ponting than under any other Australia captain. Here they celebrate one of his six at Lord's in 2005

Warne often worked hard on the opening days of the 2005 Ashes Tests. At Old Trafford he bowled twenty-seven overs for one wicket – but it was his 600th in Tests. 'I'll celebrate with fourteen hours of sleep,' he said

Above: Warne contemplates Australia falling 2–1 behind at Trent Bridge in 2005

Left: Offering his congratulations to Kevin Pietersen after his great innings at the Oval

Right: Warne drops
Pietersen on 15,
consigning Australia
to an Ashes series
defeat and himself to
another eighteen
months of Test cricket

Below: A bitter pill:
the Australian players
absorb a rare Ashes
defeat on the Oval
outfield, September
2005

Warne shows Kevin Pietersen that their friendship has been put on hold – at least until Australia have regained the Ashes – in the first Test at Brisbane, 2006

Above: Warne's relationship with England fans mixed love and hatred: here they tease him at Adelaide

Right: Warne, sporting trademark sunhat and shades, salutes the crowd on his last appearance at Perth

Left: Final ambition fulfilled: Warne and the Australian team celebrate regaining the Ashes in Perth, 18 December 2006

Below: Perfect setting: Warne claims Andrew Strauss as his 700th Test victim, on his home soil in Melbourne, Boxing Day 2006

Right and below right: Warne's ex-wife Simone smiles from the stands as Warne is chaired off at his beloved Melbourne Cricket Ground for the last time, 28 December 2006

The last hurrah, Sydney, January 2007: Warne in action during his last Test; doffing his cap to the crowd after dismissing Andrew Flintoff, his final wicket; showing off the Ashes crystal with his children; and how the *Sydney Morning Herald* greeted his departure

AUSTRALIAN PHILOSOPHIC DEBATE...

IS THERE LIFE AFTER WARNE?

to enjoy every minute of every day on a cricket field. Take that all together and that's a pretty powerful cocktail when it comes to creating a mental game plan.

But Bull denied that the subject of playing Warne had dominated his discussions with England players. 'Everyone knows he's a great player,' he added. 'But the tough players will love that challenge and will back themselves, because that is what mentally tough players do. So I wouldn't say he's been top of the list of things to discuss.'

Michael Atherton, who battled against Warne in five series, endorsed this view, saying that he personally was never fazed at the prospect of facing him. 'He's the smartest bowler I played against. He has a tremendous cricket brain, works out batsmen very quickly, and always bowls to a plan. But I never walked to the crease feeling psychologically dominated by Shane Warne. Sure, he got me out a few times, but great bowlers get wickets.' But Atherton conceded that, with Warne having so many Test wickets to his name, some batsmen might have been 'playing the reputation as well'.

Bull said that attitudes towards psychological support in sport had definitely softened. He was sure that a player who was having difficulties with an opponent would now have fewer inhibitions about asking for help than he once might have had:

If someone is having particular difficulty with their fitness, the science of medicine is on hand to help them. So, OK, someone's undergoing a bit of a confidence crisis, or struggling to get a mental game plan together for a particular bowler, then you've got the sport psychologist's support to do that. That now is just part of your preparation, part of the professional approach to the way you play the game. It shouldn't be, 'Oh no, we've got to pull in the man in the white coat. We're not going to have this guy around again until he's sorted himself out.'

Interestingly, Bull believed that had Warne appeared on the scene fifteen years later than he did, he might not have proved quite as effective, on the basis that he won a lot of mental battles before his opponents had managed to marshal their resources. 'Once you start to lose those battles, and someone else has the upper hand, then it is not an easy thing to turn around,' he added.

What is happening now is that because we know so much about sports psychology, sportsmen are learning the necessary skills at a much younger age. What I was teaching as a sports psychologist ten to fifteen years ago, well-educated and well-qualified coaches are now teaching themselves. So our role has changed. We are now working alongside coaches. If a Shane Warne came into the game today, I would like to think that the whole approach to mental game-planning would be different and we'd get on the case sooner rather than later.

But not everyone was in favour of psychological back-up. Shortly after Steve Waugh became Australia captain, in 1999, he and Geoff Marsh, the coach, brought in a pysch-ologist, Sandy Gordon, to assist the team on tour, when Waugh thought 'homesickness, staleness, personal problems and personality clashes' were liable to undermine the team unit. Waugh believed that too much emphasis was placed on physical fitness at the expense of mental fitness. 'Cricketers need to work on . . . visualizing what they are trying to achieve, to learn by asking each other questions about strengths and weaknesses, and to share insights about doubts and fears,' he said. 'There is a wealth of information stored within us all, and it's a great shame if it stays locked away, never to be used for the benefit of others.'

Waugh conceded that some of his players were not receptive to Gordon's involvement. He cited his brother Mark as one sceptic, and it would be safe to say that another was Warne, who would have preferred to work things out himself or in discussion with trusted advisers. He may have been self-absorbed, but he was not necessarily self-analytical and he probably feared that too close an examination of his motivational processes might erode the confidence he had worked so hard to build up. He was always uneasy about anyone seeking to analyse him closely. 'I don't like it how people can do books on you,' he once said. 'Anyone can write a book on anyone. I don't like that law. I don't like [it] that people can do things about your life without consent. I don't think that's fair.'

10

The Finisher

HISTORICALLY, THE SPIN bowler has always been in a unique position in Test cricket. Indeed, this very uniqueness goes a long way towards explaining why so many spinners have displayed streaks of insecurity and self-absorption. Whereas batsmen, fast bowlers and wicketkeepers might hope to play a part in the game at any stage, the spin bowler – and there was often just one of them in the team – essentially has been selected for what he might do in the second half of the match, when he is expected to run through the opposition on a worn pitch. Depending on how the game has gone earlier, the spinner may find himself working within narrower parameters than he would like: there may be few runs to play with, and the pitch may be turning less than hoped.

To an extent, the likes of Shane Warne and Muttiah Muralitharan had broadened the role of the spinner by show-ing that, such were their powers of spin on any surface, they could play a major part in the early stages of the game as well. But even for them the business end of their involvement was the second innings, when there was almost always a job to be done.

This was both an appetizing prospect and an intimidating one: appetizing because glory awaited the man who completed the mission successfully; intimidating because the result of several days of hard labour had come to rest upon one man's shoulders and one man's mind. Could he do it? The fear of finishing as Chump when Champ was so tantalizingly within reach has ruined many a spinner's career.

But it didn't ruin Warne's. It made it. To Warne, this was cricket's most fascinating aspect. The game's three measurables (runs, wickets and time) were all in play, as were the unquantifiables (how well he might bowl, how well the opposition might bat). He lived for the challenge of resolving these endgames. As far as he was concerned, the tighter the situation, and the greater the expectation, the better he performed. The message he had for his captains was simple: give me the ball and I'll finish the job for you. This was really why he didn't much like bowling with another spinner in the side, because the look-at-me quotient in potential match-winning situations was just too high. Share this with someone else? You must be joking. *C'mon, boys, on my shoulders. I'll carry you home.* His ability to win games in these most testing of circumstances had a lot to do with Australia's cricketing domination.

Even for Warne, fear of failure lurked somewhere of course, but it was nothing he couldn't deal with. In a tribute programme screened on the eve of his final Test appearance, Warne was asked by Ian Healy – who would have remembered having to convince a wavering young Warne that he was indeed capable of finishing the job against West Indies at Melbourne in 1992 – whether the expectation had ever got to him; whether he had ever lost sleep 'worrying about tomorrow'.

Warne conceded that there were times when it had, and he had. 'I might have put up a bit of bravado about those expectations, but yes,' he replied.

First of all there were your own expectations. You're a spin bowler on the last day, you've got 300 on the board, and you've got to bowl them out. Then there's everyone else's expectations. Your teammates, the public, they just think you're going to do it, because you've done it before. It's not quite that easy. There were times when you sat there at night thinking, 'Jeez, how am I going to bowl out this bloke? He's playing me well.' Or 'What happens if I do this?' You have got to think on your feet. One of the major reasons I've been successful is my attitude. At the end of the day, it's about self-belief.

He said that the expectation was wearing, but that he loved the responsibility. 'It's just something in my make up,' he said. 'The tougher it is, the better I do. I want the ball in my hand. I'm glad I'm like that. I don't think I could have given any more to cricket. I've never walked away. If I'm knackered and can't move, I've still turned up and played . . . I've given everything to the cause, and that was winning.'

Captains found it particularly hard to prise the ball from him in the second innings, when he often became totally wrapped up in the hunt for wickets. Sometimes the best thing would have been to give him a break, but that was easier said than done.

The consistency with which Warne did the job for Australia in the second innings was astonishing. Even if he didn't take a clutch of wickets – which he often did – he invariably played an important role, perhaps keeping things tight or chipping in with the breakthrough wicket that triggered the final, match-clinching, collapse. If he did fail to come up with the goods, there were usually extenuating circumstances: he was either short of full fitness, or exhausted.

With Warne in the side, the times when Australia were

beaten through failing to defend a target of substance in the fourth innings were so few as to be worth listing. All occurred on foreign soil. They were Auckland 1993 (lost by five wickets defending 200; Warne 2 for 54 in 27 overs); Karachi 1994 (lost by one wicket defending 313; Warne 5 for 89 from 36.1 overs); Barbados 1999 (lost by one wicket defending 307; Warne 0 for 69 from 24 overs); Headingley 2001 (lost by six wickets defending 315; Warne 1 for 58 from 18.2 overs); and Durban 2002 (lost by four wickets defending 334; Warne 2 for 108 from 30 overs).

And here are the extenuating circumstances. Auckland was only Warne's eleventh Test match, and the total New Zealand were chasing was quite small. In Karachi, Pakistan got home by only one wicket and off the final ball of the match, which ran away for four byes; Ian Healy missed a stumping off Warne. In Barbados, as we know, Warne was still feeling his way back from his shoulder surgery, and Brian Lara played an innings of genuine greatness. At Headingley the game was affected by rain, which meant the pitch wasn't as worn as it might have been come the fourth innings, and Mark Butcher played an innings almost as sublime as Lara's. And the match in Durban came only three days after a Test in Cape Town into which Warne put more effort than for any other game in his life, bowling 98 overs, taking 8 wickets and scoring a half-century. It took him 70 overs to chisel out the South Africans in the second innings – a marathon he compared to 'a big night out when you think you're gone several times but you get a couple of second winds'. Predictably, he carried off the match award, which was entirely appropriate as it was his 100th Test appearance and he had flown in sixteen friends and family members for the occasion. But Cape Town left him exhausted, and, with the series won, the fourth innings in Durban proved a task too many.

Warne's most eye-catching failures in Australia both came against South Africa – somewhat surprisingly given the way they generally struggled to cope with Warne. With some ease, they batted through 122 overs to draw the Boxing Day Test at Melbourne in 1997, and through 126 overs to save the game in Perth in 2005. Warne's workload was predictably prodigious on both occasions, and he bowled 35 overs on each final day alone. The escape act in Perth was more understandable in that the surfaces there were always tough for spinners. The Waca was Warne's least successful home Test venue, and its unyielding nature caused both Terry Jenner and Stuart MacGill to leave Western Australia and head for more fertile spinning pastures in the east of the country.

South Africa's saviour in Melbourne was Jacques Kallis – also a key participant in the victory in Durban five years later – who showed great composure over six hours to withstand not only Warne but concerted sledging.

'I can remember us travelling to Sydney for the next Test hardly able to believe that we hadn't won,' said Mark Taylor, who was captaining Australia.

Normally, if we gave Warney enough runs on the board on the last day, it would be all over by about 5 p.m. We got used to thinking that. But that time it didn't happen. He had bowled beautifully, but Kallis had played really well.

He didn't lose it. He didn't come into the changing room and throw things down, but I know he would have been churning inside not to have come up trumps in front of his home crowd. That would have really hurt him. But we went to Sydney and won the next game, and he bowled beautifully again after we had lost the toss and had to bowl first. What happened in Melbourne probably spurred him on.

Warne actually took eleven wickets in Sydney, the last of them his 300th in Tests. His victim, with a perfect top-spinner, was Kallis.

Warne took immense pride in his role as The Finisher, and hinted that this contributed to his decision in December 2006 to stop playing for Australia. Citing his part in Australia's sensational last-day victory over England in Adelaide two weeks earlier, when he had bowled unchanged for four hours, he said, 'If I kept going, there might be a time when I wouldn't be able to deliver like that, and people would say maybe it's time for Shane to retire.'

He wanted to quit before he lost his mastery of one of the greatest, most challenging, arts in the game.

Warne's role as Finisher proved another point of strain in his relationship with Steve Waugh after Waugh took over the Test captaincy. Whereas Allan Border and Mark Taylor took a lot of shifting from the traditional view that only in very rare instances did you depart from the time-honoured practice of batting first if you won the toss – especially given their comforting knowledge that they had Warne in their side to bowl last when the pitches were probably going to be at their worst – Waugh seemed quite willing to do without these advantages.

In his first two Tests as captain at home, against Pakistan in November 1999, Waugh caused a stir by putting in the opposition each time. Both times his move might have come unstuck. In Brisbane, Pakistan scored 367 before Australia outgunned them with 575 (Warne contributing a then Test best of 86), while in Hobart it was Australia who found themselves with the fourth-innings mountain to climb. Left 369 to win, they lost five wickets for 126 before the match was stolen from under Pakistan's noses by a spectacular sixth-wicket partnership between Justin Langer and Adam Gilchrist, the new wicketkeeper and a man who within a year would have displaced Warne as Waugh's vice-captain. Waugh had been vindicated – just. 'We believe we can win from any situation,' he said.

In his desire to dominate games from the first ball, Waugh was prepared to throw convention out of the window, and initially, at least, this seemed to involve favouring his fast bowlers ahead of his match-winning spinner. With both Pakistan and India subjected to 3–0 whitewashes during the 1999–2000 season in Australia, there were some cheap wickets on offer, but Waugh seemed to prefer that these went to his fast men, with the result that Warne's figures scarcely did justice to his contributions. Waugh was getting him to bowl at the toughest times, and against the best players, who knew how to play spin.

Overall, Waugh chose to bowl first seven times with Warne in his team – more than Border (once), Taylor (three times) and Ponting (twice) between them. With opponents naturally inclined to bat first when they won the toss (if only to avoid Warne in the fourth innings), Warne found himself bowling in the fourth innings only eleven times in his thirty-eight Tests under Waugh's stewardship. But there could be little arguing with Waugh's tactics, as he led one of the most formidable teams in Test history to nine series wins out of eleven.

Waugh's captaincy presented Warne with a huge challenge, which was another reason why he needed to reinvent the way he operated. This he did, superbly. In 2001 and 2002 he played prominent parts in five successive series wins over England and South Africa, at home and away, and Pakistan. In the space of thirteen Tests, on four different continents, he actually took the man-of-the-match award six times.

There can be little doubt, though, that he preferred the way he was handled by Taylor, Waugh's immediate predecessor, whom Warne, at the end of his career, singled out for praise as 'a good tactician and communicator'. You had to search hard for Warne compliments about Waugh – Warne even credited Border with first teaching him about the importance of the famed baggy green cap. Early on in Ponting's reign, Warne quickly assassinated Waugh the leader by commenting how nice it was to play under a captain who had faith in spin in a crisis.

Taylor could scarcely have done more to show Warne his total commitment and support. He would sometimes bat first even if conditions on the first morning favoured the seamers, and even though Taylor himself – an opening batsman – had immediately to deal with the consequences of his decision. There was a celebrated case at Old Trafford in 1997, when Australia were trailing 1–0 in the series and Taylor chose to bat first on a heavily grassed pitch in the belief that later in the game the pitch would suit Warne. But it was very tough going for the Australian batsmen on the first day – Taylor himself was out in the third over – and only a fighting century from Waugh himself, who was very uneasy about Taylor's decision, prevented the plan from badly backfiring. But Taylor's gamble paid off. The pitch eventually proved ideal for Warne, who took nine wickets in the game, and Australia emerged commanding winners.

Michael Atherton, the then England captain, remembered that Test as an illustration of just how far Australia were prepared to go to make the most of their trump card.

When I went to Australia in 1990 the first pitch at Brisbane was fairly damp and very green and the first ball from Merv Hughes took a little piece out of the pitch because it was almost wet. But the next time we went to Brisbane, in 1994, the pitch was very white. Once Warne came along and proved himself a match-winner, Australia definitely changed the way they played. Without Warne in his team, there was no way Mark Taylor would have batted first at Old Trafford in 1997. Warne dictated the way Australia went about their cricket.

It wasn't difficult to argue that Steve Waugh might have handled Warne better, and Ian Chappell – who was a close ally of Warne and no great admirer of Waugh, whom he considered too negative in the field when things were going against him – frequently did.

Waugh had reason enough for wanting to clip Warne's wings. Though Warne had won him the World Cup virtually single-handedly, he cannot have forgotten Warne's poor tour of the West Indies a few weeks earlier, or his brooding over the captaincy. And Waugh was reasonably enough anxious that no one player should become bigger than the team. And Australia did now have some other very fine bowlers at their disposal. Glenn McGrath, who had always been an immaculate operator with the new ball, was entering his pomp, and under Waugh, he would take more wickets than anyone – even Warne. McGrath was a cricketer very much in the mould of his captain: driven, with a steely focus and reluctant to take the spotlight, happy to go about his work in unfussy, unfrilly style. Waugh championed his cause, arguing that the distracting presence of Warne prevented McGrath's true greatness from being properly acknowledged. Jason Gillespie, when fit, was scarcely less of a force. And the super-fast Brett Lee had emerged and was quickly hailed by his excited captain as a 'once-in-a-generation' bowler.

Waugh's tactics, though unorthodox, could be made to work, as Australia repeatedly demonstrated. Taylor himself was happy to concede as much. 'Steve Waugh showed that if you have got three fast bowlers – Glenn McGrath, Jason Gillespie and Brett Lee – close to their prime, you can go out there and use it as an aggressive tool,' he said. 'You bowl the other side out, then bat on days two and three, and then still have Shane Warne bowling last. When you had got a big total, that worked very well.' And, with the emergence of Matthew Hayden and Adam Gilchrist, Australia's batting was to become even stronger under Waugh than it had been under Border or Taylor.

Waugh may also, in fact, have been doing his best to protect Warne, whom he had seen suffer the hardships of overwork under Border and Taylor. Warne's spinning finger and bowling shoulder had in turn collapsed under the pressure, and with Warne turning thirty in September 1999 it was not the worst idea if he was spared unnecessary strain when there were younger men willing to shoulder the burden.

There were times when Waugh asked a lot of Warne – he enforced the follow-on all five times he had the chance with Warne in his side, and it cost him dear in Calcutta in 2001, whereas Taylor declined on two of his five opportunities. But the amount of bowling Warne did fell markedly during Waugh's reign: from 307 balls per Test under Border and 294 balls per Test under Taylor, to just 254. It was, however, only a temporary respite. The figure would rise to 289 under Ponting.

On the face of it, Warne's decision to play county cricket was one of the most surprising moves of his career. Why on earth did he feel the need to commit himself to week after week of more matches, more hotels and more travelling? Was he not doing enough of that sort of thing with Australia already? Was he not satisfied with all that he was already achieving? It was an extraordinary thing, and yet before he gave up playing at international level he had put himself through four fairly full seasons in the English domestic game, in 2000 and from 2004 to 2006. Two more, in 2007 and 2008, were planned.

The only comparable case in modern times was Courtney Walsh breaking off from his duties with West Indies to bowl fast for Gloucestershire. Sachin Tendulkar had spent one season with Yorkshire, Brian Lara two with Warwickshire, but that was enough for them. And they were batsmen, not bowlers.

A variety of motives would have been at play with Warne, and money – which was always a strong factor – would have been high on the list. He had received approaches from counties during his first two Test tours of England, in 1993 and 1997, and in other circumstances he might have accepted the best of them, but the Australian board weren't keen on their prize asset subjecting his body to more wear and tear, and Warne himself knew that the board's concern was well placed. But he had almost certainly benefited financially from these overtures, because in 1997, when Sussex had invited him to return the following year to captain the side, the Australian Cricketers' Association was in the midst of tortuous pay negotiations with the Australian board and it was thought that the terms of Warne's contract were improved to dissuade him from signing up for a county.

In the absence of Warne, Sussex brought in Chris Adams from Derbyshire as captain on £85,000 per year, making him the highest-paid non-Test player on the circuit. But money was not Warne's prime motive. He could have got more than his original salary at Hampshire, which was well in excess of £100,000, from Lancashire, who were also interested in recruiting him.

The real explanation was to be found in the timing of his first contact with both clubs, which occurred during the early stages of the 1999 World Cup, well before his confidence and form picked up over the last ten days of the tournament. In other words, Warne was putting out feelers towards counties at a time when he wasn't sure whether he had a future as a Test cricketer under Steve Waugh and was unsure whether his game would ever recover its old magic. Here was Warne – the brooding, insecure Warne – making plans for what he may have suspected were his twilight years. It was another reminder that Warne, great cricketer though he was, could be afflicted by insecurities.

His choice of Hampshire was striking. He was friends with the captain, Robin Smith, whom he had opposed during his first two Ashes series, but Hampshire were an unglamorous team with little history of success and few big-name players. Most overseas stars would have regarded it as more logical to join Lancashire, where there was a tradition of winning trophies and a clutch of Test cricketers on the staff.

But why be one of the planets when you have the chance to be the sun itself? 'There was an element of him that liked being the big fish in the small pond,' Mark Nicholas, the former Hampshire captain, said. 'He liked the romance, the feeling that he could make something out of under-achievers.' Shaun Udal, who was to bowl spin alongside Warne, said, 'I think he wanted to come to us because we were a young developing side and he felt he could make a difference.'

Warne was always emotionally closest to the younger members of a dressing room. In the later stages of his career he could have retreated within himself, but he preferred to mentor the young turks, and a feature of his time at Hampshire was the recruitment of young Australians such as Michael Clarke, Simon Katich and Shane Watson, who were just setting out. When Rod Bransgrove, the new Hampshire chairman who was to forge a close friendship with Warne, went out to Cape Town in 2002 to secure Warne's signature as captain for the following year, he said to Warne, 'You're the man I want to captain Hampshire to the title.' Warne replied, 'No worries, mate, that's what I want too – and I want him [pointing to Watson] to come with me.' In the event, because of his drugs ban, Warne didn't start leading Hampshire until 2004.

His first season at Hampshire, in 2000, didn't work out as planned. Hampshire had been a strong batting team the previous year, and thought that all they needed to do to challenge for silverware was to bolster the bowling – they also signed Alan Mullally from Leicestershire. But it didn't prove that simple. Warne's presence threw things out of kilter. He once said that it had taken him a long time to realize the effect he had on other people – as a teenager, Ricky Ponting had chased the team bus to get his autograph – and Warne's nervousness when he was first introduced to his new teammates was nothing compared to how star-struck they were for the first few weeks of the season. The other problem was that, in a damp summer, they found themselves all the time playing on Warne-proof pitches. 'Everywhere we went we found greentops to nullify him and me,' Udal said. 'Well, mainly him, actually.' Hampshire ended up being relegated from the championship first division. To add to Warne's woes, early in the season the Donna Wright texting scandal led to him losing his post as Australia vice-captain.

Warne did OK with the ball in the circumstances, claiming seventy championship victims – many of them English players star-struck themselves, or exhibiting the old failings of leaden footwork or an over-reliance on the sweep. But there were precious few opportunities for him to bowl in the second innings with runs on the board and fielders round the bat. Then when he got one heaven-sent opportunity to play The Finisher he found an opponent equal to the challenge in Rahul Dravid, the masterly technician from India, who was playing a season with Kent.

On a slow, dry pitch at Portsmouth in July, Dravid gave two near-perfect tutorials in how to play Warne, and his innings of 137 and 73 not out – the latter the top score in Kent's pursuit of 205 – won his side the game. 'It was the best I have ever seen anyone play Warne in county cricket,' Udal said. 'Dravid was magnificent. He picked him early and played him very late, with soft hands. That was the thing with English players – they went hard at him. But Dravid just waited and read him off the pitch. The Indians played Warne better than anyone over the years. They were wristier, and would wait right until the end of the spin and bounce to counteract him.' Warne finished wicketless from 31.4 overs.

Warne was to rue this encounter. Eight months later, in March 2001, in a Test match in Calcutta attended by an estimated 400,000, Dravid was to put this familiarisation session to excellent use as he overcame a run of poor form – he had already been twice bowled by Warne earlier in the series – to keep V.V.S. Laxman company for 104 overs, including the whole of the fourth day, as India fought stoically to overcome a 274-run deficit on the first innings. Their partnership of 376 was the largest put together against Australia during Warne's time, and laid the platform for an astonishing Indian victory – only the third instance of a Test team winning after following on. Warne was not only restricted to one wicket but was unable to maintain his familiar control, conceding 152 runs in his thirty-four overs.

Laxman, who danced yards out of his crease on turning pitches to unerringly whip deliveries out of the rough to the midwicket boundary, was to torment Warne during this series in a way few batsmen ever did. By the time of the deciding game in Madras – where another of Warne's greatest adversaries, Sachin Tendulkar, scored a century – Laxman showed how well on top he was in their personal duel by scoring at a run per ball off him. As India chased 155 in the fourth innings, Laxman played a crucial role by hitting Warne out of the attack. In the end India got home with only two wickets to spare, and had Warne bowled more they might not have made it. But when Laxman had personally taken 26 runs from six of Warne's overs, Waugh had little choice but to pull Warne out of the firing line. It was a rare and chastening experience for Australia's champion.

But there was a rider. As on his first tour of India, Warne wasn't quite on top of his game. He was only recently back from a long lay-off after breaking his spinning finger taking a catch in a state game. He had been forced to miss an entire five-Test home series against West Indies, which

Australia had won 5–0. (MacGill, Warne's stand-in, had taken sixteen wickets.) Against batsmen as aggressive as India's, he needed confidence in his full armoury, but with time needed for his finger to function properly, he didn't have it. He provided only the odd good spell, and his ten wickets in the series cost more than 50 apiece – an embarrassing contrast to the sweeping success of Indian spinner Harbhajan Singh, who captured an astonishing thirty-two wickets in three Tests.

Sceptics interpreted Warne's poor showing as a sign that he might be approaching his journey's end, whereas in truth many heroic efforts lay in the future. But Warne's problems on that tour did not end there.

A few months after Steve Waugh had taken over from Mark Taylor, in 1999, Australia had also switched coaches. Geoff Marsh, whose last Test series as a player had been Warne's first, had stepped down after three years and had been replaced by John Buchanan, a former schoolteacher and university lecturer who had played state cricket for Queensland in the late 1970s but never reached international level. He was very much a Waugh appointment at a time when Waugh was looking at fresh ways to, in his words, 'provoke, stimulate and challenge' members of an already highly successful side.

Buchanan, who had worked successfully with Queensland and less so with Middlesex, was one of a new breed of coach who favoured new technology and left-field ideas as ways of extracting that crucial extra 1 per cent out of their players. He was big on goal-setting, and wanted the team to aspire to be as good as, if not better than, Bradman's famed 1948 'Invincibles'. In his first Test in charge, he had hung a notice up in the dressing room in Brisbane stating: 'Today is the first Test of our journey to the Invincibles.

Let's make the ride enjoyable and attainable.' He got his players to write down their aims, and would then post these on the wall too – there to be publicly lived up to.

Some of his initiatives left his players baffled, however, and Warne certainly belonged in the camp of the sceptics. To Warne – like Ian Chappell, who thought Waugh gave too much say to Buchanan – cricket was a simple game which people were inclined to over-complicate, and he found it hard to relate to Buchanan's fondness for hammering data into a laptop. Warne wasn't much interested in a computer analysis of his performances or those of opponents, saying with a hint of sarcasm, 'I still back myself to use the old brain.' Warne classified Buchanan as among the Nerds – those in the Australian camp who 'don't worry too much about their hairstyle or the latest fashions'.

Even among his supporters, Buchanan became notorious for being so wrapped up in his meticulous research that he would leave books on buses and video cameras on planes. Sometimes to his players' amusement, sometimes to their alarm, copies of various documents of his found their way into the wrong hands. In March 2000 a dossier he had compiled on New Zealand's weaknesses fell into the hands of the press. When, in July 2001, a paper he had distributed to his players extolling the tactical genius of Sun Tzu, an ancient Chinese warrior and philosopher, inadvertently became public they issued a collective sigh of relief because it enabled the press to translate it for them. 'Two things often made his assignments hard,' Waugh wrote of Buchanan in his autobiography. 'We needed the intellect to pull them off and we struggled to read his minuscule handwriting.'

How much of Australia's success was attributable to Buchanan was a moot point. Such a talented collection of players could have achieved a lot whoever was coach, and it was beyond dispute that Buchanan's communication skills faltered on the rare occasions that the team was in trouble, as happened in India in 2001 and in England in 2005. The shock defeat in Calcutta, which ended a run of sixteen Test wins in a row for Australia that dated back to the match before Buchanan took over, triggered what Waugh described as Buchanan's 'first real blunder as coach'.

After the game, Buchanan caused astonishment when, through the media, he questioned both Warne's fitness and his future place in the team. 'Warney's quite distressed when he comes off the field all the time,' he said. 'It's no secret that he's not one of the fittest characters running around in world cricket.' Asked whether Warne might be dropped for the next match, Buchanan added, 'I'm not saying he's going to be left out, he's still in the frame, but when we walk into this [next] Test we've really got to have eleven blokes who can give five days of hard cricket and not be affected by any physical limitations.'

These were heavy-handed comments about a player who only the previous year had played a crucial part in Australia's World Cup triumph and who was not long back from a two-month lay-off. If Warne wasn't in as good a shape as he might have been, that was hardly a surprise for a bowler who tended to get fit through bowling rather than training. But then Warne's general fitness had long been a contentious issue.

'He may have meant to inspire but all he did was alienate,' Waugh wrote of Buchanan's action. 'This ploy may have worked when Buck was in charge of Queensland, working with a lower-profile player on the way up who might have found such a public challenge motivational, but in Shane he picked his mark poorly.' The next day, and with the decisive match in Madras imminent, Waugh presided over a peace summit at which Warne made plain his anger at what he saw as a 'cheap shot' and Buchanan conceded he had made a mistake.

This incident had far-reaching consequences. Astonishingly, by the time Australia were touring England a few weeks later, the Australian Cricket Board had removed Buchanan from the panel of tour selectors (on tours the team was traditionally chosen by captain, vice-captain and coach) in a change that Waugh directly attributed to the coach's outburst against Warne. This was a remarkable turn of events given that Buchanan had been brought in only eighteen months earlier to support Waugh in ensuring that the team came before any individual. The decision reflected mistrust in Buchanan's ability to articulate selection issues in a sensitive manner – he was also warned to be careful about his public utterances – and a continuing anxiety to keep Warne sweet. Buchanan's remarks, though clumsy, were hardly inaccurate, but memories of Warne's sulkiness after his dropping for the Antigua Test in 1999 (when Waugh was the prime mover) would have been fresh in everyone's mind. Surely Buchanan would not have been treated in such fashion had he criticized anyone but Warne.

Whatever the rights and wrongs, the move worked. In England, Warne took thirty-one wickets and Australia took the series 4–1.

But Warne's relationship with Buchanan never really recovered, with Warne, playing the injured party, firing occasional verbal shots across the coach's bow. After Buchanan had announced his intention to step down after the 2007 World Cup, Warne called for a replacement with 'common cricket sense' and experience of playing the game at international level. He was also reported as saying, 'I'm a big believer that the coach is something you travel in to get to the game.' He subsequently said he had been misquoted, but he had another go at Buchanan after Australia lost five one-day matches in a row early in 2007, blaming the coach for driving his players too hard in training.

Inconsistent and Unsatisfactory

JOHN BUCHANAN'S REMARKS may have been insensitive and ill-timed, but if he were sensible Shane Warne would have listened carefully to what Australia's coach was saying. Fitness remained on the Australian management's agenda, and fitness – in the modern sense of being fit to pound the treadmill and pump iron in the gym – had never been Warne's strong point. When it came to fitness, he wasn't a self-starter. He tended to use the 'Who ate all the pies?' jibes from the English crowds or from Daryll Cullinan, or chiding from his mother about his double-chins, as gauges as to whether he was looking in shape or not.

To its credit, Australian cricket had always looked to push the bar higher, even though its team was indisputably the world's best. Even while Steve Waugh and his players were holding the World Cup, and winning Test series after Test series, and even while Waugh and Buchanan sought ways to enhance performance, so the selection panel of Trevor Hohns, Allan Border, David Boon and Andrew Hilditch were searching for ways to strengthen the national side. The ACB's directors may have occasionally fallen over backwards to keep prized assets like Warne happy, but the selectors were prepared to be more ruthless. They had indicated as much with their rotation policy in one-day cricket, which meant few players could expect to play every game. No one was to assume their place was safe.

It seemed that Warne was indeed sensitive to which way the wind was blowing – either that or he had listened to the hecklers in England – and towards the end of 2001 he sought to do something about improving his condition by living on a spartan diet of cereal, baked beans and water. It didn't do much for his cricket in the Tests against New Zealand, who quite successfully deployed frustration tactics against him, but he once again fed well on South African prey during the 2001–02 Australian season.

Not for the first time, his timing proved good. The selectorial axe was being raised, but not above his neck.

Early in 2002, Australia surprisingly failed to make the final of the triangular one-day competition they hosted, for only the third time in twenty-three years. It was a close-run thing – they finished level on points with New Zealand – but enough to prompt the selectors to take drastic action just twelve months before Australia's defence of the World Cup in South Africa. Eight days after Australia's untimely exit, Steve Waugh was replaced as captain of the one-day side by Ricky Ponting (Waugh would remain in charge of the Test team for another two years) and also removed as a player; his twin brother, Mark, was also dropped. Neither had been in great form, and in the case of Steve his fitness had also been an issue: he had been troubled by various muscular strains.

Warne was stunned. He felt that if Steve Waugh, a World Cup-winning captain, could be treated in such a manner, then no one in the side was safe. Everyone needed to be on their mettle.

He worked on his physique with renewed vigour. He looked slimmer than of old during the tour of South Africa, where he performed strongly in the Tests, notching his

100th appearance and finishing as the leading wicket-taker, before returning to Melbourne for the Australian winter, which he spent training hard and pushing himself through another crash diet. His weight fell to 84 kg – almost as low as it had been before he left for his first Test tour of Sri Lanka in 1992 – and he claimed he was the fittest he had been since then. By the time he returned to action at the Champions Trophy in Sri Lanka in September 2002 he was barely recognizable from the old Warne, striking a remarkable figure with slimmed waist and broader chest.

He went straight from there into a Test series with Pakistan, where despite gruelling heat he showed himself at the peak of his powers, snaring twenty-seven wickets in a three-Test series – an Australian record, nearly half of them with lbws, testimony to the efficacy of his new slider. Going into the final day the first Test lay in the balance, with Pakistan requiring 137 with seven wickets in hand, but Warne swiftly settled matters in his side's favour with the wicket of Younis Khan, and the spirits of his opponents never recovered.

Two months later, on 15 December 2002, with Warne having played a full part in Australia retaining the Ashes in just eleven days of cricket, he dislocated his bowling shoulder diving to stop a ball from Craig White during a one-day international in Melbourne. Plainly in agony, he was stretchered from the field and rushed to hospital, where he was examined by the surgeon who had operated on the shoulder four years earlier. Scans confirmed ligament damage.

It was a cruel blow. Warne was lying just nine short of his 500th wicket in Tests – a target he had had a chance of reaching in the forthcoming Boxing Day Test at the MCG – and Australia's World Cup campaign was just over eight weeks away. Having fought so hard to be fit enough to be selected for the tournament, he would have been desperate to play. And, with memories of the time it had taken him to regain his form after his 1998 shoulder surgery, he would have been desperate to recover as fast and smoothly as possible.

In the event, he narrowly beat predictions of a six-week lay-off, returning to face England in the triangular one-day series finals thirty-nine days later. He bowled with no apparent loss of power and took a couple of match-turning wickets in the second final to help snatch a dramatic five-run win. The way was clear for him to go to South Africa after all.

The injury was another blunt reminder of his cricketing mortality, however, and on 22 January 2003, the day before his comeback, he held a press conference to announce that, at thirty-three, he would be quitting one-day cricket after the World Cup in an effort to prolong his Test career by 'five or six years'. Three days later he was chaired from the field in Melbourne after what was anticipated would be his last ODI on his home ground.

Again, a major injury had triggered an emotional, possibly theatrical, response.

At 6.30 a.m. on 10 February 2003, on the eve of Australia's opening World Cup match, Warne took a call at his hotel in Johannesburg from John Mendoza, the head of the Australian Sports Drug Agency, telling him that a drugs test he had undergone before the triangular finals had shown up positive.

Warne had created some shocks in his time, but as a bolt-from-the-blue this news – which broke the next morning – was right up there with relevations of his dealings with John the bookie. Within hours, having issued a statement to the media, he was on a plane back to Melbourne, out of the World Cup and once again firmly in disgrace with his countrymen.

Warne had tested positive for a diuretic. Diuretics were on the list of prohibited substances for sportsmen because of their capacity to act as a masking agent for steroids.

Warne – who in the next fortnight would give three press conferences plus the now traditional mea-culpa television interview with Channel Nine – repeatedly expressed his shock at what had happened and denied that he had ever taken performance-enhancing drugs. He insisted that he had taken a single tablet, which he had believed was merely a fluid-reduction tablet and not a prohibited substance, because he had wanted to look good on television for the announcement of his intended retirement from one-day cricket. His mother, Brigitte, always anxious for her son to look his best, had given it to him. In other words, he had taken the pill purely out of vanity. He claimed he was the victim of 'anti-doping hysteria'.

However, the story was not quite as straightforward as Warne would have had everyone believe. Fresh details emerged from an Australian Cricket Board tribunal, the Australian Sports Drug Agency, and newspaper investigations that cast doubt on his version of events.

A major divergence concerned the number of Moduretic tablets he had taken. Warne publicly insisted he had taken just one, but in front of the ACB's three-person tribunal – consisting of Queensland judge Justice Glen Williams, Dr Susan White, a sports drugs specialist, and rather bizarrely Peter Taylor, the former Australia spin bowler whose Test place Warne had taken eleven years earlier – he admitted that he had 'got some of the drug on two occasions from his mother'. He said his mother had given him 'sheets of tablets', something she herself confirmed under questioning. The tribunal concluded that Warne had taken at least two tablets, something the quantity of diuretic found in his urine sample made self-evident. But it clearly could have been many more.

Afterwards, the tribunal publicly stated said that it had 'grave doubt that it has the full information on his use of Moduretic'. It stated that Warne had given 'vague, inconsistent and un-satisfactory' evidence and that it did not accept that he was 'entirely truthful'. It was dismissive of Warne's claims that he could not read the warnings on the Moduretic packaging because of 'torn flaps' and that he was unaware of the consequences of cricketers having prohibited substances in their bodies. It also found Brigitte Warne's evidence 'vague and unsatisfactory as to the number of tablets she had given him'. One question that never got answered was why Warne had taken a sheet of Moduretic tablets with him to South Africa if his only reason for taking the tablet (or tablets) had been to look slimmer on TV back in Australia a few weeks earlier. (He had surrendered a sheet, with two tablets missing, to Errol Alcott, the team's physiotherapist, in Johannesburg the day he learned of his positive test.)

But this was not all. It transpired that the Australian Sports Drug Agency had first tested Warne back in mid-December, just before his shoulder injury, and that that test, also, had contained evidence of a diuretic, though in insufficient quantity to trigger a positive result. This had led the agency to seek to test him again the next time he played, although because of his injury lay-off it had had to wait almost six weeks for the chance.

Then, the day before the tribunal sat, another damaging claim was made. The Melbourne *Age*, which appeared to have had sight of an eighty-page scientific analysis of Warne's positive test, reported that traces of drugs other than diuretics had been found in his urine sample, though the levels of these drugs had been below the threshold necessary for him to test positive for them. What drugs these were was not stated.

These two points – the December test and the traces of other substances – changed the landscape of the story as presented by Warne and his supporters. The December test appeared to give the lie to his original claim that he had taken just one tablet in January; it also confounded the suspicion that his sole purpose had been to use drugs to speed his recovery from his injury, tempting though that might have been given the history of his shoulder. The traces of drugs six weeks apart suggested a pattern of consumption, with the most likely motive the desire to make himself look slimmer and fitter than he was, to preserve his one-day place and forestall another public barb from the likes of Buchanan.

Once again Warne had failed to know where to draw the line in life off the field. Once again he seemed incapable of taking responsibility for what he had done. Once again he appeared guilty of vanity.

But, if he had committed grave misjudgements, he wasn't alone. The way the Australian Cricket Board handled the matter was little short of scandalous. According to guidelines established by the World Anti-Doping Agency, Warne ought to have received a two-year ban from all cricket. As it was, the tribunal – perhaps suspecting that a two-year ban would drive Warne into premature retirement – gave him merely a twelve-month suspension. It cited in mitigation the evidence of the ACB's medical officer, Dr Peter Harcourt, that there was no direct evidence of steroid use. This was nonsensical: the point about diuretics was that they masked steroids; this was why they were prohibited in the first place, and why WADA deemed that they merited a two-year ban.

It was a decision that was every bit as self-serving as the board's refusal in 1995 to suspend Warne and Mark Waugh for their dealings with John the bookie so that the two of them could take part in a crucial tour of the West Indies. As usual, it seemed that winning was viewed as far too important to come second to principle. Dick Pound, the chairman of the World Anti-Doping Agency, accused the tribunal of 'stepping right up to the edge of the cliff, but not jumping off'.

But the most opprobrium was saved for Warne. He had often said that he objected to the judgemental, moralistic attitude of Australians, but he kept getting into scrapes that invited them to judge him unfavourably. Even his team-mates found it hard to express much sympathy for a colleague who had so carelessly jeopardized their World Cup prospects, though in fact they went on to win the tournament without losing a match. Personal sponsors reviewed their positions and it was estimated that Warne's earnings in Australia dipped in 2004 to around £600,000, behind those of Ponting and Adam Gilchrist.

'For all his cricketing genius, Shane Warne is immature, rather naive and probably vain enough to think that he can get away with just about anything hamfisted,' said John Benaud. 'He will be proclaimed the greatest leg-spinner of all time, but sadly there will always be that qualifier about his absolute stupidity.' Peter Roebuck reckoned that this scandal marked the low point of Warne's career: '[Of all his misdemeanours] he was least forgiven for his drug-taking before the World Cup and the way he blamed his mother. When it became clear that more than one substance had been found in his body, many people concluded that he wasn't telling the truth.'

Warne initially declared himself shocked at his suspension, but he must have known it could have been worse. On reflection, he might have realized that the Australian board had once again looked after its Chosen One as best it could. Perhaps remembering the old Australian maxim about copping it sweet, he didn't appeal.

As was the case when he was dropped from the Australia side four years earlier, privately Warne didn't take his demotion well. Indeed, it was accompanied by another personal crisis, although of a different sort from the previous time, when he was preoccupied with fears that his cricket career might be coming to an end. Now there was to be media coverage relating to allegations of extramarital affairs. There were claims of harassment, which led to a South African woman being found guilty of trying to extort money from an associate of Warne's and of a relationship between Warne and a lap-dancer from his home city of Melbourne.

This last was different from previous reports of Warne's infidelity, because pleas of mitigation due to loneliness on tour couldn't be made. This was an affair seemingly conducted on his own doorstep, during an enforced lay-off when family demands might have been expected to be uppermost in his thoughts, and it reportedly lasted three months, not one or two nights. 'We'd meet up, go out to clubs and meet up with his mates,' Angela Gallagher, who at thirty-eight was a few years older than he was, claimed. 'He seemed to make no secret of me.' Gallagher said that Warne had told her he had an open marriage. Here perhaps was a prime example of Rod Bransgrove's theory that away from the pitch Warne seemed to think himself invisible. But he wasn't, and Gallagher eventually sold her story to *New Idea*, an Australian publication, and also relayed it to viewers of Channel Seven, rivals to Warne's friends at Channel Nine.

Several months into his ban, Warne's marriage was near to breaking point. Simone had long been exasperated by the stories of infidelities, but the allegations concerning Gallagher suggested the cruellest betrayal. To escape another media frenzy outside the new family home in Brighton, Melbourne, the couple fled to Europe with their three young children to try to sort out their difficulties, and ended up spending several weeks in Spain, where Bransgrove had a property they could use as a home away from prying eyes. Exhausted by the relentless attention, Warne was so disenchanted with Australia that he told friends – perhaps only half-jokingly – that he was thinking of emigrating and qualifying to play cricket for England. It was not a practicable suggestion, but it showed how desperate he had become.

Later, he and Simone announced through a joint magazine interview that they intended to stay together: Simone, it seemed, had found it in her heart to give him another chance. Warne struck a contrite figure, a man seemingly humbled at the realization that he had again not just pushed life's rules, but broken them. 'I think this is my last chance at everything,' he told Australian *Women's Weekly*. 'We've all got choices and I've made a few too many bad ones.'

Significantly, one reason why Simone took him back, it seemed, was because she had seen how distressed her husband was. 'I saw how upset he was when he told me about it all,' she said. 'He was pretty much at the lowest point in his life. I think he doesn't ever want to feel that again.'

This episode may have been bad for Warne's marriage – which was to hit further trouble within two years – but it may not have been bad for his cricket. The chaos of his domestic life probably served only to further drive him to get back to doing the thing he did best; only intensified the ache to return to the one stage where he knew he could still do things right. Egocentric behaviour may be disruptive to normal life, but it doesn't necessarily run contrary to being a highly successful professional sportsman. Assured of Simone's continued love, Warne prepared to go out and create good headlines again.

Some had questioned whether he could cope with a year on the sidelines. Steve Waugh, his Test captain, had feared that he might give it all up. 'I'm sure that Shane will initially say to himself, "I want to get back in there and back on the field," but as time goes by his mind will be in different places . . . he has got to have the motivation to continue,' he said. 'To train for twelve months without playing, that has to be very difficult.'

And frankly Warne had achieved everything he could have hoped for in cricket, and more. Australia had been at or near the top of world cricket throughout his time, and he had to his name a tally of Test wickets that most bowlers could only fantasize about. If he'd never bowled another ball, his niche in the game's history was assured. If he'd said he was throwing it all in for a career in the broadcasting box alongside Ian Chappell, Richie Benaud and Co. no one could have blamed him. As the end of the suspension loomed, the critics seemed uncertain what to expect. Michael Atherton argued that it was an 'impossibility' for Warne to return to his best form; that his best had long been behind him.

But even before the Angela Gallagher story emerged,

Warne would not have wanted to leave the game on such an off note as a drugs ban. Quitting would have been to endorse disgrace and accept defeat, which was unthinkable for a man who had fought so hard to earn a reputation as a winner. He had shown many times in his career that he viewed any setback, whether it be an injury, a bad personal performance or a team defeat, merely as a fresh challenge. And, like Simone, many of his friends in cricket were standing by him. 'As long as he still wants to come, we'll have him,' said Bransgrove, whose plan to have Warne captain Hampshire in 2003 was scotched by the ban. 'I'm convinced he didn't take performance-enhancing drugs. He's been stupid, but we should keep this in perspective. It was a minor indiscretion.' Channel Nine gave him commentary work.

Waugh had predicted that Warne would find it hard to train for twelve months without playing, and of course Warne didn't train for all that time. But about ten weeks before the end of the ban he embarked on a strict regime to get himself back in shape. He started off training at the St Kilda Saints ground, before hiring a personal trainer to put him through a punishing schedule of boxing, jogging, cycling and weights. He went on another special diet, at the end of which he was back down to around his optimum weight.

As it happened, an enforced rest proved to be by far the best thing that could have happened to Warne. Had he continued playing, he would certainly have retired earlier, very probably more than twelve months earlier. As it was, a year of rest revitalized his mind and body, and rekindled his enthusiasm, in a way no one could possibly have foreseen.

'Prior to my twelve-month ban, I was getting to the stage where my body was about to give up,' he reflected near the end of his career. 'I had so many operations and I was about to pack it in. I was just about burned out. The year off did me the world of good.'

Yet again, he'd got lucky.

12

Lonely Everest

THERE WAS ANOTHER motive behind coming back. Warne had been halted within tantalizing distance of the world Test wicket-taking record, the Everest of bowling and well worth him trying to plant his flag – if not Australia's on the summit. The record lay in the hands of the beanpole Jamaican fast bowler Courtney Walsh, whose 519 wickets was achievable with a few productive matches by Warne, whose tally stood at 491.

It was just the sort of thing to get his competitive juices flowing. The Australians always prided themselves on putting winning first – team before self, and all that – and they could be scathing in their condemnation when they saw foreign players chasing records, but their stance was slightly disingenuous. They liked a CV-enhancing record as well as the next man. During Warne's lay-off, in October 2003, Matthew Hayden had plundered 380 off a Lilliputian Zimbabwe attack in Perth to break the record for the highest Test score; given the context, it was an obscene act of gluttony.

And there was no doubt the bowling record was on Warne's mind: when he had announced his retirement from one-day internationals, he had said he wanted to play on in Tests and become the leading wicket-taker of all time. The last Australian to hold the record was Dennis Lillee, back in the eighties, and another Australian, Clarrie Grimmett, had been the only leg-spinner to hold the prize, from 1936 to 1953.

To add spice to the situation, during Warne's absence Sri Lanka's Muttiah Muralitharan had raised his wicket haul to 485, and Australia and Sri Lanka were due to face each other in Sri Lanka in March 2004, the month following Warne's scheduled return, so the stage was set for an exciting race between the two to knock Walsh from his perch.

It was a duel guaranteed an extra edge, too, because love had never been lost between the Australians and the Sri Lankans. Australia were bitter at their shock defeat in the World Cup final of 1996, and had never liked Arjuna Ranatunga, the former Sri Lanka captain, who delighted in antagonizing them. The Sri Lankans took exception to Australian sledging that they felt went beyond the bounds of decency, and were unhappy at Murali's treatment by Australian umpires. Warne was often a generous opponent, but he seemed to make an exception in the case of Murali, whose record he rather damned with faint praise, citing the many 'easy' wickets he had taken against Bangladesh and Zimbabwe. 'We get on OK but it is not a close friendship,' Murali once said of Warne. 'We say hello to each other but conversation never goes much further than that. I don't compete with him but he might feel the other way.' But their friendship warmed after they both became involved in charity work following the tsunami in December 2004.

Graham Thorpe, who scored Test centuries against both, had no doubt that Warne was the greater bowler, and most who faced both would probably have agreed – though Murali took his wickets more cheaply and at a fractionally faster rate. 'Warne was always varying the degree he spun the ball, while Murali generally just tried to spin the ball as much as he could,' Thorpe said. 'Warne kept on developing during his career, changing his game plans for each batsman, trying subtle new ways of getting you out. Murali was less sophisticated. There were fewer mind games.'

Fortunately for Warne, with the pitches in Sri Lanka bound to favour spin, Australia would have wanted to take two specialist spinners, so provided he could show even moderate form he was a near-certain pick. As usual, Stuart MacGill had acted as a very capable understudy during Warne's time out, taking 65 wickets in 12 Tests, but without Warne and the injured Glenn McGrath the attack had lacked control and, frustratingly, Australia had just been held to a 1–1 draw on home soil by India, whose batsmen had made hay.

In short, Warne was needed, and in the event the Australian selectors appeared to have no hesitation in recalling their favoured son on what for any other player would have been regarded as flimsy evidence of form. Everyone, it seems, was in a hurry to get him back. On the day his ban was lifted he stepped into a Victoria second-XI match that had begun the previous day; a crowd of 1,000 turned up to watch him at the Junction Oval, while up the road the full Victoria side performed in front of a smaller gathering at the MCG. On the final day, Warne was unable to prevent the academy successfully chasing 306 as he leaked 120 runs in 19.5 overs, but within a few days he had been restored to the state team and was providing something like normal service as he smothered Tasmania's pursuit of 440 with four cheap wickets. The next day he was named in the Test squad for Sri Lanka.

The series proved a triumph for Warne – and for Australia in their first Test series under Ricky Ponting. Fears that they might lose their edge without Steve Waugh were confounded as they battled back with Waugh-like grittiness to overcome first-innings deficits in all three games, mounting imposing totals of 512, 442 and 375. The way their batsmen used nimble minds and feet to counter Murali was a key factor in the 3–0 scoreline, but so too was Warne's bowling. With Ponting winning the all-important right to bowl last in each game, Warne came up trumps every time. Without him, Sri Lanka might have hung on for draws in Galle and Colombo – where he snatched four wickets in the last scheduled session – and sneaked a win in Kandy, where they made a bold attempt to chase 352. Warne's removal of Tillkeratne Dilshan late on the penultimate evening was a crucial moment, and next morning Australia emerged narrow winners. Warne was named man of the series.

But he was to be thwarted in what turned into a drama-filled race with Murali. Both of them were the dominant bowlers for their sides, but, with Murali due to play his next series first, Warne really had to overhaul Walsh before the end of the Sri Lanka tour. He needed 29 wickets to do that but could manage only 26, while Murali, needing 35 for the record, took 28. In any case, both were exceptional hauls for a three-match series; indeed, Murali's was the biggest by someone finishing on a losing side.

Six weeks later, in May 2004 in Harare, Murali duly overtook Walsh to take the record. Warne might have deposed Murali within a matter of days in the same city, but two Tests that Australia were due to play in Zimbabwe were scrapped at the eleventh hour when the Zimbabwe Cricket Union voluntarily withdrew from Test cricket rather than resolve a bitter dispute with its white players as the ICC wanted it to. MacGill had refused to join the tour in protest at Zimbabwe's humanitarian crisis, but he was the only one;

Warne and the other Australians spent uncomfortable hours in Harare insisting that their focus didn't go beyond playing cricket.

However, Warne's time came before his comeback year was out – though not without further turbulence. Murali's action had become the subject of fresh controversy, with Chris Broad, an ICC match referee, calling it into question. When Australian prime minister John Howard joined the ranks of Aussies knocking the bloke who'd pinched the record from under the nose of their man and labelled Murali a 'chucker', Murali had had enough and announced he was withdrawing from Sri Lanka's reciprocal tour of Australia. Warne called him thin-skinned for pulling out.

Warne needed eleven wickets from two matches but, in a rare failure to live up to the preferred script, finished with ten, giving him merely a share in the world record with Murali. Warne, it has to be said, wasn't always at his best when pursuing a personal milestone, and his hunt arguably cost Australia victory in the second Test in Cairns. They had 85 overs to dismiss Sri Lanka on the last day, and Ponting gave 37 of them to Warne, who bowled unchanged for five hours but, striving too hard, delivered only four wickets. Sri Lanka secured the draw with their ninth-wicket pair at the crease. There had been a Test at Auckland in 2001 when Warne was pushing to overtake Lillee as Australia's leading wicket-taker and Steve Waugh, judging that Warne 'appeared distracted by the attention his chase was getting', had preferred to turn to his other bowlers to do the donkey work. In the end, Waugh had brought on Warne to dismiss the last man and 'get the record out of the way'. But the suspicion was that Ponting – five years younger than his bowler, rather than four years older as Waugh had been – never had that degree of control over Warne.

Thanks in part to further trouble befalling Murali, who was sidelined by shoulder surgery, Warne eventually made the record his own three months later, in October 2004, when he dismissed India's Irfan Pathan in Madras. Warne acknowledged the feat by holding up the ball to all sections of the crowd, which included his wife, Simone. 'I would have been happy to take one Test wicket when I started my career,' he said afterwards. Anyone who had spent an afternoon watching him work an umpire might have begged to differ.

The series in India, of course, was about a lot more than Warne's world record. India was a place where Australia had not won a series in more than forty years; it was the one blemish on their modern record, and Steve Waugh had labelled it 'the final frontier'. But part of the reason behind their defeats on their last two tours was that the series had been played after Australia's domestic season, and fatigue had taken its toll. This time the Australians managed to negotiate that the tour took place before their home matches; they also secured a seven-day break between the second and third Tests, and an itinerary free of one-day matches. It made all the difference. Australia's superior organization paid off and they emerged deserving 2–1 winners.

Warne himself was in much better shape than he had been in India in 1998 and 2001, when he had been neither fully fit nor in form against gifted players eager to exploit any weakness. Now he was hungry for success and much fresher after his year out, even though he had recently spent most of the English summer captaining Hampshire in passionate, combative style. He had made amends for the relegation suffered during his previous season, and his no-show in 2003 because of his drugs ban, by seeing them restored to the championship first division.

By his own standards, he played a relatively small part in the Indian triumph, but there were extenuating factors. He broke his right thumb in the nets on the eve of the final match in Bombay, where he would certainly have taken many wickets on a grossly underprepared surface, while unfathomably a green seamer had been prepared in the previous match in Nagpur, on which the Australian fast bowlers were predictably dominant. Warne was also deprived by rain of a classic last-day, fourth-innings battle in Madras, where India needed another 210 runs with all wickets in hand. India were favourites, but on the fourth night Warne was spikily confident of pulling another rabbit from his conjuring hat. And who would have dared bet against him?

Aside from his world record, Warne would have perhaps got most personal satisfaction from having thrice dismissed cheaply Laxman, his old nemesis.

During Australia's rather soulless trouncings of New Zealand and Pakistan at home in the 2004–05 season, Warne built up a sizeable lead over Murali which was still intact on the day he retired from Test cricket. His return from his ban had been a triumph and he was once again king of all he surveyed. When he arrived in England in April 2005, to lead Hampshire for two months before a keenly awaited Ashes series against a rejuvenated England side, he seemed as content as he had ever been.

'It doesn't really matter how many Test wickets I end up with,' he told me one day in Southampton. 'I don't think it matters if I take any more. I've made my niche in the history of the game in what I've achieved and the way I've gone about it. I absolutely love the game, because every match something different happens. That's its beauty.' He had signed a new contract with Hampshire, and spoke of bringing his family to live in England, the plan being that he would captain Hampshire for two seasons after he had stopped playing for Australia. He believed he could deliver them the championship.

He had previously spoken about carrying on with Test cricket for several more years, but he was now starting to think that the time to step down was fast approaching. There weren't many suitably big stages on which to bow out, and he privately came to the conclusion that he would go at the end of the Ashes.

But, as he said, the fascinating thing about cricket was that something different always happened. And something different was about to happen now that was to force him to tear up his plans.

The Ashes series of 2005 proved the ultimate test in Warne's career, and the ultimate vindication of his greatness. He found Australia in the unusual position of being badly up against it for most of the time, and his personal life – not so unusually – in turmoil. Things could not have been stacked more against him. And yet, despite his team struggling and his marriage failing, his all-round game was more potent than it had ever been. In terms of both wickets taken (40) and runs scored (249) it was the best series he ever had. Once again, he had found inspiration within desperation.

He was, in many senses, a man apart. He was the oldest man on either side, yet his enthusiasms, off the field as well as on, suggested the opposite. His closest friend on the Australian team was Michael Clarke, who was twelve years his junior, and on the England side Kevin Pietersen, who was eleven years younger. Teammates who were more his age seemed to prefer to keep their distance lest they be tainted by the alley-cat antics. His relations with the coach, John Buchanan, remained cool.

Yet he was approaching the finish, and willing to make peace. Having spent years fighting tooth and nail for every tiny advantage, he wanted the end of competition to be amicable. He had the appropriate stage on which to go out. He wanted the goodwill too.

When opponents such as Pietersen or Andrew Flintoff performed well, he was prepared to congratulate them in full view of cameras beaming the scenes back to Australians no doubt uneasy at this apparent acquiescence to English success. He seemed equally comfortable with the partisan English crowds, who, sensing their team finally had a chance of regaining the Ashes after sixteen years, baited, goaded and mocked the Australians at every turn. But, Warne being the star they had long loved to hate, he had been used to this treatment for years and took it in his stride; many of his teammates were taken aback at the febrile atmosphere and were thrown off their games. Warne, in any case, was this time largely spared. As he fought heroically to keep his side afloat, the English were prepared to acknowledge his champion status. Their chants of 'We only wish you were English' went to the heart of Warne's popularity with the enemy; England followers admired him largely because he represented what they hadn't got, what they'd never really had – a world-class leg-spinner.

When the series was lost, though, Warne felt the backlash from those Australians who thought he was too matey with the Poms. Even his old mate Merv Hughes had a go at him.

The Australians were in trouble even before Warne joined them from Hampshire ten days before the series. The one-day squad had been playing for five weeks, and signs of complacency and disorganization were already evident. In the space of seven days, they lost four times. They were dismissed for 79 by England in a Twenty20 match, and raised the eyebrows of the cricketing world by losing to Bangladesh in a full one-day international — a game which one of their players, Andrew Symonds, missed because he had stayed up all night drinking. Their cricketers, it seemed, had grown as weary of winning as their public, who had stayed away in droves from home matches during the 2004–05 season and left the Australian board nursing a substantial loss. Australia had failed to appreciate how much England had improved, and how much Jason Gillespie, the leading bowler in India, and Michael Kasprowicz had declined. 'I've hardly been able to stop at a traffic light without somebody winding down a window and shouting, "79 all out!" ' Warne commented. But, as ever, he remained optimistic that Australian superiority would tell in the end.

And sure enough, when Australia overcame a fighting start from England to decisively take the first Test at Lord's in July, it appeared that the normal order had been restored, and that another Ashes series was set to assume the usual course.

It was with their next move that the Australians made their decisive mistake, and it was one born out of arrogance. When Ricky Ponting won the toss at Edgbaston, the logical thing to do was ignore the clouds overhead and bat first on an excellent batting surface that would only get worse. To bowl first went against logic and against the first principle of Australian cricket, which was to give Warne the fourth innings to finish the job. In such circumstances, even Steve Waugh would probably have batted first. To make matters worse, that morning Glenn McGrath had trodden on a ball in practice and put himself out of the game. And Ponting had still wanted to bowl first.

After England had rapidly posted 407 on the first day, there were reports that Ponting and Warne had argued in the dressing room about the decision to bowl. Australian denials did little to stop the speculation. But Warne had been against the decision, as Ponting later conceded. 'It's absolute garbage that there is a problem between me and Warney. He just didn't agree with the decision to bowl first. He was the only one. Everyone else was on side.'

From that day on, the momentum was with England, and arguably only Warne's amazing efforts prevented them from winning four matches. He made England fight every inch for their victories at Edgbaston and Trent Bridge, as he battled in the second halves of the games to make up for Australia's deficits in the first: six wickets and 42 runs in Birmingham, 45 runs and four wickets in Nottingham. In the end, England got home by just 2 runs and three wickets respectively. At Old Trafford, where Australia held on for a draw with their last pair together, it was his batting that did most to deny England: he scored 90 and 34, and was at the crease more than four and a half hours in total. With Australia needing to win the final game to level the series and retain the Ashes, no one could really blame Warne that they failed: he dropped a crucial catch, it's true, but he did take twelve wickets. In most circumstances he would have been a shoo-in for the man of the series award, but that justifiably went to Flintoff, who scored 402 runs and took twenty-four wickets.

Nothing articulated Warne's never-say-die attitude better than his defiance with the bat. As if carrying the bowling wasn't enough of a task, he repeatedly tried to repair the damage done to Australia's batting by a formidable pace quartet of Flintoff, Steve Harmison, Simon Jones and Matthew Hoggard. In the early part of his career Warne had not been much of a batsman, and if he had made runs it had usually been because the bowling had been softened up first.

Interestingly, he had started to make more of his batting only after his big shoulder operation: ten of his twelve Test fifties came from 1999 onwards. Just as his bowling became cannier and more resourceful, so too did his batting. That was when he first started scoring runs when they were needed to boost his team, not just his average. He was happiest in conditions where the bounce was good and true, such as Adelaide and Brisbane, and he could step back and carve the ball backward of point; he didn't like grafting for runs, was over-excitable against spin, and never reached 40 in Asia. He preferred to save the intense concentration for his bowling. But he loved batting – it was, after all, what he had first shone at when he was young – and with the end in sight he gave a lot to every aspect of his game. Earlier in the 2005 season, in his 321st innings for Hampshire, he had finally recorded a coveted maiden first-class century. Five matches later he had added a second.

That Warne could focus so totally on giving so much to the team cause while his marriage had humiliatingly collapsed just a few weeks before seemed barely credible. It was as though the cricketer performing the Herculean feats could not be the same person as the man plastered across the front of Britain's Sunday tabloids. But, distressingly for Shane and Simone, he was.

Unsurprisingly after the problems in Australia two years earlier, the first story to break, in the *Sunday Mirror* on 19 June, was enough for Simone to demand a divorce. Once again, a young woman – this time twenty-five-year-old Laura Sayers – claimed to have had sex with Warne. Six days later, Simone and her husband issued a joint statement announcing that they were to separate. They fled to Spain, but this time there was no reconciliation. Such an outcome was hardly possible as more allegations of Warne's liaisons emerged. In the *Daily Mirror* Julia Reynolds, a blonde promotions model, even claimed to have spent two nights with Warne during the fourth Test in Nottingham. With Warne getting out for nought, she felt she had 'done my bit for England'. England might have been spared some anxiety had she spent more time with him.

As he must have known he was on a last warning from his wife, it was surprising Warne seemed so willing to court danger. It may have been simply that he thought he could get away with it: it was reported that his UK agent had employed the publicist Max Clifford to try to keep stories about him out of the papers. It may have been, too, that he could not help himself. In some of his franker interviews, Warne spoke of perhaps needing to 'see people' to prevent himself making 'poor choices'. But, while part of him wanted to grow up, another part didn't. 'The problem is there's still a big kid inside me who likes to have fun,' he told *GQ* magazine. 'I am passionate about my cricket and I love my family, but I'm also a kid, and maybe I need to grow up . . . And maybe I don't. Life is not a rehearsal, it's about having fun.'

The bottom line was probably that Warne, like many before him, found fame a lonely place. It was a view that Terry Jenner seemed to support. 'Shane's a very sensitive soul and he cares what people think of him,' he said. 'His insecurities come from him wanting people to like him.'

Warne was devastated at the separation, but had little choice but to accept it. Some in the Australian media denounced him for potentially destabilizing the team ahead of a big series, but Warne dismissed such talk, saying that he had repeatedly shown he had the mental strength to focus on the job at hand whatever was going on in his private life. 'I think all the guys are happy to have me back, contrary to what some people think,' he said at a pre-Ashes press conference. 'I won't let you guys know if I'm happy or sad, I will just be me. That is how it has got to be. I'm actually doing OK. And England and Australia is what it is about.' On another occasion he said that having broken his marriage, the need to make a success of his cricket became even stronger: 'I'm not going to lose both,' he said. 'I've got to make this [my cricket] a winner . . . There's no other way.'

England fought a brilliant tactical campaign, at the heart of which was a plan to counter the threat of Warne. By picking off the weaker members of the Australian attack – Gillespie, Kasprowicz and Brett Lee, who played all five matches but conceded more than 800 runs – England believed they could undermine Warne and McGrath, who for years had given their side control.

The whole thing worked far better than England could have hoped, partly because their initial targets wilted under fire, partly because McGrath missed two matches through injury. All this heightened the pressure on Warne, who, instead of entering the attack prepared for the kill, with England already on the defensive, found himself coming on trying to stem a flood of runs and often with England's openers still at the crease. It didn't help that Australia bowled first in every Test after the first. At Edgbaston, Warne began his first spell with England 56 for 0 after 13 overs. At Old Trafford, he started with England 130 for 1 after 33 overs and, although Warne took only one wicket (as it happened, his 600th in Tests), Ponting gave him a spell of 27 overs. 'I'll celebrate with fourteen hours of sleep,' Warne said wearily that night. At Trent Bridge, he came on with the score 74 for 0 after 17. By the Oval, The Finisher was getting used to his role as The Starter; after coming on at 61 for 0, he quickly claimed the first four wickets of the game, the first time in his career he had done that. This was the novel life he led in England in 2005.

Before the series, Warne had reasonably claimed, 'I know the England guys and the way they play and I have a general idea about their psyche.' But the psyche of this England team was different. In the past against Warne, England teams had tended to hang in the crease, leaden-footed and tentative, unsure of their scoring options. But now, under the captain—coach partnership of Michael Vaughan and Duncan Fletcher, the policy was one of far greater aggression.

Fletcher, a resourceful one-day player with Zimbabwe back in the eighties, before their promotion to Test level, had been brought in as coach in 1999 with two main aims: to improve England's play against spin and to regain the Ashes. With Fletcher's guidance, the technique against spin had improved greatly, and England had won back-to-back series on the Asian subcontinent in 2000–01. More recently, England had used a spin-bowling machine called Merlyn to help them prepare for facing Warne. Jenner had said that a machine couldn't get inside a batsman's head the way Warne could, and likened it to making love to a robot, but there was no doubt that Merlyn helped the England players familiarize themselves with the degrees of turn Warne could generate and devise counter-strategies. Above all, Fletcher demanded a positive approach against spin. He encouraged the sweep and the slog-sweep, saying there was no point being timid against a spinner as good as Warne, who would prey on uncertainty.

That was why England's performance in the first Test at Lord's had been such a disappointment. They had been far too cautious. Afterwards, Fletcher and Vaughan had got together to review tactics. 'We chatted especially about Shane Warne,' Fletcher wrote in *Ashes Regained*. 'We needed to be more hungry for runs against him. The mindset of the batsmen needed to be changed . . . so that we looked to score off every ball . . . You cannot let such a great bowler dictate. We could not let any of their bowlers dictate.'

And England's blitzkrieg on the first day of the second Test at Edgbaston, when they smashed 54 fours and 10 sixes in 80 overs, was a clue as to how they intended to play things from there on. Andrew Strauss had greeted Warne's first over by hitting him straight over the top for four, and he followed up with two more boundaries in his second over. In Warne's third over, Marcus Trescothick had hit him straight down the ground for six. During the rest of the series, the two left-handed openers remained positive against Warne, scoring faster against him than anyone but Pietersen, but they paid a heavy price. Trescothick was out to Warne five times in all, Strauss six. It showed that there was a limit to what could be achieved, that Warne was simply too good to allow many liberties to be taken. Most of his plans seemed to work, but overall he conceded runs at 3.15 per over, which was high by his standards, and he even resorted to time-wasting as England pushed for a declaration at Old Trafford.

Vaughan was at the heart of the whole process, as dictator of policy and exemplar of how things should be done. He had been a member of the England team that had lost the series heavily in Australia in 2002–03, but had enjoyed huge personal success, scoring a fluent century against Warne in

Adelaide and two more, after Warne had withdrawn injured, in Melbourne and Sydney; Warne said later that he'd run out of ideas as to how to bowl at him. This time Vaughan played only one major innings – his 166 at Old Trafford was the biggest score of the series – but he was always positive, and his brisk 45 on the tense last morning at the Oval had given England crucial momentum. He was out to Warne just twice.

Warne held Vaughan in high regard, as he did any batsman who played him really well, and the respect was reciprocated. 'The way he changes the field, the way he changes the angle of delivery, opens you up then bowls a tad faster,' Vaughan said, 'you know you need to score off him or you can just get stuck, so he gives you opportunities to do so. But those opportunities also carry a risk. He is a wily old fox.' But Vaughan also believed that Warne preferred bullying to being bullied himself, and he determined to ruffle Warne's feathers when he came out to bat, sending him sprawling with a shy at the stumps at Lord's and sledging him from the slips at Old Trafford.

Of all the one-on-one duels, Warne versus Pietersen was the most captivating. Flintoff actually took as many runs off Warne's bowling as Pietersen (they both scored 153), but Flintoff wasn't really a great player of spin: he wasn't nimble on his feet, and went at the ball with hard hands. Pietersen was in a different class altogether. The fact that they played together at Hampshire and were firm friends only added spice to Pietersen's combat with Warne, but the real magic came from two cricketing geniuses pitting their wits against each other. Pietersen put his eye and his build to excellent use by reaching down the pitch to smother Warne's spin or to slog-sweep him through midwicket. Like the Indians, he had terrific wrists. Like the Indians, too, he targeted the on side as the region where runs against Warne were safest. He hit him for eight sixes in the series: two straight, six slog-sweeps.

Pietersen was the clear winner, losing his wicket to him only three times. He was bowled by Warne just once, on the first day at the Oval, and stared at the pitch in disbelief as though he simply couldn't believe that his eye, or some gremlin in the turf, had betrayed him. On the fifth day, with the Ashes at stake, Pietersen played the innings of his life to make the match, and the series, safe for his side. 'He started out by faffing around against Warne,' Trescothick, who was batting at the other end, said. 'Then suddenly he went six, six. I walked down and said, "Well played," and he said, "Yeah, I've had enough of blocking. I'm gonna smash it." ' Soon Warne was forced into defensive mode, bowling round the wicket at Pietersen's legs. It was a huge moral victory and played the major part in England restricting Warne to four wickets in thirty-three overs on the fifth day.

While the Oval became the tumultuous epicentre of English celebrations, the Australian dressing room became a scene of desolation, all the more eerie for the situation being so unfamiliar. Warne was bereft, utterly devastated for the second time from a loss he never expected (divorce being the first). Although he had had a wonderful series, in the final analysis he was highly culpable in the loss because he had dropped Pietersen 15 runs into his great innings of 158: standing at slip, he had got a good sight of the ball and got both hands in front of his face to take the catch, but it had dipped on him at the last moment. It was a major surprise: if Warne was not as good in the position as the exceptional Mark Waugh, who had retired in 2002, he was still a very fine first slip and missed little.

The English crowd predictably taunted Warne as the

day, and the full significance of the error, unfolded, chanting, 'You've dropped the Ashes!' But Warne wisely took it in good part. 'When you get a hard time in another country,' he said later, 'the secret is to get along with them [the public]. Don't fight it or get grumpy, because they'll be more on your back. Let the cricket do the talking and have some fun with it.'

After the game, Warne pulled back from announcing anything firm about his future. There had been speculation that he might be about to retire, but at a press conference he equivocated. 'You can't just say, "I want to keep playing." You've got to weigh up the whole package, and at the moment my kids are the most important thing to me. I haven't seen them for lengthy periods and I am really missing them. Hopefully, if I'm still around in eighteen months I'd love the opportunity to try and get the Ashes back. If not, cricket will move on.'

He even declined to discuss whether he was available for the forthcoming Australian season, which was only a few weeks away. But deep down, he must have known there and then that he could not stop. This was not the sort of finish he had wanted or imagined. It had been the right stage but the wrong result.

After the defeat, recriminations in Australia were soon in full flow and Ricky Ponting was peppered with more flak than most. He had been out-thought by Vaughan, and his tactics were widely criticized as lacking imagination. Dennis Lillee, among others, called for him to be replaced as captain by Warne.

There was, of course, no realistic chance of this happening. Ponting was there for the duration, and in any case within weeks he was supervising a strong Australian revival with largely the same group of players. A few were dropped, but most soon fought their way back. Losing the Ashes had remotivated all of them. Great cricketers had great reputations to restore. South Africa defied Warne and held out for a draw on a dead pitch in Perth in December 2005, but otherwise Australia went steadily about the business of sweeping all before them. The theory that Warne was the best captain Australia never had was to remain just that – a theory.

Warne should probably have been grateful that the idea never got off the ground. Towards the end, he insisted he had no regrets about never leading his country, and he may even have meant it. Possibly he came to accept that the post would indeed have demanded of him a discipline and responsibility he didn't really possess. His time leading Hampshire from 2004 onward certainly provided clues that that might have been the case.

In many ways Warne was an inspirational county captain. Displaying a warmth and affection for the whole project that weren't always evident in his dealings with Australia, he brought energy to a young side not blessed with extraordinary talent and turned them into a competitive outfit. Under him, an old-fashioned club threw off its inhibitions and played with a real verve and hunger for success.

In 2004, his first season as captain, Hampshire won promotion from the second division of the championship. In the next two years they challenged for the title, only to finish second, then third. But for Kent striking a poor deal in negotiating a run chase against Nottinghamshire, which gave Notts a win they might not otherwise have achieved – much to Warne's chagrin – Hampshire might have been champions in 2005. They were a potent force that same year in one-dayers too and won the C&G Trophy, although Warne's involvement in the Ashes kept him out of the later rounds. His gambler's instinct brought outrageous victories at Taunton in 2004 and at Trent Bridge in 2005, when the opposition respectively got to within 51 and 49 of victory with seven wickets in hand, yet lost. Overall, Hampshire won half their championship matches in which he led them.

Rod Bransgrove, the chairman, was understandably delighted. 'He was a special leader,' he said. 'I once heard him say some amazing things in a pre-season talk, reminding his players to be sure to thank staff like the dinner ladies. Most people would never think of things like that, but he saw it as important. He was always very grounded. Of all the cricketers I've dealt with he is easily the most impressive.' Others acknowledged his leadership qualities. 'He has got a saying that you can't pick and choose what games you play or what days you want to be ready to play,' said Dominic Thornely, an Australian batsman who played under Warne at Hampshire. 'That's your job. You've got to be ready to play. That's the attitude that makes him the world's best.'

'Young players looked up to him,' Peter Roebuck said. 'There was a tremendous aura about him. He was a champion cricketer who carried a packet of fags and lived the life. He was what a lot of young players aspired to be. People like Kevin Pietersen beat a path to his door, joining Hampshire largely to play under him.' Nasser Hussain had played against Warne in his last season for Essex, in 2004, and had been amazed at how much the occasion had meant to Warne: he remained utterly committed. Nick Knight, leading Warwickshire, concurred: every game meant something to the Hampshire captain.

But Warne's diplomatic skills left something to be desired.

His team never featured well in the fair-play league – something he was mischievously rather proud of – and if things didn't go his way he tended to sound off against umpires or would publicly denounce opponents as overly cautious. He was docked three penalty points after an altercation with Somerset's Peter Bowler, and almost incurred further punishment after a finger-wagging exchange with umpire Alan Whitehead during a defeat to Surrey; only an evening pilgrimage to the umpires' room saved him.

Opposing captains caught the brunt of his fire. He got into an ugly spat with Ronnie Irani, the Essex captain, during a match Hampshire lost heavily, which resulted in both men being warned by the umpires about their future conduct. Irani issued a statement denying Warne had called him a 'son of a whore'. Another time, instead of calming an already tense situation following an incident between Simon Katich and Sussex's Matt Prior, he harangued Prior himself. 'To try to publicly humiliate young players in the opposition is disappointing,' Chris Adams, the Sussex captain, said at the time. 'Matt Prior came in for quite a lot of verbal abuse. I have lost a lot of respect for him [Warne] because of the way he behaved.' But Adams said later that he himself had been trying to gain an advantage and was at fault: he had apologized to Warne, and things had been smoothed over between them.

To Warne, these skirmishes were all part of the landscape of county cricket, necessary milestones on the road to the negotiated third-innings declarations that sometimes determined the fate of championship points. When Lancashire, with whom Hampshire had been battling for the runners-up spot, failed to show an interest in setting a target in the last round of matches in 2006, Warne showed his displeasure by bowling a series of stratospheric full tosses.

He did not care if some thought his actions undignified or unbecoming. All he was interested in was a contest, another me-versus-him situation. But while he always backed himself to the hilt, others weren't always as confident in their own abilities in a showdown with Warne.

But would Australia have lost the Ashes in 2005 had Warne, and not Ponting, been captain? Probably not. Warne would never have bowled first at Edgbaston. Nor would he have ever underestimated the opposition, or overestimated himself.

13

The Hollywood Finish

LOSING THE ASHES in 2005 had been a hammer blow to Warne's pride, but it did provide the opportunity to script a magical conclusion to the story of his extraordinary career. With England due to tour Australia late in 2006, he had a mission worthy of one last great effort – regaining the Ashes in one of the most eagerly anticipated Anglo-Australian contests of all time. If that was accomplished, he could bid a triumphant farewell to the game in front of his home fans. What could be better? 'I like to go out on top,' he would say later. 'I think I've earned the right to go out on my terms.'

It must have been obvious to him that he was approaching the end as a Test player. There had been speculation that he might go on until 2009 – Richie Benaud had said that he thought Warne was capable of playing until he was forty – but Warne's responses about his future were guarded. He wasn't sure how much more punishment his body could withstand, and was anxious to quit as a long-overdue gesture of commitment to his family. Although officially divorced, he and Simone said they had resolved their differences and she had agreed that he could continue living in the family home whenever he was in Australia, giving him hope that one day there might be a full reconciliation.

Finishing on a high was non-negotiable: it simply had to

happen. But the details couldn't be pre-ordained. He was going to have to see how things went. However, the forthcoming Ashes presented a golden opportunity. After that, Australia hadn't got another Test series for ten months. That was at least one more crash diet away.

As it was, his bowling shoulder was groaning. It had caused him trouble during the one tour he had made after the Ashes, a seven-week stint in South Africa and Bangladesh in March and April 2006. The Bangladesh leg was inconvenient but unavoidable: Australia were obliged by the ICC's tours programme to go there, but kept their stay to the bare minimum. Five days after completing a 3–0 whitewash in Durban, the first Test began in Dhaka; the players were so exhausted they could barely keep awake on the coach to the ground. And they very nearly came unstuck: Bangladesh won the toss and batted well into the second day for a score of 427; Warne's analysis – no wickets for 112 from 20 overs – was one of the worst of his career. Only a captain's innings from Ricky Ponting at the last gasp delivered the expected victory. The shoulder continued to play up when Warne was with Hampshire and he had to fly to Australia for treatment in June 2006.

He had also renewed his difficulties with the Australia coach. Buchanan had organized a boot camp in the Queensland jungle as a bonding exercise for the team. Afterwards, most of the players acclaimed it a success, but it was the last thing Warne wanted. He hated organized fitness work at the best of times, and this also took him away from a crucial championship match with Hampshire, which they narrowly lost. Warne described the camp as 'one of John Buchanan's wonderful, mastermind things that keep everyone stumped' and pointed out that the Ashes were still three months away. He reportedly made some other unflattering remarks about Buchanan, and had both coach and captain demanding explanations. 'I just wish he'd just play the game and keep his mouth shut,' one former Australia player said. 'It would be so much more beneficial for the country as well as for him.' Whatever he thought of Buchanan, Warne probably knew there were things he could get away with under him that a new coach might not tolerate. It was another reason to tie things up as fast as he could.

More encouragingly, England were in grave trouble. They had not so much gone overboard about winning the Ashes as keelhauled themselves in champagne. Every member of the team had received an OBE or MBE, even Paul Collingwood, who had made only one appearance, at the Oval, and scored 7 and 10 (albeit a gritty seventy-minute 10). And within weeks of winning the Ashes a plague of mishaps befell the squad that was to undermine the build-up to the Australia tour: several key players, including Michael Vaughan and Andrew Flintoff, were afflicted by chronic injuries while Marcus Trescothick was suffering burnout. So, as the Ashes approached, the hopes of Australia – and Warne – steadily rose.

But there was an additional consideration. Warne being Warne, he would have liked to announce his retirement in advance, so that his exit from the big stage could receive a full media and public fanfare. Ideally he wanted the sunset finish at the last two Tests of the Ashes series, in Melbourne (his home ground) and Sydney (the place where his Test career had begun). Apart from anything else, the more ideal-ized the finale perhaps the better his chances of winning back Simone. But he knew too that the team had to come first: he must not detract from the team effort. Three years earlier Steve Waugh had announced beforehand that the home series with India would be his last, and he had been criticized for created a distracting sideshow.

The bottom line was this: Warne would not be able to announce he was retiring before the Boxing Day Test at his beloved MCG unless Australia had won the first three Tests of the series; only then would the Ashes already be back in Australian hands. So that became Warne's target and was perhaps what was going through his mind as he discussed his retirement plans with Michael Clarke in Brisbane, where the first Test was played, and with his parents in Adelaide, scene of the second.

It represented one hell of a task, but to Warne it was perhaps only like doing what he had done countless times before when he had bowled his side to victory on those tense fifth afternoons: the clock ticking, runs at a premium, wickets to be taken. It was going to need everything to go his way. He might just have to make a few things happen, just push things that little bit harder. It was audacious, even outrageous. But if anyone could do it, Warne could.

Of course, Warne and Australia pulled the whole thing off: not just three wins in three, but a historic five out of five – the first 5–0 Ashes whitewash in more than eighty years. Pride was more than salvaged. Warne – once again a central player in the drama, with twenty-three wickets – got to announce his retirement when he wanted, got to lap up the world's applause, and got walk-on parts for Simone and the kids in Shane Warne: The Farewell. Australia loves to salute a hero, and with Glenn McGrath and Justin Langer also retiring from Test cricket the three of them got the full soft-focus, sugar-coated treatment. In front of a packed house, the tributes never seemed to end on that final sentimental afternoon in Sydney in January 2007.

It all turned out far better than even Warne could ever have dared hope. Journalists attending his retirement press conference even abided by a request to confine their questions to his cricket and not exhume the old scandals. They not only obliged, they greeted him with a round of applause.

As chance would have it, too, he went to the MCG – where he had watched and played sport for twenty-five years, and where he got an adrenalin rush simply from the noise of the vast crowd – needing just one wicket for his 700 in Tests. This he duly took – Andrew Strauss beaten through the air and bowled – on Boxing Day, the biggest social day in the Australian cricketing calendar, once again giving the people what they had wanted on a stage that couldn't have been bettered.

And yet it could have been different. It was a close-run thing at times. His bowling only just held together, and he did indeed have to push things. He worked the umpires as hard as he had ever worked them, and won from them some generous decisions and a fair bit of slack when it came to gamesmanship. There was artistry in his game, but also ugliness. But this was no time for niceties: the stakes were too high for that. And he was no more easy on his body, which he pushed beyond what seemed possible for a man with more than 6,500 Test overs on his clock. He bowled long spells, but doubtless at his own bidding – Ponting would have been brushed aside had he suggested Warne took a breather. There were times when he was plainly sore and stiff, but who cared? For once, he was prepared to gamble as much as he liked with his fitness.

To keep the dream on course, in Adelaide he produced one fantastic four-hour spell to turn what looked a certain draw into an astonishing victory. It was an effort that encapsulated his genius. Out of nowhere, he raised the intensity of his cricket to such a level that the opposition's morale simply imploded. That he had struggled to make any impression earlier in the game, producing the most expensive analysis of his career and inviting speculation that he was finished, only heightened the sense of shock. It was like a horror movie where the corpse reaches out of the grave to strangle its unsuspecting victim. After that, England were never the same again.

Warne's ruthless competitiveness, his love of conflict, was never more in evidence. Responding to criticism that he had been too friendly to England in the previous series, he had said: 'I want to win the Ashes back in a good, hard-fought social series.' But in fact his behaviour was purely antisocial. The England players were harried by him from start to finish; it must have felt like the vengeful Furies were constantly swirling round their heads.

Abandoning the idea of going out on a tide of goodwill, he sledged the England players mercilessly. When Paul Collingwood scored a double-century, Warne told him bluntly he'd had 'arse' (i.e. luck) and wouldn't make runs later in the series when batting conditions were tougher. He was right. He mocked Collingwood for having been given an MBE for scoring 7, cleverly picking on the smaller of Collingwood's two innings at the Oval. He belittled Ian Bell as 'the Shermanator' and Geraint Jones as 'the club pro'. But if England's fielders dared to sledge him – as Collingwood did when Warne began batting in Adelaide and Sydney – he theatrically stopped the game and waved his arms as though he couldn't possibly be expected to bat until all was calm. 'You're making me concentrate, mate,' he had said, turning to Collingwood, standing at slip. You'd got to admire his cheek. Who else would have dared pull such a stunt and keep a straight face? But after he'd said he was going, he was pretty much free to do what he liked. What were they going to do? Suspend him again?

Warne wasn't alone, of course. The entire Australian squad seemed intent on withholding all credit from everything their opponents did. When England made a big score in the first innings in Adelaide, the Aussie camp denounced them – after the game was won, of course – for scoring too slowly; Pietersen, at least as good a player as most of the Australians, was labelled selfish by Buchanan without any real evidence. So once again the Australian public was left contemplating the price of victory. 'It portrays a tiresome arrogance,' one newspaper stated of the national team. 'It's great to win but to win with integrity and grace is even better . . . A touch more humility is needed.'

Warne's first act as bowler was telling. In his opening over of the first Test in Brisbane, he fielded a ball from Kevin Pietersen and fired it to the wicketkeeper just inches from Pietersen's head. It was a clear sign that he was putting their friendship on hold. Pietersen let the matter go, but in the second innings Warne had another go, throwing in another fast return to Adam Gilchrist, only this time Pietersen had to evade being hit and an angry exchange of words followed.

'I knew things were different [before the match],' Pietersen said. 'He was calling me by my full name. He was calling me Kevin. He wasn't calling me KP or PK as he normally does. I'd see him in the [hotel] lobby or the dressing room and he would call me that in front of the team, in front of the other Australians. It was the start of the psychological warfare, but it probably made me play better. I enjoyed it. It was a battle.'

Not everyone responded as positively, but generally the England team played Warne well in the first Test. When he bowled on or around leg stump they looked to use their feet, show the full face of the bat, and hit him through mid-on. It proved a safe and productive approach, and Warne didn't like it. He was forced to resort to some of his variations, but they didn't come out particularly well. In fact he didn't really bowl well at all, and one of the reasons he had a second go at Pietersen was that Pietersen had just hit him for three straight fours in two overs. Warne's best moment was when he cleverly tossed one up outside off stump to Collingwood on 96, inviting him to go for the boundary that would bring him his hundred. He beat him through the air, and Gilchrist completed the stumping. But Collingwood and Pietersen shared a stand of 153, and England – set a mammoth 648 to win – actually took some heart from their fourth-innings total of 370 and Warne's match figures of 4 for 149.

Reasonably enough, Duncan Fletcher said afterwards that his team had played Warne well. But Warne couldn't allow this – it was too near the truth – and he publicly issued a rather fanciful rebuttal of the England coach's claim. 'Kevin Pietersen was the only one who played me well,' he said. 'It shows just how worried they are about spin. There are no secrets about England. Duncan is trying to back up a few players who aren't convinced and are really worried about me . . . I don't think anything has changed. All I see is the same stuff.'

Privately, though, he wasn't feeling anything like as confident as he sounded and arranged a remedial net session with Terry Jenner before the second Test. His right shoulder was dropping in his delivery and this was putting more demands on his sore fingers. Jenner worked on correcting his alignment, even putting markers on the ground to help him. When the two of them broke off, Warne still hadn't come to terms with the new alignment, but amazingly, if utterly predictably, he had got things right by the time he began bowling in the match. 'He'd worked it out,' Jenner recalled with an admiring shake of the head.

His first ball . . . he was straight through the crease. It was beautiful . . . up in the air, landed, spun . . . It was just gorgeous. I don't know anyone else that can do that. That's the reason he's a genius. I coach young kids who can't think about what they do from one day to the next, even though their career depends on them improving. Yet Shane, we talk, he listens. If it's what he likes he goes with it. If it's not, he asks more questions. Once he accepts it, away he goes. But it doesn't always bring immediate wickets.

And it didn't bring immediate wickets now. On a typical Adelaide feather bed, England spent the best part of two days building an imposing score of 551 for 6 declared. Again, the bulk of the runs came from Pietersen and Collingwood, who shared a massive partnership of 310. Warne bowled much better than in Brisbane, but without luck, as the methods that had worked for the England pair before were deployed to good effect again. Warne was reduced to posting four men on the boundary and bowling round the wicket at Pietersen's legs. With Pietersen eschewing all risks, it developed into an undignified stand-off that didn't reflect well on Warne's reputation as an attacking bowler; nor did final figures of 1 for 167 from 53 overs. Umpire Rudi Koertzen called one leg-side wide, and there was slow hand-clapping from the crowd.

'He rang me up at the end of the first day and said, "What am I supposed to do?" ' Jenner recalled. 'I said: "Just do it again . . . It was beautiful. Poetry to watch." He couldn't have bowled better than that. He had got none for 85. Collingwood had played and missed fifteen times, he wasn't even close to edging them; KP had skied one. You won't see many better performances than that for none-for. I had to talk him up because he'd outperformed the batsmen but had nothing to show for it.' It was the last great motivational talk Jenner delivered to Warne and would reap rich dividends. But the media were starting to have their doubts about Warne's future. 'Is time fraying the spinner's web?' asked Greg Baum in the Melbourne *Age*. Adelaide's *Sunday Mail* commented, 'For the first time in his life, Shane Warne has stumbled across an English batsman he does not know how to deceive. Kevin Pietersen has become the first English batsman to truly emerge from the thirteen-year shadow cast by that first delivery to Gatting.'

However, boosted by Ricky Ponting being dropped 35 runs into his innings of 142, and a doughty 43 from Warne, who posted a seventh-wicket stand of 118 with Michael Clarke, Australia got within 38 of England's score. This left the game intriguingly poised. England were in an awkward position. There wasn't really enough time for them to force a win themselves, so all they could do was play for a draw – but the danger was that they would lose momentum. Australia had been in a similar position on the same ground against India two years earlier and ended up losing, so they knew exactly how England might trip up. Warne, moreover, was a master at preying on indecision. If England looked hesitant, he'd be sure to pounce.

England got through to stumps on the fourth evening with the loss of only one wicket, partly because Warne was still stiff after his first-innings marathon. But the next morning he was very upbeat, determined that England should be made to fight for every run. Gilchrist recalled how Warne had had a real spring in his step, how vocal he had been, how he had energized the team. 'He led us and we all followed,' he said.

Sure enough, the England batsmen sleepwalked their way to disaster. Whereas before they had looked to be positive against Warne, and used their feet to negate the spin, now they were caught on the crease again. It was like the bad old days of the nineties.

So supine were they that they barely deserved better than the poor luck they got in the first hour. The collapse started with Mike Hussey and Warne screwing out of umpire Steve Bucknor a woeful bat–pad decision against Strauss that Hussey surely must have suspected was dubious from his position at short leg. In Warne's next over a panicky Ian Bell ran himself out, and in his over after that Pietersen was freakishly bowled round his legs missing a sweep at a full-length ball. It was a bad error by Pietersen, but Warne had been clever: he had left a gap backward of square leg, inviting the easy single, inviting the shot.

After that, Warne never stopped harrying England. He put absolutely everything into his bowling. Some of the England players had never seen anything like it. Warne was swerving the ball through the air like in the good old days, and his accuracy was astonishing. There was simply nothing to hit. Backed up by a fine spell of reverse swing from Brett Lee, he kept Australian fingers so tight on English throats that mistakes were bound to come. And he just kept on bowling, over after over, as though the long, fruitless hours of labour in the first innings had never happened. He had no intention of giving up until the job was done, and by the time it was he had bowled unchanged for four hours and taken 4 for 29 from 27 overs. It was scarcely credible that England – the same England that had scored faster against Australia in 2005 than any side in modern times – had spent two sessions adding just 70 to their score. It was nothing like enough to avoid defeat, and Australia won by six wickets with something to spare. Even the one England batsman who didn't lose his wicket was traumatized by his experience: Collingwood had stayed in for more than three hours for just 22, and then entered a slump in form so profound that it lasted eight weeks.

Warne was euphoric. At the post-match press conference he again ridiculed Fletcher's claim that England had been playing him well, and declared Adelaide to be the greatest victory of his career. When Ponting, who was sitting beside him, sang his praises, tears visibly welled up. Perhaps it was dawning on him that his final mission was very nearly accomplished, that the end really was in sight.

When he got to Perth for the third Test, he sought out Ian Chappell for a beer and confided in him his plans. He knew Chappell would know whether he was doing the right thing, and Chappell supported his decision. 'He just said: "It's better they say, 'Why are you going?' rather than 'Why don't you?' " I thought that was spot on,' Warne recalled.

The eighty-five overs he had bowled in Adelaide had taken their toll. His back was stiff, and he was quite quiet for the first three days in Perth as Australia pushed for the series-clinching result. But his team looked to him once again to finish the job when England were left the near-impossible task of batting just over two days to score 557 or hold out for a draw. He got through thirty-one overs on the fourth day, but was plainly battling fatigue. Bell played his first spell with embarrassing ease, and although Warne eventually had his revenge – having Bell caught at cover – it was to be his only success of the day. When he prepared to resume bowling after tea, Ian Chappell, on Channel Nine commentary, couldn't help saying how long it was taking Warne to get himself warmed up – it was the nearest anyone came to letting out Warne's secret that he was planning to retire. Fortunately, late in the day, Glenn McGrath nipped in with two wickets to keep Australia on course for victory.

It would have been a blow to Warne's pride had Ponting had to call on his fast bowlers to finish Warne's work for him, but with an English coffin almost sealed there was no chance of keeping him away from the hammer. Ponting gave the opening bursts to his quick men on the final morning, but when they failed to deliver a hit he whistled up Warne. It took him just fifty balls on either side of lunch to dismiss Flintoff, Harmison and last man Monty Panesar. The Ashes were back in Australian hands after just fifteen months.

As the Australian dressing room embarked on what turned into an all-night celebration – they not only had recovered the Ashes but also now, uniquely, held every trophy available to them in international cricket – Warne took Ponting to one side and told him he was planning to quit. His first words were 'It's my time.' Ponting asked him if he was sure he was making the right decision, but did not attempt to dissuade him.

Three days later, on 21 December, Warne publicly revealed he was finishing. It was a decision that took many by surprise and left them asking – as Ian Chappell had said it would – why he was going now.

Warne spent a lot of his press conference explaining why. 'Since 2005 it has been a mission of mine to get the Ashes back,' he said.

> I would probably have retired at the end of the 2005 Ashes
> if we had won. I felt that would have been a pretty good
> time to go, but there was some unfinished business to do.
> The urn is something special to me and I saw how much
> we hurt as a team after that series . . . No matter how long

it took, it was my mission to get that urn back. That's how much it meant to me. I think you can tell by the way we've played this series and the way I've gone out there and bowled, I've been pretty determined. It's been hard work at times, and the body will enjoy not playing after Sydney for a while, but when the game has been on the line we've been able to deliver.

There was one other message he was anxious to get across. In paying tribute to those who had helped him in his career, he raised the name of Simone. 'She has been my rock,' he said. 'I come home from a bad day, feeling sorry for myself, and Simone and the kids are there to cheer you up. She's been outstanding support for me over a long period. Who knows what the future holds there? I'd like to thank her. She's been my best friend for a long time.' Right to the end, Warne was living out his life on a very public stage, using a televised press conference to try and win back his wife. Who indeed knew what the future held?

Warne, high on the excitement of his 700th wicket, bowled brilliantly on the first day at the MCG, again turning the ball prodigiously. By rights he shouldn't have had much to do on the opening day, because the pitch heavily favoured the seam bowlers, but after being introduced into the attack just before 3 p.m. he had simply bowled too well to be taken off. He had bowled eighteen overs off the reel, with Strauss's wicket coming with his twentieth delivery.

But in truth the Tests in Melbourne and Sydney were disappointingly lopsided affairs – over in three and four days respectively. In any case, Warne was in party mode after Boxing Day and in the last three innings of the series he took just four wickets – although the ball that claimed his 708th and last, to have Flintoff stumped on the fourth evening in Sydney, was a peach. Not that he was really needed: the fast men did the work well enough. He seemed more in the mood to have fun with a bat in his hand. Curiously, Warne had not made many Test runs on either ground before, but now he infuriated England with an unbeaten 40 in Melbourne and, surviving an undetected catch off the glove, 71 in Sydney, both valuable in their contexts. He was named man of the match at the MCG, and was chaired from the field on the shoulders of Matthew Hayden and Andrew Symonds, who had scored centuries in the game.

Poor England – tormented and teased to the end.

Few cricketers had experienced quite such adulation as Warne. He had tasted the downside of fame, but even when he was in trouble he was still front-page news. People always wanted to hear what he had to say. Articulating what was happening in his life became part of the ritual of his existence. But how was he to feel when the cameras and microphones were switched off?

The successful professional sportsman faces a profound challenge coming to terms with the afterlife of competition, not only what he does with himself – media work perhaps, or a sports-related business of some kind – but in coping with the knowledge that nothing he does in future can be as exciting, or probably as significant, as what he has done already. At a stage of life when many people's careers are still on the way up, he has to start afresh.

The fact that Warne played for so long, and played so much, suggested that he didn't want to let go, that he feared missing the game and missing the fame. Like Sir Steven Redgrave and Pete Sampras, he just wanted to carry on, finding reasons to have one more go. And who could blame him when others spoke so eloquently of the pain of retirement?

When Kathy Freeman retired in 2003, she said that her future stretched out before her 'like a wilderness'. Ted Dexter said that after he stopped playing cricket it took him seven years before he knew what to do with himself. 'I missed it dreadfully,' he said. 'You lose something in your life that can never be replaced.'

No wonder some retired sportsmen fall prey to depression, alcoholism, drugs or domestic violence. It's not just the lionizing they miss: some footballers have said they miss the abuse of rival fans too. Others pretend that nothing has changed and carry on the champagne lifestyle until the money runs out, or the wife walks out. 'All the things that make you great as a sportsman can be hard to deal with in normal life — that cut-throat competitiveness where you'd die to win; the "me, me, me" that sport is about,' Colin Jackson said. 'They make sportsmen great, but they don't necessarily make you a great person. There's a process of adjustment which is quite a big deal.'

Others walk away from their sport altogether, sick of the whole routine of training, playing, watching, talking. Jimmy Connors said he didn't watch five minutes of tennis in the ten years after he gave up the game. Jürgen Klinsmann went to live in Calfornia, where football meant little to people. 'It was perfect, because it was so nice not being recognized,' he said. Others still, such as Eric Cantona, Johnny Weissmuller and Vinnie Jones, went on to live out fresh fantasies by turning their hands to acting. Not the route, probably, for Warne. His theatrical side had been fully extended already.

Australians despaired of Warne because of all the dumb things they said he had done. But he was one of the cleverest cricketers, and part of his cleverness lay in his understanding of people. In this sense, he remained very grounded. He never overestimated himself, or underestimated his opponents, and by remaining true to himself he gave himself a good chance of surviving the erosion of his celebrity. He was still a big kid at heart. One of the last things he wanted to do before he died, he said, was to race a Formula One car.

'I started playing almost twenty seasons ago,' he said when he retired from international cricket. 'That's a lot of life to give to cricket. The next half [of my life] is exciting. I don't know what the future holds, though I've got some ideas. I'd like to think there are various opportunities.' Australians wouldn't have been overly happy at one of the first opportunities he availed himself of, as he planned to spend 2007 and 2008 playing for Hampshire, which was to arrange for his children to be educated in English schools during those years.

Warne will be OK in the sporting afterlife. The artistic streak within him that helped shape his career, and control his fame, will see to that. He could have stopped playing in 1999, when his body seemed to be hinting that enough was enough, or in 2003, when he was suspended for a year. But he didn't, because it would have meant an unsatisfactory finish, and he could not tolerate that. If Warne has had one knack in life it is for scripting happy endings.

Statistics

1. How Warne performed against each country

Country	Tests	Wickets	Average	Best	Won	Lost	Drawn
v. England	36	195	23.3	8–71	24	7	5
v. South Africa	24	130	24.2	7–56	15	4	5
v. New Zealand	20	103	24.4	6–31	12	1	7
v. West Indies	19	65	30.0	7–52	10	7	2
v. Pakistan	15	90	20.2	7–23	11	2	2
v. India	14	43	47.2	6–125	8	4	2
v. Sri Lanka	13	59	25.5	5–43	8	1	4
v. Bangladesh	2	11	27.3	5–113	2	0	0
v. Zimbabwe	1	6	22.8	3–68	1	0	0
v. ICC World XI	1	6	11.8	3–23	1	0	0
TOTALS	145	708	25.4	8–71	92	26	27

Warne missed 32 Tests through being dropped (3), injured (15) or suspended (14). Of these, Australia won 19, lost 6 and drew 7. With him, their win percentage was 63.5, without him 59.4.

2. How Warne served his captains

Captain	Tests	Wickets	Average	Balls per match	Won	Lost	Drawn
Allan Border (1992–94)	26	116	24.0	307	12	6	8
Mark Taylor (1994–99)	42	199	25.6	294	23	11	8
Steve Waugh (1999–2002)	38	175	26.6	254	27	6	5
Adam Gilchrist (2001–04)	5	18	33.8	240	3	1	1
Ricky Ponting (2004–07)	34	200	24.3	289	27	2	5
TOTALS	145	708	25.4	283	92	26	27

Warne's balls per match averages exclude one match under Taylor in which he didn't bowl because of injury. When Warne retired, in January 2007, he had bowled more balls (40,705) and taken more wickets than any other bowler in Test history.

3. How Warne influenced the toss

Generally, Australia wanted to bat first and bowl last, when Warne would be at his most dangerous. Of the sixty-nine times they won the toss with Warne in their team, they chose to bowl first and bat last only thirteen times (under Border once, Taylor three times, Steve Waugh seven times and Ponting twice). The tactic usually worked, presumably because early conditions favoured the seamers: Australia won ten times and lost once after putting in the opposition.

The surprise is that opponents, who won the toss seventy-six times, were prepared to risk Warne bowling last twenty-five times. (New Zealand opted to do so six times in twelve; Sri Lanka four times in six.) It rarely paid off for them – Australia were beaten just three times – but Warne's influence on these matches was relatively slight, his 91 wickets costing 30 apiece. Presumably again, many of them were seaming pitches; hence the decision to bowl first.

4. How Warne influenced the game

Warne's involvement can be broken down into five different scenarios in the 144 Tests in which he bowled. In one match, in which Pakistan were beaten at Hobart in 1995, he could not bowl because of injury.

(a) Australia bowling in the first or second match innings only

Nine times: Australia won 0, lost 2, drew 7.

These were some of Warne's most undistinguished games. The opposition batted only once either because they amassed a big first-innings total or because the game was affected by rain. Six of these games took place in the first three years of Warne's career; the last occurred in 2001.

Warne's record: 8 wickets, average 92.5.

(b) Australia bowling in the first and third match innings

Sixty-two times: Australia won 43, lost 9, drew 10.

Early in Warne's career, Australia generally preferred to avoid this scenario, as it exposed them to a fourth-innings run chase. They were shaky at these under Border and Taylor. After 1998, they lost only one run chase, and that was by two runs at Edgbaston in 2005. Warne played a large part in keeping Australia's average target down to 208 on the 41 occasions they were required to bat in the fourth innings.

Warne's record: first match innings: 150 wickets, average 27.6; third match innings: 178 wickets, average 22.2.

(c) Australia bowling in the second and third match innings

Thirteen times: Australia won 10, lost 1, drew 2.

These were times when Australia batted first, made a big score, and enforced the follow-on. Making the opposition bat again straight away was risky because it might fatigue Australia's bowlers and Australia might be left with a tricky run chase in the fourth innings. But Australia's average first-innings lead in these games was 337, so the dangers were not great. Taylor was the only one of Warne's captains who decided against enforcing the follow-on (both times at Brisbane, with leads of 259 against England and 202 against West Indies; each time Australia won anyway).

Australia were twice thwarted by individual double-centuries in the follow-on: from Salim Malik in Rawalpindi in 1994, which earned Pakistan a draw, and from V.V.S. Laxman at Calcutta in 2001, when India overcame a deficit of 274 to pull off a sensational win by 171 runs.

Warne's record: second match innings: 42 wickets, average 17.5; third match innings: 37 wickets, average 24.4.

(d) Australia bowling in the second and fourth match innings

Fifty-nine times: Australia won 38, lost 13, drew 8.

This was usually the dream scenario for Australia, and Warne rarely let them down when it came to finishing the job with any sort of total to defend in the fourth innings. But credit is due to the batsmen for building big leads; when Warne retired there had been only three instances of sides other than Australia scoring more than 350 in the final innings to win a Test. Eight of Australia's defeats came when the opposition was chasing fewer than 160.

Warne's record: second match innings: 145 wickets, average 28.1; fourth match innings: 140 wickets, average 23.7.

Listed overleaf, in order of ascending target, are Warne's performances in the fifty games in which he bowled in the second and fourth innings, with Australia leading by more than 100 going into the final innings:

	O	M	R	Wkts	O	M	R	Wkts	Target	Result
v. E, Edgbaston, 1997	35	8	110	1	7.3	0	27	0	118	Lost by 9 wkts
v. I, Madras, 2001	42	7	140	2	6	0	41	0	155	Lost by 2 wkts
v. SL, Colombo, 1992	22	2	107	0	5.1	3	11	3	181	Won by 16 runs
v. NZ, Auckland, 1993	15	12	8	4	27	8	54	2	201	Lost by 5 wkts
v. WI, Antigua, 1995	28	9	83	3	7	0	18	0	257	Drawn
v. NZ, Auckland, 2000	22	4	68	3	20.3	4	80	2	281	Won by 62 runs
v. NZ, Brisbane, 2001	18	2	61	0	18	2	89	3	284	Drawn
v. E, Sydney, 1999	20	4	67	1	19	3	43	1	287	Won by 98 runs
v. NZ, Hobart, 1997	27	4	81	1	28	6	88	5	288	Drawn
v. NZ, Perth, 1993	37.1	6	90	1	13	6	23	0	303	Drawn
v. WI, Barbados, 1999	15.5	2	70	1	24	4	69	0	308	Lost by 1 wkt
v. SL, Darwin, 2004	6.5	1	20	3	19	2	61	0	312	Won by 149 runs
v. P, Karachi, 1994	27	10	61	3	36.1	12	89	5	314	Lost by 1 wkt
v. E, Leeds, 2001	16	2	49	0	18.2	3	58	1	315	Lost by 6 wkts
v. P, Colombo, 2002	24.3	7	94	7	30.3	3	94	4	316	Won by 41 runs
v. NZ, Brisbane, 1997	42	13	106	4	25	6	54	3	319	Won by 186 runs
v. SA, Adelaide, 1994	44.2	15	85	1	30.5	15	31	4	321	Won by 191 runs
v. SA, Cape Town, 2002	28	10	70	2	70	15	161	6	331	Won by 4 wkts
v. SA, Durban, 2002	13	4	33	4	30	6	108	2	335	Lost by 5 wkts
v. WI, Sydney, 1996	35.2	13	65	3	27.4	5	95	4	340	Won by 124 runs
v. SL, Galle, 2004	42.4	9	116	5	15	5	43	5	352	Won by 197 runs
v. SL, Kandy, 2004	20.1	3	65	5	21.1	2	90	5	352	Won by 27 runs
v. SL, Cairns, 2004	38	7	129	3	37	14	70	4	355	Drawn
v. ICC XI, Sydney, 2005	12	3	23	3	19	4	48	3	355	Won by 210 runs
v. WI, Melbourne, 1992	24	7	65	1	23.2	8	52	7	359	Won by 139 runs

	O	M	R	Wkts	O	M	R	Wkts	Target	Result
v. SA, Melbourne, 2005	21	7	62	2	28	7	74	4	366	Won by 184 runs
v. SL, Colombo, 2004	36	7	115	2	33	11	92	4	370	Won by 121 runs
v. I, Adelaide, 1992	7	1	18	0	16	1	60	0	372	Won by 38 runs
v. SA, Adelaide, 2001	39.4	9	113	5	29	7	57	3	375	Won by 246 runs
v. I, Melbourne, 1999	24	5	77	1	26	7	63	1	376	Won by 180 runs
v. SA, Melbourne, 1997	42	15	64	3	44	11	97	3	381	Drawn
v. E, Melbourne, 1994	27.4	8	64	6	13	6	16	3	388	Won by 295 runs
v. E, Manchester, 1993	24	10	51	4	49	26	86	4	390	Won by 179 runs
v. I, Adelaide, 1999	42	12	92	4	10	6	21	2	396	Won by 285 runs
v. SL, Adelaide, 1996	26	4	74	0	27	11	68	1	401	Won by 148 runs
v. SA, Durban, 2006	25	2	80	2	35.5	9	86	6	410	Won by 112 runs
v. WI, Brisbane, 1996	27	3	88	2	41	16	92	2	420	Won by 123 runs
v. E, Lord's, 2005	7	2	19	2	20	2	64	4	420	Won by 239 runs
v. E, Nottingham, 1997	32	8	86	4	16	4	43	3	451	Won by 264 runs
v. E, Perth, 1995	23	8	58	2	7	3	11	0	453	Won by 329 runs
v. I, Bangalore, 2004	28	4	78	2	32	8	115	2	457	Won by 217 runs
v. E, Brisbane, 2002	26.5	4	87	1	10.2	3	29	3	464	Won by 384 runs
v. NZ, Adelaide, 2004	28	5	65	1	27.3	6	79	2	464	Won by 213 runs
v. E, Manchester, 1997	30	14	48	6	30.4	8	53	3	469	Won by 268 runs
v. SA, Perth, 2005	29	4	92	3	47	21	83	3	491	Drawn
v. E, Brisbane, 1994	21.2	7	39	3	50.2	22	71	8	508	Won by 184 runs
v. WI, Brisbane, 2005	28	9	48	5	2	1	1	0	509	Won by 379 runs
v. I, Nagpur, 2004	23	8	47	2	14.3	2	55	2	543	Won by 342 runs
v. E, Perth, 2006	9	0	41	1	39.2	6	115	4	557	Won by 206 runs
v. E, Brisbane, 2006	9	0	25	0	34	7	122	4	648	Won by 277 runs

(e) Australia bowling in the first and fourth match innings

One time: Australia lost 1.

Only once were Australia forced to follow on during Warne's career – at Trent Bridge in 2005, when England led on first innings by 259. England gambled that they wouldn't need many runs batting last on a wearing pitch. They didn't, but Warne still made them fight every inch for victory.

	O	M	R	Wkts	O	M	R	Wkts	Target	Result
v. E, Nottingham, 2005	29.1	4	102	4	13.5	2	31	4	129	Lost by 3 wkts

5. Warne's best matches

12–128 (7–56 and 5–72) v. South Africa, Sydney, 1994	Lost by 5 runs
12–246 (6–122 and 6–124) v. England, Oval, 2005	Drawn
11–77 (7–23 and 4–54) v. Pakistan, Brisbane, 1995	Won by an innings and 126 runs
11–109 (5–75 and 6–34) v. South Africa, Sydney, 1998	Won by an innings and 21 runs
11–110 (3–39 and 8–71) v. England, Brisbane, 1994	Won by 184 runs
11–188 (7–94 and 4–94) v. Pakistan, Colombo, 2002	Won by 41 runs
11–229 (7–165 and 4–64) v. England, Oval, 2001	Won by an innings and 25 runs
10–155 (5–65 and 5–90) v. Sri Lanka, Kandy, 2004	Won by 27 runs
10–159 (5–116 and 5–43) v. Sri Lanka, Galle, 2004	Won by 197 runs
10–162 (4–116 and 6–46) v. England, Edgbaston, 2005	Lost by 2 runs

The only other occasion on which Warne took seven wickets in an innings was 7–52 v. West Indies at Melbourne in 1992.

6. Highest innings against Australia with Warne playing

Score	Match innings	Batsman
281	3	V. V. S. Laxman, India, Calcutta, 2001
277	2	Brian Lara, West Indies, Sydney, 1993
237	3	Salim Malik, Pakistan, Rawalpindi, 1994
226	1	Brian Lara, West Indies, Adelaide, 2005
213	1	Brian Lara, West Indies, Jamaica, 1999
207	2	Nasser Hussain, England, Edgbaston, 1997
206	2	Ravi Shastri, India, Sydney, 1992
206	1	Paul Collingwood, England, Adelaide, 2006
180	3	Rahul Dravid, India, Calcutta, 2001
177	1	Sachin Tendulkar, India, Bangalore, 1998
177	1	Michael Vaughan, England, Adelaide, 2002
173 not out	4	Mark Butcher, England, Leeds, 2001
167	3	V. V. S. Laxman, India, Sydney, 2000
166	1	Michael Vaughan, England, Manchester, 2005

163 not out	2	Mohammad Azharuddin, India, Calcutta, 1998
158	3	Kevin Pietersen, England, Oval, 2005
158	1	Kevin Pietersen, England, Adelaide, 2006

In all, 84 hundreds were scored in innings in which Warne bowled, by 57 batsmen. Of these, 56 were scored by right-handers and 28 by left-handers. Those who scored the most were Lara and Tendulkar (5) and Jacques Kallis and Graham Thorpe (3). Nineteen were scored for England, 12 each for India and West Indies, 10 each for New Zealand, Pakistan, South Africa and Sri Lanka, and 1 for Bangladesh. Thirteen centuries were scored against Warne in the fourth innings, two of them by Sanath Jayasuriya of Sri Lanka.

7. *Those batsmen who did best against Warne*

Innings v. Warne*	Runs v. Australia	Average	Hundreds	Out to Warne	Batsman
35	1,834	55.6	5	7	Brian Lara (WI/ICC)
44	1,438	33.4	0	10	Michael Atherton (Eng)
22	1,209	60.5	5	3	Sachin Tendulkar (India)
45	1,206	29.4	0	14	Alec Stewart (Eng)
35	1,188	38.3	3	7	Jacques Kallis (SA/ICC)
29	1,149	46.0	3	9	Graham Thorpe (Eng)
33	1,128	35.3	2	5	Gary Kirsten (SA)
33	1,075	35.8	2	11	Nasser Hussain (Eng)
20	963	53.5	2	5	Kevin Pietersen (Eng)
30	947	31.6	1	7	Herschelle Gibbs (SA)
27	930	38.8	1	7	Nathan Astle (NZ)
22	918	41.7	2	6	Graham Gooch (Eng)
28	902	33.4	1	7	Mark Butcher (Eng)
26	898	34.5	0	8	Marcus Trescothick (Eng)
20	893	44.7	2	5	V. V. S. Laxman (India)

*Innings v. Warne denotes innings in which Warne bowled.

Asanka Gurusinha, of Sri Lanka, scored 410 runs in nine innings in which Warne bowled, averaging 51.3, and was never out to him.

8. *Those batsmen with the worst records against Warne*

Out to Warne	Innings v. Warne	Percentage	Batsman
11	18	61.1	Ashwell Prince (South Africa)
5	10	50.0	Tillekeratne Dilshan (Sri Lanka)
6	13	46.2	Hashan Tillekeratne (Sri Lanka)
8	20	40.0	Andrew Strauss (England)
6	15	40.0	Brian McMillan (South Africa)
8	21	38.1	Hansie Cronje (South Africa)
8	22	36.4	Craig McMillan (New Zealand)
8	24	33.3	Rahul Dravid (India/ICC)
11	33	33.3	Nasser Hussain (England)
5	15	33.3	Shivnarine Chanderpaul (West Indies)
7	22	31.8	Andrew Flintoff (England/ICC)
5	16	31.3	Mark Ramprakash (England)
14	45	31.1	Alec Stewart (England)
9	29	31.0	Graham Thorpe (England)
8	26	30.8	Marcus Trescothick (England)

Minimum five dismissals; specialist batsmen only

Sources

I would especially like to thank the following for their assistance:
Michael Atherton, John Benaud, Richie Benaud, Greg
Blewett, Rod Bransgrove, Steve Bull, Mark Butcher, Gary
Frances, Ian Healy, Murray Hedgcock, Rodney Hogg, Nasser
Hussain, Terry Jenner, Darren Lehmann, David Lloyd, Mark
Nicholas, Jack Potter, Peter Roebuck, Chloe Saltau, Bob
Simpson, Peter Sleep, Max Suitch, Mark Taylor, Graham
Thorpe, Shaun Udal and Craig White.

Thanks too to David Luxton for his help with the original
idea of the book, and to Roland Philipps, Rowan Yapp and
James Spackman at John Murray's; also to Edward Faulkner.
And to Philip Brown for his excellent photographs.

Shane Warne himself was routinely helpful in his many press
conferences and interviews.

The following books were useful:
Ashes Victory by the England cricket team (Orion, 2005)
Spun Out: The Shane Warne Story by Paul Barry (Bantam, 2006)
Ashes Regained by Duncan Fletcher with Steve James (Simon
  & Schuster, 2005)
TJ Over the Top by Terry Jenner with Ken Piesse (Information
  Australia, 1999)
Gazza: The Gary Kirsten Autobiography by Gary Kirsten with
  Neil Manthorp (Don Nelson, 2004)

Worth the Wait by Darren Lehmann (Methuen, 2005)

Twenty20 Vision: My Life and Inspiration by Mushtaq Ahmed with Andy Sibson (Methuen, 2006)

Warne's World by Louis Nowra (Duffy & Snellgrove, 2002)

The Complete Shane Warne by Ken Piesse (Viking, 2000)

Crossing the Boundary by Kevin Pietersen (Ebury, 2006)

Coming Into Play by Andrew Strauss (Hodder & Stoughton, 2006)

My Autobiography by Shane Warne with Richard Hobson (Hodder & Stoughton, 2001)

My Illustrated Career by Shane Warne (Cassell, 2006)

Out of My Comfort Zone by Steve Waugh (Michael Joseph, 2005)

Michael Davie wrote an excellent article on Warne's background in the Melbourne *Age* on 28 January 1995, and Jana Wendt published an insightful interview with Warne in *The Bulletin* on 5 April 2006. *Goodbye Warney*, a programme broadcast on Channel Nine on 1 January 2007, contained excellent interviews with Warne and his teammates.

Thanks also to the Melbourne *Age* for its articles on Warne's drug offence and to the *Sydney Morning Herald* for permission to reproduce the cartoon in the inset section; to the *Wisden Cricketer* for permission to reproduce extracts from an article by Ashley Mallett in March 1998, and to Michael Joseph for permission to reproduce extracts from Steve Waugh's autobiography.

Read more . . .

Harry Thompson

PENGUINS STOPPED PLAY: ELEVEN VILLAGE
CRICKETERS TAKE ON THE WORLD

**It seemed a simple enough idea at the outset: assemble a
team of eleven men to play cricket on each of the seven
continents of the globe**

Except – hold on a minute – that's not a simple idea *at all*. And when
you throw in incompetent airline officials, amorous Argentine
colonels' wives, cunning Bajan drug dealers, gay Australian waiters,
overzealous American anti-terrorist police, idiotic Welshmen dressed
as Santa Claus, Archbishop Desmond Tutu and whole armies of pitch-
invading Antarctic penguins, you quickly arrive at a whole lot more
than you bargained for.

Harry Thompson's hilarious book tells the story of one of those great
madcap enterprises that only an Englishman could have dreamed up, and
only a bunch of Englishmen could possibly have wished to carry out.

'As funny as you'd expect from the writer of *Have I Got News For You*'
Daily Express

'Rare, clever, creative . . . A maverick, pushing boundaries with
outrageous jokes' *Guardian*

'Crammed with sharp observation, comic and cruel characterisation
and a great many very good jokes . . . Gloriously funny and life-
affirming' *Daily Telegraph*

*Order your copy now by calling Bookpoint on 01235 827716 or
visit your local bookshop quoting ISBN 978-0-7195-6346-1
www.johnmurray.co.uk*